GRAND PRIX PEOPLE

GRAND PRIX PEOPLE

PEOPLE

Revelations from inside the Formula 1 circus

GERALD DONALDSON

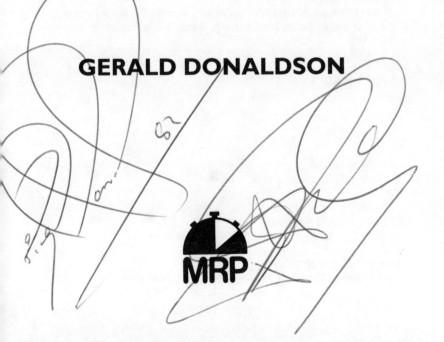

MRP

MOTOR RACING PUBLICATIONS LTD
Unit 6, The Pilton Estate, 46 Pitlake, Croydon CR0 3RY, England

First Published 1990

British Library Cataloguing in Publication Data

Donaldson, Gerald *1938–*
    Grand Prix people: revelations from inside the Formula 1 circus.
    1. Formula 1 racing cars. Racing. Races. Grands Prix
    I. Title
    796.72

    ISBN 0-947981-53-5

Typeset in Great Britain by
Ryburn Typesetting Ltd, Halifax, West Yorkshire

Printed in Great Britain by
The Amadeus Press Ltd, Huddersfield, West Yorkshire

CONTENTS

2: VIEWS FROM THE PRESSROOM

3: OBSERVATIONS IN THE PADDOCK

ACKNOWLEDGEMENTS

I wish to thank Motor Racing Publications for conceiving and commissioning this book, all the Grand Prix people herein for their co-operation, Peter Dick and Ultra Word Processing for helping transcribe over 40 hours of taped interviews, and Elizabeth and Anny.

I would also like to express my thanks to Dave Kennard for shooting and supplying the vast majority of photographs used to illustrate this book.

Gerald Donaldson

At each of the 16 events in the FIA Formula 1 World Championship series up to 3,000 people have the prized credentials which entitle them to move freely inside the privileged confines of the Grand Prix circus.

They are a disparate lot, a group of strong personalities from many cultural and social backgrounds, united in a common cause: the quest for success at the pinnacle of motorsport. There is a great deal of camaraderie among them but, since the essence of this sport is competition at the very highest level, there is inevitably conflict and controversy among its players. There is also a great deal of humour and, perhaps surprisingly in such a mechanically oriented endeavour, some very deeply felt human emotion.

The Grand Prix People include the famous drivers and the racing team personnel, the high-profile owners, managers and designers, as well as those who work behind the scenes to field the exotic machinery; the members of the FIA and those who provide organizational services, people who are often hard-pressed to maintain law and order in such an aggressive environment; the sponsors and trade suppliers whose enormous financial investments make this the most expensive sport in the world; the people in public relations and hospitality who labour to bridge the gulf between the commercial and sporting aspects of the series; the assorted VIPs and guests who either contribute to the sport's celebrated glamour and mystique, or they search for it; and the largest group of all, the members of the media, whose efforts are largely responsible for making Formula 1 racing such a hugely popular global spectacle.

The 110 personalities profiled in this book are positioned in the Pit Lane, the Pressroom and the Paddock, according to where they can usually be found, the number of persons in each section reflecting the proportion of people who work in that area. The individuals were chosen variously for the importance of their position, their influence on the sport, their contribution to it, their success in it, or their human interest factor. Such is the volatility of the world they live in that several of them changed their circumstances after they were interviewed.

This is by no means a definitive list, or a Who's Who of Formula 1, though it is often a Who Thinks What of Who. The majority of those included have never before had a chance to publicly express their feelings about their peers and the state of the sport in general. Their strongly held opinions and often pithy observations offer unique insights into Formula 1 racing. Above all, the candid revelations in the following pages provide fascinating portraits of the intriguing international cast of characters who are the Grand Prix People.

1
PERSPECTIVES
ALONG THE PIT LANE

CESARE FIORIO finds directing Ferrari's race team a pressure job, but he works well with ALAIN PROST.

DEREK WARWICK, one of the most enthusiastic of all the Grand Prix people, remains a realist and an optimist.

A conversation with Jimmy Clark inspired PETER WINDSOR to turn his racing passion into a way of life which led him to Ferrari.

Former stockbroker SHERIDAN THYNNE finds the money for the Williams team and ANN BRADSHAW provides the link between the sponsors and the press.

McLaren's TYLER ALEXANDER thinks Formula I is like an overbred cocker spaniel.

PATRICK HEAD sketched racing cars in his schoolbooks long before he met Frank Williams.

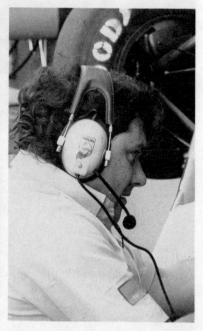

BOB DANCE has been with Team Lotus for more than 30 years, but once he used to make model racing cars go faster.

After going racing with Lotus for eight years CHRIS DINNAGE doubts he could ever be content with an 'outside' job.

NIGEL MANSELL

*"I think that some people here get out of bed in the morning,
and no matter what hat they wear or whatever coat they put
on, some of them think their job is to be a pain in the arse to
everybody!"*

"Absolutely, 100 per cent, NO!" That would be Nigel Mansell's
response should one of his sons wish to become a Formula 1
driver. And midway through the 1990 season Mansell abruptly
announced his imminent retirement from the sport that made him
rich and famous. His decision caught everyone, including all the
Grand Prix people, completely by surprise.

The father of little Leo and Greg Mansell was at the very
pinnacle of his profession: arguably the most exciting driver of all,
idolized by millions of fans around the world, driving for Ferrari,
the most illustrious team in racing, and earning more money in
one year (probably close to $10 million) than most people ever
will in a lifetime.

But few drivers paid heavier dues than Nigel Mansell. He came
up the hard way, without any money, literally breaking his neck
and his back en route to Formula 1. When he finally got there his
ability was often questioned, he seemed accident-prone, there
were feuds with his peers (he attacked Senna physically after they
collided at Spa in 1987) and his teams (Peter Warr at Lotus said he
had "limited capabilities" and Frank Williams said he was "a pain
in the arse"). During much of this time the press, especially in
England, tended to rubbish him, labelling him ill-tempered and a
chronic complainer. They wrote him off as a loser and there were
often jokes made at his expense along the pit lane.

It took him six difficult years and 72 Grands Prix before he
finally reached the top step of the victory podium (at Brands Hatch
in 1985). Becoming a winner (15 times to mid-season 1990)
changed both the man and his reputation. Mansell, the winner, was
more mellow and mature and better able to manage the fires of
ambition which, he admitted, occasionally burned out of control.
If Mansell became a new man, those who wrote about him also
underwent a remarkable transformation. To the Italians he became
an heroic figure, in the Villeneuve mould, and 'Lion Nigel' was

perceived as the prototypical Ferrari *pilota*. Many of the British journalists began to consider the mustachioed driver with the Union Jack on his helmet a thoroughly decent bloke. Some who formerly villified him began to regard him with what seemed akin to affection, a word that 'Our Nige' felt was not too strong when speaking about the journalistic reversal of form a few months prior to his retirement announcement.

"In the past three or four years I've consolidated my position in Formula 1 whereby even my worst enemy in England, from the press point of view, has got to acknowledge that I've at least cracked it. I've won a lot of races, I'm one of the fastest drivers in the world and I was even voted by *Autocourse* (the Formula 1 annual, edited by Alan Henry) as being the number one driver in the world in 1989 (Senna was second, Prost third). I think there's been a bit of a turnaround on both sides. I understand them more. They understand me, and we do get along pretty well now. In one word, we respect one another."

Mansell's bravery, toughness and fierce, British bulldog determination had always been respected. Born on August 8, 1954, at Upton on Severn, he first drove a car (an Austin Seven) in a nearby field at the age of seven. That same year he watched Jimmy Clark in a Lotus win the 1962 British Grand Prix at Aintree. There and then young Nigel resolved to one day follow in the great Scot's footsteps, an ambition no doubt entertained by countless other small boys around the world. It's unlikely any one of them would have persevered through Mansell's coming misfortunes.

After considerable success in kart racing as a teenager, he won 30 of 41 Formula Ford races to capture the 1977 Brush Fusegear Championship, despite suffering a broken neck in a late-season testing accident at Brands Hatch. When a backmarker cut him off Mansell's Crossle went backwards into a bank and the whiplash "snapped my neck in a couple of places". He was diagnosed as having come perilously close to becoming a quadraplegic.

"They told me that I'd never drive again and that the shortest time I could expect to be in hospital was six months. So I told a nurse I had to go to the loo, I packed my things and walked out of the place. Within five weeks of discharging myself I was racing again."

He had qualified as an engineer with Lucas Aerospace, worked 15 hours a day to finance his racing passion, then resigned from his job to devote his life to his sport only three weeks prior to the neck-breaking incident. Previously, he had also sold his gun collection and some paintings to get into Formula Ford. Next he sold his house to finance a move into Formula 3.

In 1979, an Oulton Park shunt (with Andrea de Cesaris), sent Mansell's March airborne and he was considered lucky to survive the huge cartwheeling crash. He was again hospitalized, this time with broken vertebrae. Shortly after this, Colin Chapman summoned him for a Formula 1 test at Paul Ricard, and Mansell, stuffed with painkillers and hiding the extent of his injury from onlookers, performed well enough to be given a Lotus test contract.

As he sat on the starting grid for his Formula 1 debut, at the Austrian Grand Prix in 1980, Mansell felt a burning sensation on his backside: "I had reached the point, the very minute I had worked towards all my life – and there I was getting my arse burned!"

Fuel had spilled out when the tank was being topped up and Mansell was given the option of not starting. He declined, the Lotus mechanics splashed water over him and he set off. Forty painful laps later his race was mercifully terminated by a blown engine and he was pulled from the cockpit with first and second degree burns to his buttocks.

Mansell became very close to Colin Chapman and was devastated by his sudden death in 1982, a year that Mansell calls "horrendous". He had grown to like and admire Gilles Villeneuve and was deeply shocked by his death at Zolder. After Riccardo Paletti was killed in Montreal and the race restarted, Mansell's forearm was badly sprained in a collision with Giacomelli. Then he witnessed Pironi's career-ending crash at Hockenheim. For Mansell, "those awful events created a terrible feeling inside me".

Even when the winning started, in Williams-Hondas in 1985, Mansell continued to suffer. A crash at Detroit gave him a mild concussion, and two weeks later a 200mph accident at Paul Ricard (a tyre exploded and a wheel hit him on the helmet) resulted in a severe concussion. Another incident left him with painfully torn chest muscles for the last half of the season, but he won two races.

In a span of 18 months he scored 11 victories, yet lost out on two World Championships he was poised to win. In 1986 a burst tyre in Adelaide destroyed his season at the last possible moment ("the lowest point in my career"). In 1987 it was a serious qualifying accident at Suzuka that injured his back again (a spinal concussion, more painful even than his back-breaking F3 injury) and handed the title to his hated Williams 'team-mate' Piquet (who called Mansell "an uneducated blockhead" and took verbal shots at his wife).

There was little joy to be had in 1988 when Judd power proved to be inadequate in the Williams cars, and Mansell kept his spirits up with memories of some of those winning performances. He makes no secret of being an emotional man, and that first Grand Prix victory, in front of his home fans, brought tears to his eyes. Even more rewarding was his scintillating late race charge to beat his least favourite Brazilian at Silverstone in 1987. He was simply unstoppable, setting lap records 11 times in the final minutes as he reeled in the other Williams. Thousands of stiff British upper lips were quivering with emotion when he took the chequered flag. And on his victory lap Mansell stopped to kiss the pavement at the spot where he'd overtaken Piquet.

His 1989 debut with Ferrari, when he won at Rio, suggested he might have used up all his bad luck, though there was more controversy at Estoril, where he failed to heed a black flag, then collided with Senna and was suspended by FISA for the next race at Jerez. At that point an angry Mansell hinted that he was considering retirement, but few took him seriously. During the rest of the season, as long as his Ferrari was in good running order, he kept it right up at the front, darting about with a stylish abandon reminiscent of Villeneuve that endeared 'Nigelo Manselli' to the fanatical Italian *tifosi*. His brilliant victory over Senna's more powerful McLaren at the Hungaroring (after he had qualified a lowly 12th), accomplished by one of the great passing manoeuvres in recent racing history (when he darted past Senna as they were lapping Johansson), was one of the finest drives of his career.

At the beginning of the 1990 season a serious shot at the World Championship beckoned and Mansell seemed to have everything going for him. Still, many of the scars from his previous misfortunes remained. The years had taken their toll and he wondered if it had all been worthwhile.

"It's a question I ask myself year by year. The answer is ultimately found when you're in the car and you're racing and driving for a great team, like I am now for Ferrari. The answer is ultimately 'Yes'. That's why I'm still here. Beyond that I've got a lot more things into perspective now and I'm able to enjoy myself more than probably I've ever done before."

Mansell's main source of enjoyment is his family. He describes his wife Rosanne (who has been with him through thick and thin since the Formula Ford days), daughter Chloe and the two boys as "my backbone. My family is incredibly important to me." They live in the lap of luxury in a sumptuous home near Port Erin, on the Isle of Man, and have a holiday house on the Mediterranean island of Ibiza. Mansell has all the trappings of success (including the requisite jet and helicopter) and business interests that include a new Ferrari dealership in England and a golf and country club in Portugal.

Golf is Mansell's other passion (son Greg is named after his good friend, the Australian golfer Greg Norman) and he plays at a semi-professional standard (he competed in the 1988 Australian Open). He also helps to "keep my feet on the ground" by serving as a Special Constable on the Isle of Man police force. "I've done it for over three years now and enjoy it. I've also done a lot of promotions, launching campaigns for safety and car theft, and so on. Police work gives you a better perspective of life, and I hope to help by setting an example. The IoM welcomed us with open arms, it's a fabulous place to bring up a family, and if I can give something back to my society through my police work then I'm happy and proud to do it."

So Nigel Mansell was reasonably content with his lot in life and grateful for what the sport had given him. But he remained ever mindful of what it had taken out of him and, besides the danger, there were certain things about Formula 1 that he wouldn't want his sons exposed to. He pointed to the unpredictability of the sport and the anxiety it can cause. Then there's the constant intensity and frequent ruthlessness. "Sometimes it gets to me. There's very little morality in Formula 1 and there are no prisoners taken.

"For my boys, I think there are better and easier ways to make a career. I wouldn't dissuade them from being sportsmen. What I would try and do is put them into golf or tennis, into a sport where it's more the person. We're sometimes called gladiators to drive Formula 1 cars. Maybe we are and maybe we're not. But basically we're so dependent on the teams, the engineers and mechanics and manufacturers, that it's very difficult at times. But if you're a tennis player or golfer you make it on your own, near enough, and your talent can cover up for your golf clubs."

Mansell might one day pursue golf more seriously but, for the moment, it seemed, the Formula 1 positives still outweighed the negatives. "There are highs and lows at every Grand Prix. Sometimes the little things can get to you, like when there are too many people forcing their way into the garage and actually standing between the mechanics and the cars, so the mechanics can't work on the cars. Then the mechanics start throwing wobblies. Our lives are in the mechanics' hands and some people are totally unreasonable. It might be press, it might be photographers, it might just be autograph-hunters. But there is a job to be done by professionals and to me the garage is sacrosanct on Grand Prix weekends."

Professionalism is a prominent word in his vocabulary, and he considered keeping his body and mind in fighting trim an essential part of the business of racing. Few drivers concentrated as much on fitness and endurance (in 1981 he saved Lotus manager Peter Collins from drowning in the surf at Rio) and Mansell pushed himself through a vigorous training regimen. To keep his head in shape he got rid of a host of personal sponsors (at one point he had 14 of them) to give himself more private time for relaxation. He felt he'd educated himself to be a realist and he tried to maintain a positive attitude, a task that was made easier when his prancing horse machinery was in good fettle.

"Whatever happens, I try and be very professional and treat every Grand Prix with the same amount of urgency as I can. If the car is working reasonably well, more often than not you're in a good disposition. If you're struggling, you can't get the balance of the car, and so on, then everything seems to get on top of you: cameras and tape recorders always in your face, autograph-hunters hounding you, and so on. Amazingly enough, it can all turn around on race day, and it can become one of the most fantastic days of your life!".

Mansell had few more of those days as the 1990 season progressed and his World Championship hopes dimmed as his Ferrari was seldom around at the finish. Meanwhile, a more circumspect Prost racked up the points in an identical machine. Or was it? Mansell began to express doubts about that and there was increasing tension in the Ferrari team. Mansell drove harder than ever and distinguished himself with at least one memorable moment in every event. In Mexico (where he finished second to his team-mate Prost) he passed Berger on the outside of one of the fastest, most dangerous corners of all, an experience that left even him breathless . . . perhaps a bit frightened?

"Motor racing is pretty frightening, period. And just looking at a Formula 1 car, let alone getting in one, can be unsettling. And then it can bite you in the arse. I will say, the manoeuvre I did outside Gerhard at Mexico, yes, that was frightening. Because, you see, I had to force my right foot to stay on the deck, and I didn't brake going into the corner. I went in there flat, and it's a pretty shitty corner at the best of times. And, yeah, I was wondering halfway around whether the car would slide just that tiny bit too much and I would go off. But it was a calculated risk and all of motor racing is a calculated risk."

At this point, Mansell was speaking only three weeks before his sudden retirement announcement. He seemed preoccupied with a summing-up of his racing life and the current situation in Formula 1. He talked about the fans who pursued him, noting that some of them "were trembling with excitement" when they met him. "I feel very sympathetic toward them. I think it is important that if they think that much of you, no matter how much in a rush you are, even if it is only 30 seconds, you should bring yourself to just give them that little bit of time for a signature or pose for a photograph. And even at times a second photograph, and then you draw the line, as it might get out of hand if you don't.

"I admire people too, but I don't worship them. Admire people for what they do and achieve, yes, that is one thing, but to be totally enthralled by an individual, overawed by them, is perhaps not a healthy thing for anybody. I've certainly never thought of myself as a hero. And it is very strange for me to think about that. I never stood still long enough to appreciate where I am now in the eyes of some people. I've only ever thought I was just doing my job. I only ever drove as hard as I know how.

"On the actual circuit I think I can, and do, deliver as good, if not better than, any other driver in motor racing today. What I am not good at is the politics off the circuit . . . the underhanded, back-stabbing manipulation which is done by some of the people who do succeed. I simply can't compete in that arena. If I can win the World Championship simply by who I am and what I am and what I do, fine. But I just won't compete in all the polemics.

"I think what spoils Formula 1 for me now is the peripheral things. The barbed wire fences, the over-zealous security people, the hassles which interfere with you doing your own job. And the easiest part for me still, the most enjoyable part, is when you're driving. But as soon as you step out of that car, sometimes it's so trying, it's unbelievable. And for no fault of your own.

"You can blame progress, you can blame the amount of money in the sport now, you can blame lots of things. But I believe if people were just a little bit more sensitive, no matter what position they held, everybody in Formula 1 could enjoy themselves so much more. I think that some people here get out of bed in the morning, and no matter what hat they wear or whatever coat they put on, some of them think their job is to be a pain in the arse to everybody!"

Then came Mansell's favourite race, his home Grand Prix at Silverstone. In qualifying, spurred on by the motivation of thousands of his fans, he turned in a scintillating pole-setting performance which he called "the lap of my life". In the race, in fighting form as usual, he led for awhile, but once again was forced to park his failed Ferrari. On his walk back to the pits Mansell symbolically tossed his driving gloves and balaclava into the adoring crowd. While his team-mate Prost was spraying yet another bottle of champagne from the victory podium Nigel Mansell was announcing that at the end of the season he would retire from the sport. He had added up his wins and losses and decided to quit while he was still ahead.

ALAIN PROST

"For sure, the pressures here make some people behave badly."

The most successful Grand Prix driver of them all first got behind the wheel of a car in 1963, when he was eight years old. It was his father's Citroen, and after Alain Prost tried a kart, on a family holiday at Antibes when he was 14, he embarked on an amazingly successful racing career, zipping through the lesser formulae with ease and entering Formula 1 in 1980, winning all the way.

When he broke Jackie Stewart's record of 27 wins, at Portugal in 1987, Prost said it was his most memorable racing experience. But there were many more milestones to be counted, and soon after the 1990 season began, he scored his 40th victory in Brazil, and there were more to come. In almost every recent season he has been a main contender for the driving title, a feat he first accomplished in 1985, repeated the next year and won again in 1989. All three World Championships came while he was driving for McLaren. Then came his celebrated personality conflict with team-mate Senna, which caused Prost's defection to Ferrari.

Even in the paddock on a Grand Prix weekend, Prost is more often than not a winner in the card games he plays with friends, mainly several French journalists. One of his intimates is Jean-Louis Moncet, who co-authored the Prost memoirs in a book they called *Life In The Fast Lane*. Prost's life away from racing is based in Switzerland, where he resides with his wife Ann-Marie and their two sons. He runs a successful business enterprise, Pole Promotions, a company which, among other ventures, stages the annual Pau Formula 3000 race.

A studious and analytical approach to racing has caused Prost to be nicknamed 'The Professor'. He always drives with his head, instead of his right foot, and feels that "some people are born winners. I do not say that for only Formula 1, but for life in general. I think you should consider life as a game and play it that way.

"To win, your motivation must be very high. My motivation goes up and down according to whether the car is competitive, or some places where you may feel more comfortable, and so on. I did not enjoy 1989 at all, and that is why I almost retired. But my motivation is very high again at Ferrari because I have a fresh mind and a new challenge and the ambiance is good. I feel very comfortable. And that's what is so fantastic about this job, you know. From one year to the other you can change completely – different team, different motivation.

"The people who know me well know that I'm never depressed but the thing is, if I'm not very happy or something is wrong, I can't hide it. That's the problem. It shows and I can't hide it, even after 10 years here. But I'm never depressed. In fact I always find a way to come back if I want, like I did after my 1989 season. But, on the other side, I much prefer when everything goes well around me, and in that way I'm much, much stronger now than ever before.

"When I started in Formula 1 my pleasure in driving was about 90 per cent of the time. But I was also thinking about Formula 1 99 per cent of the time, which was not so good. At the moment, my pleasure is still about 90 per cent, and I think I work at it even much more than before. But the only difference is, when I don't work in Formula 1, I can think about something else. I can switch it off, and this is much better for me.

"Often, for me, the best moments are when I'm sitting in the car. The worst part is all the time spent with people outside the racing programme. Because on the Grand Prix weekend you would like to be concentrating on doing your job. So, you must be able to enjoy the racing, because all the rest of it is sometimes very difficult.

"I sometimes think it's a shame the way some of the press writes about us. Before the 1990 season, for example, in testing we did a very good job and worked very hard, but all the newspapers wrote only about the Senna and Balestre affair. And I think it's bad, the more you give importance to this kind of thing. Honestly, I think the problem is the sports press. Maybe it's the problem to sell newspapers, that we see they're more interested about scandal.

"It's like when some people talk about the money in Formula 1, it looks like the money is bad – Formula 1 is all sponsoring and all publicity. But, for me, this kind of publicity in Formula 1 is much better than sometimes what you can see on TV advertising, or on posters along the road. If you want to talk money, you talk real business. And it's about the same for the personalities. In Formula 1 it's very difficult because of the so different personalities, but if you want to make a bad story you make a bad story. If you want to make a good story you make a good story.

"For sure, the pressures here make some people behave badly. I think that is right. That's the first reason people write about personalities. The second reason is the big, big difference between the technology of Formula 1 and the capacity of the people following Formula 1 to know what we are doing. Because if you stand here in the pits, stand here all day, you still won't know what we do. So, in fact, the only thing you can care about are the characters and personalities. You can't talk about the technology because you don't know it. That creates a big problem."

RICCARDO PATRESE

"It's a different world, this Formula 1 . . . You can have the very best life here."

Surely no-one looks more like an Italian racing driver than Riccardo Patrese. But the handsome native of Padua's claim to Formula 1 fame goes far deeper than his classic Latin countenance. With over 200 Grand Prix starts under his belt he is the most experienced driver in the history of the sport. Now more competitive than ever, and a highly respected member of the Grand Prix establishment, Patrese's staying power is testimony to the truth in the old adage: if at first you don't succeed, try, try and try again. During his eventful career he has also lived through the truth of another dictum of motor racing: the highs are higher and the lows are lower than in any other sport.

At Imola in 1990, Patrese wept tears of joy when he won the San Marino Grand Prix, his first victory in seven years. But if that was one of his finest days, the tragic Monza race in 1978 was undoubtedly his worst. There, Patrese's Shadow was judged to have triggered the multiple crash that claimed the life of the Swedish driver Ronnie Peterson. The Italian rookie, in his second season, was branded a 'killer' by the press in his own country. Equally devastating, from Patrese's point of view, was the reaction of his peers who banded together to teach him a lesson. Previously, he had developed a reputation for being dangerously aggressive, and now the other drivers demanded that he be banned from the next race, at Watkins Glen, or they would boycott it.

Patrese accepted his punishment with grim resignation, then suffered through four tormented years of waiting while the matter of his guilt or innocence was deliberated in the Italian courts. The verdict, which found him completely blameless, was bitter-sweet. By then Patrese had retreated into himself, adopting a public pose of frowning petulance. He tried to protect himself with "a wall of arrogance. I was also a very shy person, which increased the opinion that I was a harsh and unfriendly man".

Patrese raced on, driving away his frustrations, and finding comfort in his growing family. His wife, Susi, has always stood by him. "She was born in the racing way with me. I met her when I was just a karting driver, she saw all my racing life, and because of that she got used to this way to live. She is really very good from this aspect because she never asked me to stop and she is able to stay beside me without giving me any pressure. Or giving me some pressure if I need it. She understands in which way to act, not to disturb me, but at the same time if she has to push me a little bit she does that. She is not, how you say, oppressive?"

So Patrese persevered and became a respectable journeyman driver, capable of scoring points whenever his equipment was worthy of it. He kept out of trouble on the track, avoided the politics off it, and with the passage of time his tarnished reputation was repaired. He admits to undergoing a personality transformation and believes this was a result of a combination of his increasing maturity and familial developments that changed his perspective of life.

"When I came to Formula 1 I was 22. I was a boy. I changed and learned to be better with people. Probably my approach with the people and journalists became different. And I think that mainly after '84–85 my attitude with the Formula 1 world changed quite a bit. Because until that moment, if things were wrong, they were affecting me a lot privately. I was unhappy, unsatisfied. And because of that also, with people, I was not very good. Then something changed in my private life. I had twin daughters born in '85, and so I said, 'OK, fine, motor racing is very important', but when I'm out from that world, I have another life – quite a good life. I can enjoy that, so I could relax a little bit more in myself, because of that."

Thus, the arrival of little Beatrice and Maddelena Patrese changed their father's life. With their mother, and their older son Simone, Riccardo found rewards unobtainable behind the wheel of a racing car, yet that contentment contributed to making him a better driver. A more balanced life made him less intense about his racing. It didn't slow him down any, but the speed became tempered with judgment. Though he is now a regular frontrunner, he feels he has not yet plumbed the depths of his talent.

"I think, from a driving point of view, since the beginning I showed quite good speed. But mainly in the last few years, definitely my maturity in driving improved and I'm a better driver. But even now that I'm the driver with the most Grand Prix starts I think I still have more to learn from Formula 1. You never stop learning and the more I learn, the better I become."

Patrese tempers his steady diet of driving with other distractions to help recharge his racing batteries. He has a keen ear for music, particularly the works of Beethoven, though at his homes, in Padua and Monte Carlo, he listens to everything from Antonio Vivaldi to Tina Turner. In the ski season the Patreses retreat to their chalet in Cortina, in the Dolomites, where Riccardo resumes the sport he excelled in as a teenager. Now, in the 35 to 40-year-old masters category, he admits to occasionally donning his helmet for downhill races. "My sponsors are not supposed to know! But anyway, I think always I do it in a very safe way, because on skis I'm quite good and my limit is always below the percentage that can be dangerous."

A less dangerous hobby, and even more of a Patrese passion, is his collection of model trains. He has nearly 100 of them, including a range of Marklin models made in Germany late in the 19th century. He spends hours tinkering with his trains (Susi jokes that he wears a trainman's cap when thus engaged) and his concern for mechanical perfection extends to racing cars, which makes his abilities as a test driver particularly valuable to the Williams team and to Renault.

If Riccardo were to establish a collection of the racing machinery he's driven it would be a sizeable one. He won his first kart race at the age of 10, was Italian Karting Champion in 1972 and World Champion two years later. The switch to cars proved equally successful. In 1975 he was second in the Formula Italia series, then drove a Formula 3 Chevron to win the Italian and European Championships in 1976. After a short stay in Formula 2, again in a Chevron, he was drafted into the Shadow team to make his Formula 1 debut at Monaco in 1977.

When the Arrows faction split away from Shadow Patrese went with them, and the team very nearly became the Cinderella story of 1978 when Patrese led the South African Grand Prix in a brand new car until a few laps from the finish. That ended in tears with a blown engine, then Shadow won a court case against Arrows over alleged plagiarism in the design of the car. The replacement chassis was not up to par, and then came the grief of Monza. Patrese languished with Arrows until 1982, when Bernie Ecclestone signed him to partner Piquet at Brabham. During that two-season sojourn he won at Monaco (1982) and South Africa (1983), but his move to the all-Italian Alfa Romeo effort "for sentimental reasons" found him near the back of the grid in uncompetitive cars for two years. A spell in Lancia sports cars in endurance racing during this period was more successful.

Patrese's return to Brabham in 1986 was marred by the death of his team-mate and good friend Elio de Angelis in a testing accident at Paul Ricard. He describes that as the lowest period of his career. "Never before have I had the urge not to race. It was a stupid death, unexpected and cruel." After another season with Brabham, Ecclestone, who was about to sell the team, helped Patrese get a ride with Frank Williams for 1988, and that partnership has been the most fruitful of his lengthy career.

Becoming a potential winner and a regular visitor to the podium was like bathing in the fountain of youth for the veteran. "My motivation is high because I enjoy what I'm doing. I love the sport and especially now that I am back to high standard, being a protagonist with all the top drivers, it is very easy now. It's much more difficult to keep the motivation when maybe the car is not competitive, you have problems with the team, and all this kind of thing. But because everything is going quite well, I'm quite satisfied with myself, the team and everything else.

"Since I came to Formula 1, technically it has changed a *lot*. But you cannot say that the effort you were putting in in 1977 is much different from the effort that we are putting in now. The only difference is that, of course, there is more possibility for teams because there is more money to have better development because of better technology. And also because of this, for a racing driver it's a bit more complicated. Before it was enough to be just a racing driver, and concentrate in the car, and that was it. Now, you have really to be also a public relations man because the sponsors require you a lot, and you must also be a public man for this reason."

Now that he is at ease with himself, Patrese's natural charm, together with his prototypical racing driver persona, fits neatly into the requirements of the public relations side of his profession. And with all those years of struggle behind him and the future full of promise, he enjoys nearly every aspect of his racing life. Despite having experienced it over 200 times before, he looks forward to each Grand Prix weekend with great anticipation.

"For me the best time of a Grand Prix weekend is when you have pole position on Saturday afternoon and the car is going well for Sunday – but it's not very often happening! I think there are some moments that are very difficult . . . the waiting. The moments that you wait to go testing, that is mainly Thursday afternoon. Then there is Friday, which usually is the most important day to sort the problems. Then you have all Friday evening to think about what you can do to improve the car. And you can experiment on Saturday morning. If all goes well, Saturday afternoon is more relaxing because you should already have a very clear idea of what you need for the race. But after Saturday qualifying it can also be very difficult. If you want to change something you don't know if it's going to be good or bad, because in half an hour on Sunday morning it's very difficult to understand if it works. And then, after the race, it can be quite nice. If you finish the race in a good position, there are very good moments. I should say that you live very intense all the weekend.

"It's a different world, this Formula 1. It's nothing you can compare with. You go around the world, you visit many places, it's a very active life. But to be on the top is very difficult, and to *beat* these drivers is very difficult. But I should say, with the speed, then with application, and with the knowledge of the circuits, and the world generally, you can improve yourself quite a lot. You can have the very best life here."

JEAN ALESI

"I try to be a calm person. Sometimes when I am very angry I want to explode, but I try to remember the English way."

At the opposite end of the spectrum from the Formula 1 veterans is Jean Alesi, a young driver who seems destined to make a significant mark on the sport. With his audacious debut in France in mid-season 1989, when he finished a fighting fourth, and his subsequent charging displays of aggressive motoring, Alesi very quickly jumped to the front of the queue of newcomers who aspire to replace the superstars.

In his room at his parent's home there is a life-size poster of Gilles Villeneuve, and Alesi's rapid progress has been reminiscent of his boyhood hero. Besides a press-on-regardless style of driving, Alesi also possesses a Villeneuve-like candour and lack of pretension.

"To be honest, when I was a boy I never thought I would be in Formula 1. Because I was sure it was too difficult for me. I thought it was only for a bigger person. Like Villeneuve."

Alesi followed the adventures of his racing heroes closely and, like millions of racing fans around the world, he mourned the death of Villeneuve at Zolder in 1982, and of Elio de Angelis four years later, at Paul Ricard, near Alesi's home town of Avignon. After de Angelis' accident Alesi changed the colour scheme on his own helmet to resemble that used by the Italian driver. And Alesi's Italian heritage is very important to him.

Jean Alesi was born in Avignon in 1964, a couple of years after his parents arrived there from their native Sicily. As a result of his heredity and his environment Jean is bi-cultural, but, it would seem, his loyalty is not necessarily divided. "All my family is Italian. We speak Italian when my grandfather and grandmother are with us because they don't understand French. But the food and the mentality is always Italian in my house.

"When I began my career in racing I was a Frenchman, but the French sponsors said to me, 'Oh, you are not French, you are Italian. So you have to go back to your own country to race'. And now they want me. But they are not honest. And I am happy to see, at Imola and Monza, there are some big signs 'Forza Alesi!'"

His first sight of competition was in the club events, rallies and hillclimbs his father contested, and he still values the advice Franck Alesi can give him. "I was raised very close to racing. My father has a body shop, and when I was very small, after school, I was always at the garage. My father prepared his own cars and only stopped racing because it was very difficult to have free time. He was a very good driver and I still need him. When I speak with him he has very good information, not about the technical side of Formula 1, but about driving the difficult parts of the circuits."

With his father's encouragement, the junior Alesi began competing in karts in 1981 and immediately showed an aptitude behind the wheel. He won seven of 20 races in his first season, and nearly every event he entered in the next one. In 1983, a corner of the Alesi workshop was set aside to prepare a Renault 5 for Jean to race in the R5 ELF Cup series. A win at Nogaro and strong showings against more experienced opposition prompted a move into single-seaters.

Alesi, having set his sights on the route taken by such as Didier Pironi, Patrick Tambay and Alain Prost, enrolled in the Winfield School for drivers, where he finished a close second to Eric Bernard (another French driver to eventually graduate to Formula 1). In his two seasons of Formula Renault the Alesi name was not particularly prominent, but a move up the ladder into Formula 3 in 1986 saw him win at Le Mans and Albi, and the following year he won seven races to become French Formula 3 Champion.

In all but that 1987 season, when he drove for an established French equipe, Alesi ran his own team, with headquarters in his father's garage. Home was a caravan behind which he and a friend towed the racing machinery around France. Jean remembers those nomadic times fondly. "My mechanic was a good friend. He was 50 years old, so he was also like a father to me. And it was very funny because he was also our chef. Those years, '83, '84, '85 and '86, they were my best time in racing. It was so great to live like that, in a caravan, to stay very close to the team, which was my very own team. It was fantastic!"

Alesi parlayed his reward for winning the French Championship, a tryout in a Formula 3000 car, into a ride in that series for 1988, with the same team that entered him in Formula 3. Alesi calls that season (when he finished 10th overall) "a disaster. It is so easy to say the team was shit. But it is true! All the year was very difficult. But in 1989 I had the big opportunity to come to Eddie Jordan."

With Eddie Jordan Racing, Alesi won races on the streets of Pau and Birmingham and in the wide open countryside of Spa to become the International Formula 3000 Champion. Until mid-season, when he was well on the way to clinching that title, Ken Tyrrell, who was experiencing contractual difficulties with his regular driver Michele Alboreto, knew nothing about Jean Alesi. But when Tyrrell spotted his name at the head of the Formula 3000 standings he signed Alesi as a replacement for Alboreto. Tyrrell's invitation proved to be Alesi's passport to prominence in Formula 1, but he also feels particularly indebted to Eddie Jordan.

"For me, Eddie Jordan did a fantastic job, because he tried to give me the English mentality. It is very different from the Latin, like me. The difference is like . . . if you remember a long time ago when Jesus Christ came to Nazareth. When he first came, everyone said he was fantastic. Four days later he was crucified. That is the Latin mentality. Up and down. Too much.

"Inside, I am still a little bit like that. But for one year I also lived with an English family (in Oxford) to try to understand the language and the mentality. For me, this was a very good experience. I try to be a calm person. Sometimes when I am very angry I want to explode, but I try to remember the English way. I try to stay quiet and try to understand what happens around me."

Only one thing about his early Formula 1 experiences makes Alesi's Latin blood boil. "It was in France, and I spoke with this journalist who came to see me in a hotel. He wanted to know about my contract with Tyrrell and a lot of other things and I tried to explain it honestly. Two days after, when I read the newspaper, it was completely different. He changed completely my responses. That is very bad. When I read it I was very, very angry. Now I feel I have to be careful of journalists all the time.

"I'm just not happy when they try to find some problems when the problems are not there. They look for scandal and politics. I think that is very bad because it creates a bad mentality in Formula 1. That is the reason why the top drivers, like Senna, you can't speak with them. They don't want to speak and all the time they stay in the motorhome or in the hotel.

"The problem is that some people come to me and say, 'Oh, we hope you will stay like you are. You are not like the normal drivers'. I am not sure that I am very different. Sometimes I am very happy, sometimes I am very angry. Before, I did not have problems with journalists. Maybe because I was not quick enough!

"Now I must try to change a little bit my job at the race track. I want to do everything there and when it is finished I want to go away to my hotel and be quiet. At the circuit I will be more professional. I will always work hard with my team. With the fans I am now a little bit more popular and they want more autographs. I will do that because it is part of my job, and without these people we can't race. I will work with my sponsors for the same reason. I will speak with journalists also. But when I leave the circuit I want to be in another world."

Jean Alesi's other world is populated mainly by his parents, his brother Jose, who is also his manager, and especially by Laurence, his girlfriend, who has accompanied him on much of the long journey he has travelled in so short a time.

DEREK WARWICK

"Sometimes I shout in the cockpit. When I've done a good job and come past the finish line, I shout. I'm so happy!"

One of the favourite drivers from a journalistic point of view is Derek Warwick. He is regarded as a 'thoroughly decent bloke', always willing to talk about what he does for a living, and always doing so with infectious enthusiasm. In fact, he is one of the most enthusiastic people along the pit lane.

"People often ask me why I'm a racing driver. Well, first of all I *love* motor racing. I love *everything* about driving. Even now, after well over 100 Grands Prix, I come into the paddock and just look at the Camel Team Lotus transporter and I get excited. I look at the racing car and I get excited. I'm still a racing driver from the heart.

"Sure it's financially rewarding, but there are other motives. I love being noticed by the fans. I love signing autographs. I love talking to journalists, giving my points of view. I love doing TV. I love talking to the mechanics, the marshals, everybody. I don't even mind all the travel. I'm lucky because I travel at the sharp end of the aircraft, instead of the blunt end, so I'm rather spoiled.

"There's not much I don't like about it. But to be honest, I suppose the disappointments are the lowest point. You know I always think there are two sides to motor racing. First of all, about 95 per cent of the time, you have the lows. And the remaining 5 per cent of the time you have the highs. But that 5 per cent of highs outweighs the lows 100 per cent.

"It all started when I was 12 and began racing go-karts in England, then three years later I raced stock cars, the old crash, bang, wallop stuff. You were supposed to be 16 to get your licence, but I forged my birth certificate. I raced against my father, Derek, and my uncle, Stan, who own the Warwick Trailer company. We made our own chassis, single-seat open-wheelers, in our shop. Those were good times.

"The main ambition for me then was to work in the family business and go after the Super Stock World Championship, which I did win in 1971. We won hundreds of races and toured around Europe, even to South Africa, flogging around on dirt and tarmac oval circuits. Then I needed a new challenge.

"My real hero was Jochen Rindt. He was fast, a charger, a glamorous character, and he enjoyed himself. I admired people like Rindt and Villeneuve. Now I will never be a Gilles Villeneuve or a Jochen Rindt – I've never really had their flamboyant style – but I think I get the same values as them from motor racing. That is, they were chargers, they had 110 per cent commitment, and they enjoyed their motor racing. But they enjoyed their own lives as well. And that to me is very important in the overall make-up of a Grand Prix driver.

"Now you take someone like Ayrton Senna. He's achieved 1,000 times more than I have. He's won Grands Prix, been World Champion, he's in the top team and making over $10 million a year. So he should be much more content and happy with life than I am. But he hasn't got an eighth of what I've got. He's not even in the same world as I'm in. I really feel sorry for him. And that's a shame. It really is. I think he needs educating about life. Life is very short. Not just because we could die tomorrow.

However long it is, it's still very short. So enjoy it while it's here.

"Anyway, I went Formula Ford racing in 1975, at first against my father's will. His idea was for his son to run the family business and do a bit of stock car racing on the side. But Uncle Stan and I dragged him up to the Racing Car Show in London and, of course, when we got him into the exhibition hall he was sold, and we bought the car there and then. Coming from stock car racing, Formula Ford was like heaven, more sophisticated.

"We ran the car from a corner of the workshop, myself and two of the company mechanics who helped out. But I was the only guy who could change the gears on the car. In 1976 I won 33 races from 62 starts, won the European Championship and was second in two British Championships. I only crashed two or three times. It was a good year. Yeah, '76 was fantastic, because I also got married to Rhonda during that hot summer. I'd met her at a stock car race in '71 and we've been together ever since.

"I also did well in Formula 3. In 1978 I won something like 12 races and Nelson Piquet won 13. I won the Vandervell Championship and he was second. He won the BP and I was second. But the next year was a big disaster when we tried to do Formula 2 on a shoestring budget with a car that was one of the worst March ever made. I was still working in the trailer business about 12 hours a day, running the whole show, so it was all very difficult.

"But 1980 in Formula 2 was the first time I actually felt like a racing driver. It was great. We had a two-car Toleman team with BP sponsorship and I won two races and was second in the Championship to my team-mate Brian Henton, who was the lead driver. After that I had a chance to sign with Arrows, but went into Formula 1 with Toleman instead.

"But 1981 was a disaster. The Hart turbo was a complete disaster, though it was a good engine later on, and the Toleman chassis was bad. We called it the Flying Pig. But I still had faith in the team and in myself. In my own mind I was still the greatest thing in the world! So I stayed with Toleman and things improved, and we finished in the points regularly by the end of '83.

"By now I was sort of branded as the great white hope from England. I had offers from Lotus and Renault, and it was a great day for me when I signed for Renault for '84. That was a good year for me. Michele Tetu was a good designer, Gerard Larrousse was the team manager, and everything was good. I led two or three races, finished second twice and had two third places. It was an excellent season, really.

"Renault offered me a lot of money to re-sign for the next season. I also had strong contact with Williams, then Lotus offered me $1½ million. But I still felt Renault was the way to go. Unfortunately I was dead wrong, and 1985 was one of the worst years of my life. I was discouraged, upset, confused, the lot, and it was very difficult to survive.

"Tetu left and Larrousse was fired, others left and the car that came out of Renault for '85 was a complete disaster. It was so frustrating because the team had so much money and resources and just didn't use them properly. It was a huge disappointment to me.

"Near the end of the season I had a couple of offers, the most interesting one being from Lotus to join Senna. I put a lot of effort into joining them. Then, just before Christmas, Senna appparently made a stipulation that he did not want me in the team. I'd already accepted to be his number-two. But he didn't even want me there as number-two. He thought I would be a threat to him.

"He said it was because he didn't think Lotus could prepare two cars equally, but I think it showed his insecurity. I felt I could have given him more than I could take away, because of my experience and the way I go about life. I think I could have helped Ayrton a lot in '86. I felt very bitter, and the amazing thing was he sent me a Christmas card, wishing me all the best for '86. I don't bear any grudges, but my wife's reaction was not quite the same! But you know, I admire him for sticking to his guns, because he got some awful press about what he did.

"At the time I felt very upset, very discouraged, very disillusioned. For the first time in my whole life I could not do what I wanted to do. Up until then I had gone in whatever direction I wanted, and it was a good feeling. Suddenly, everything was taken away. All the good drives were gone and I was left without a seat in Formula 1. That for me was the worst Christmas and the worst time in my life. I just felt . . . incomplete.

"I felt nobody had faith in my ability. I found for the first time I took a knock inside, you know? I felt maybe I wasn't as good as I thought I was. Then Tom Walkinshaw offered me a seat at Jaguar and that taught me there *is* another life. All of a sudden I was in sports cars and Formula 1 looked very pathetic from where I was sitting. It didn't look so important. The people in it looked very insecure. Very petty.

"Driving for Jaguar was one of the biggest things in my life. I was very proud to be part of that first win at Silverstone, and just racing at Le Mans for Jaguar in '86 was something that I will go to my grave with. I mean it was fantastic, amazing! I actually cried just before the start. I had tears coming down my face because I have never had such emotion put through me in all my life. The fans waving the Union Jacks, the shouting, the chanting of my name. I mean even now I'm tingling just thinking about it.

"Then, unfortunately, I got back into Formula 1 after poor Elio de Angelis had the accident testing at Ricard. And you know a lot of people rang up Brabham, even on the day of his accident, to ask about getting his drive. I never made any contact with Brabham. They contacted me, and that wasn't until 10 days after Elio's death.

"Bernie Ecclestone told me that nobody but me was ever on his mind. But, out of respect for Elio, he felt it wasn't right to contact me immediately. And that meant a lot to me. That was my first introduction to Bernie Ecclestone and everything that happened from then on changed my opinion about him.

"I had heard a lot of bad things about him, that he was devious, only interested in money, and so on. But that's completely untrue. What I realized is that Bernie is basically just a frustrated racer. He simply loves motor racing. Yes, he's a good businessman, but Bernie is a *racer*. And his racing team meant a *lot* to him.

"Now I know Bernie as well as anybody and have the highest opinion of him. Without Bernie Ecclestone we wouldn't have Formula 1 the way it is now. It would be roughly where Formula 3000 is now and that would be bad. Bad for the sponsors, bad for the teams, bad for the journalists, bad for us all.

"Anyway, Bernie offered me the same contract as Elio. He actually showed me his contract and offered me a very good deal. I was amazed by that. I mean, he could have got me for the rest of the season for nothing. I was prepared to do anything to get back into Formula 1. Yet my time with Brabham was also very disappointing because the car was obviously very bad.

"When I joined the team I thought, with Gordon Murray around, with his magic, all of a sudden a new chassis would come out and Zap! – I'd be winning races. Of course that didn't happen. I think Gordon was already winding down and had lost his motivation. Fortunately, I was still having good races for Jaguar. We won two races and I only missed winning the World Sports Car Championship by one point in '86.

"But one of my great racing memories was experiencing the power of the BMW engine in the Brabham. I will remember qualifying at Monza for the rest of my life. Because at Monza I had 5½ bar boost, from a 1,500cc engine, and we had *1,300* horsepower! A seven-speed gearbox and I was still on the rev limiter in top gear! It was like being in a bloody rocket!

"I've never been in a rocket but it's how I imagine it must be. It was a lay-down car, so your head was tilted way back. I remember when I started the qualifying lap, with a seven-speed box remember, and I could not change gear quick enough before I was on the limiter. And going through the chicane I'd already gone 500 metres on the limiter and thought I was on a *perfect* lap. It was wonderful. But we'll never know because going into the Parabolica the thing just self-destructed. I mean the engine just blew to pieces. Threw the crank, pistons and everything right out the sides. It was one of the BMW hand grenades. But what a ride that was!

"After Brabham I had three years with Arrows. We had our ups and downs, but those were good years, really. We had some difficulties at first, then I got along well with Eddie Cheever. I think you have to enjoy your team-mate. You're only in the car about 5 per cent of the time. The other 95 per cent you're out of it, working with your team-mate, the team, with the sponsors. So if you can't enjoy that 95 per cent, the 5 per cent looks pretty lean.

"A good sponsor is one that understands those mathematics. At Arrows the USF&G people understood that and they were very easy to work with, among the best I've ever had. They treated us like stars, which is nice for the drivers. At every race there would be 30 or 40 USF&G people over from the States and we'd eat with them one evening during the course of a Grand Prix weekend. But that wasn't a bind. It was fun.

"The Americans have a different attitude from the Europeans. They're much more casual and they put themselves on the same level as us. The trouble with some Europeans is that they put you up on a plateau and then begrudge it. They resent that you're up there, so there's no relationship. But I haven't put myself up there, they've put me up there in their minds.

"I think that there's a lot of fake glory and razzmatazz about Formula 1, and a lot of drivers listen to their own press and they get very big-headed. And I suppose a lot of sponsors and people in the paddock do exactly the same. That could never happen to me. My family, my father and mother, uncle, brothers and sisters, they would kick six pounds of shit out of me if I became big-headed.

"My wife wouldn't allow it, either. She's a very level-headed person. To my daughters, Marie and Kerry, I'm just 'Dad'. I take them to the horse events. I'm the guy who shovels the manure out the back of the horse box. Sure, they're very proud of their dad, but they don't put me up on this enormous pedestal.

"I consider myself very fortunate, really. I'm married to a gorgeous woman. I have two fantastic children. I live on an island that's just heaven. My job is something I love, and I get paid very well for doing it. And I've got great friends.

"I've always said that it doesn't matter whether you are the local refuse collector or the Lord Mayor of London – I can enjoy an evening with you. I've got some friends in Jersey who are worth millions. I've got others who are just normal, hard-working people. I don't associate with people who are 'rich' or 'poor'. I am friends with good people. Period.

"There's a lot of people in Formula 1 who are complete arseholes. I mean, they're as big an arsehole as you will find in this world! There are some people you can't trust. Some people who have got daggers in every single pocket they own. But there are some genuine people, too. There are some people that want to help. There are some people who are here for the right reasons.

"But some of the so-called nasty guys have also had to survive, and maybe that's what made them nasty. You've got to be aggressive and hard in this business. I think a lot of people would say that I've been too much of a nice guy. Well, all I can say to that is the only reason people can say that is because I've never been in the right position to win. Otherwise people would be saying you can be a nice guy and still be World Champion. I think I can still change that saying, that nice guys finish last. But I'm also a realist. I'm running out of time.

"Winning is what motor racing is all about. I've done a whole lot of Grands Prix with no wins. Sometimes that gets to me, inside, though I don't lie awake at night worrying about it. I've put it all into realistic perspective. I'm not over-anxious, but I know that if we do a good job I can race to the rostrum, and if we get things right on the day, we can be lucky. I'm a realist and an optimist. In fact, I'm more motivated now than I've ever been.

"No matter what you are in Formula 1, you are the best. All the people here are at the top of every single field, whether you're a driver, a truckie, mechanic, sponsor – even a journalist! You have to be the best, otherwise you're just not here. That brings a lot of problems, because all these people have egos and ambitions. Sometimes that makes for a difficult mix, but somehow we all gel together.

"I get along well with most of the journalists. They're like the drivers, owners, sponsors. You've got some that you trust, some that you don't. You've even got some that you dislike, but you still have to put up with them because they can do a lot of damage to you. I respect people like Roebuck, Henry, Hamilton, Jeff Hutch, Pino Allievi, Giorgio Piola. Jenkinson . . . well Denis is an excellent journalist, but I think maybe he's in the wrong decade. He has some strange views.

"You know, people don't realize it, but to win a motor race is often easier than to finish seventh. Finishing seventh can be bloody difficult when the car you're in shouldn't be in seventh. I also think that when you're giving 100 per cent in a bad car, you're more likely to have a shunt than giving 100 per cent in a good car. I've had some pretty heavy shunts, and I'm glad they weren't in a car from past decades, when a couple of them would have been very severe. I also think if you're good in this life, certain people will look after you.

"I've been lucky, and maybe I've used up all my accidents. Eddie Cheever has a great way of putting it. He says that having an accident is like paying your bills with a credit card. It's fine all the time the credit card is working, but at the end of the day you have to pay the money you owe on the credit card. I'm never frightened, but sometimes, after a shunt, I get back to the hotel room, speak to my kids and my wife, and I think, 'Oh shit, that was a big one. I was lucky there'.

"Driving a Grand Prix car is bloody hard work. I've done hard graft in my life. I've sweated buckets working with welding plants in the workshop at Warwick Trailers, and come out of there after 18 hours, physically and mentally exhausted. But that's only 10 per cent of the pain that you go through in the cockpit of a Grand Prix car. In training, I get up at 7 o'clock in the morning and run, sometimes 10 miles, at a pace that is crucifying for me, and that's *nothing* compared to the suffering in the car.

"You hurt all over. Your neck seems like it's falling off, your legs are numb or in pins and needles, your hands hurt because at Monaco you've done 4,000 gear-changes and it's gone through your gloves, and now your hands have just blown up. Your feet hurt where you brake so hard on some circuits that they've just gone numb. It's just amazing pain.

"But there's also the unbelievable elation. There's pleasure in a Grand Prix car like nothing else on earth. That absolutely fantastic feeling when you put the ultimate qualifying lap together. Getting the lap right, getting the corner right, knowing that nobody else could have done better than you in the car. Sometimes I shout in the cockpit. When I've done a good job and come past the finish line, I shout. I'm so happy!

"You know, I think deep down there's a few people within my family who'd like to see me stop. I'm a million miles away from that, but I'm preparing for life after Grand Prix racing. I've got Honda dealerships in Jersey and we're opening more in England and France. I'm also getting more involved with the family business. I've got property. I'm also helping my little brother Paul in his racing career. He's very important to me and I think he's a very good driver. So I've got plenty to do when I stop racing.

"Still, I think it's going to be a problem to replace everything I get out of Formula 1. But then maybe it won't. Maybe by the time I retire I'll have satisfied all my racing ambitions and I can relax back into reality. Because Formula 1 is unreal."

AYRTON SENNA

"So it is very difficult to find someone in this environment with whom you can have a constructive conversation."

He is undoubtedly one of the greatest racing drivers in history, and one of the most controversial. Everybody has an opinion about him, invariably a very strong one. Yet the man himself remains an enigma. He's the subject of endless speculation and, it would seem, considerable misunderstanding. This is mainly because he seldom speaks publicly, which is a great pity, for Ayrton Senna has a great deal to say.

He is a complex man – intense, introspective, sensitive, private – and very intelligent. He is probably the most intellectual of all the drivers and, if Alain Prost is The Professor, Ayrton Senna should be The Philosopher. Noted for his fierce commitment to racing, and his penchant for taking risks, it may really be his intellect that most sets Senna apart from his peers.

He is remarkably articulate (even in English, a language far removed from his native Portuguese), though talking about any superior talents he might have makes him uncomfortable. "To say that I am better than most drivers is something you have to discuss, to see if it is really true. If it is true, it is for me an uncomfortable feeling. It is in a way pleasant, of course, but talking about it publicly, just being open and natural about the subject, is difficult for me.

"I do try very hard to understand everything and anything that happens around me. Not only in the car, but in my behaviour as a professional on the circuit, outside, in the garage, and so on, and it takes a lot of energy. At the end of every day I feel very tired, because I just give everything I have. It drains me completely.

"Sometimes I think I know some of the reasons why I do the things the way I do in the car. And sometimes I think I don't know why. There are some moments that seem to be only the natural instinct that is in me. Whether I have been born with it, or whether this feeling has grown in me more than other people, I don't know. But it is inside me and it takes over with a great amount of space and intensity."

Behind the wheel he constantly strives to combine his

metaphysical inquiries with his natural instincts to make a supreme effort. But sometimes he finds himself in the grip of an unknown superior force and Senna becomes a passenger on a surreal ride into unexplored nether regions – beyond his normal limits, beyond his understanding. It's an experience that can be frightening.

"When I am competing against the watch and against other competitors, the feeling of expectation, of getting it done and doing the best and being the best, gives me a kind of power that, some moments when I am driving, actually detaches me completely from anything else as I am doing it . . . corner after corner, lap after lap. I can give you a true example I experienced and can relate it.

"Monte Carlo, '88, the last qualifying session. I was already on pole and I was going faster and faster. One lap after the other, quicker, and quicker, and quicker. I was at one stage just on pole, then by half a second, and then one second . . . and I kept going. Suddenly, I was nearly two seconds faster than anybody else, including my team-mate with the same car. And I suddenly realized that I was no longer driving the car consciously.

"I was kind of driving it by instinct, only I was in a different dimension. It was like I was in a tunnel, not only the tunnel under the hotel, but the whole circuit for me was a tunnel. I was just going, going – more, and more, and more, and more. I was way over the limit, but still able to find even more. Then, suddenly, something just kicked me. I kind of woke up and I realized that I was in a different atmosphere than you normally are. Immediately my reaction was to back off, slow down. I drove back slowly to the pits and I didn't want to go out any more that day.

"It frightened me because I realized I was well beyond my conscious understanding. It happens rarely, but I keep these experiences very much alive in me because it is something that is important for self-preservation."

In that 1988 Monaco Grand Prix Senna was leading his team-mate by nearly 50 seconds when he crashed – inexplicably. While Prost went on to win, Senna did not return to the McLaren pit. He walked the short distance to his flat and promptly went to sleep. He later acknowledged that he lost concentration when his pit ordered him to slow down. The accident was a major turning point in his inner life.

"I am religious. I believe in God, through Jesus. I was brought up that way, was maybe drifting away from it, but suddenly turned the other way. Things that have happened in my racing career contributed a lot to my change of direction. It was a build-up of things that reached a peak, and then I had a kind of crisis. Monaco was the peak and it made me realize a lot of things.

"It is something that is difficult to talk about, very touching for me. But it is something unique in life, something that can hold you, can support you, when you are most vulnerable. It has made me a better man. I am a better human being now than I was before this. I am better in everything I am and everything I do."

There have been other changes in his attitude toward life. Much has been made of Senna's absolute single-mindedness, how he divorced his wife because he was so consumed by his racing passion. He has always been deeply devoted to his family, but now he feels the need for a more balanced life, and to share it with another person.

"Time shows us, as we progress, different perspectives of life. And a few years ago I had no time for anybody or anything other than racing. Today I not only have the time, but I *need* the time for my family, my friends, and particularly for my girlfriend. And it is something that I fight for and I organize my life in order that I can get the right balance between the private life, the personal life, and the professional life. Because only that way, having the equilibrium between both sides of myself, can I perform to my best.

"Now, even when I am doing my job, the need for somebody to be by my side is great. It gives me something I don't get in any other activity in life. You know, I think when you love a woman you feel more human. You feel stronger, a better man, more macho, and at the same time you feel inner peace because it fulfils the empty space that you have, that we all have in us, and that only love can fulfil."

Little Ayrton Senna was only four years old when he first drove a go-kart, and as a schoolboy his head was filled with heroic visions of the exploits of Stewart, Lauda, Villeneuve. The highlights of his life were Grand Prix mornings in Sao Paolo when he awoke, trembling with anticipation at the prospect of watching his heroes in action on television. He remembers that just before the start of the race the palms of his hands were wet.

"Now, before the start of the race, I have still a lot of expectation – tension – when I am waiting. My hands still perspire a bit, but I have other feelings. Like an empty space in my stomach, a feeling of wanting to sleep . . . there are several conflicting emotions."

Senna admits he brings a high degree of emotional intensity to his racing, but it goes beyond his profession. "I am intense about everything I do. I have an attitude about life that I go deeply into it and concentrate, and try to do everything properly. It's part of my personality."

His public personality has been called remote, ruthless and arrogant, accusations that began shortly after Ayrton Senna da Silva came to England at the age of 20, following several successful years in kart racing. He soon shortened his name (in the interests of brevity and clarity for journalists), and his reputation for a willingness to sacrifice anything on the altar of motor racing began with his divorce in 1982.

When he came into Formula 1 with Toleman, in 1984, appreciation of his obviously superlative skills were leavened by those detractors who maintained he was prepared to win at any cost. He was accused of reneging on his Toleman deal (he bought out his contract) to join Lotus, where he refused Derek Warwick as a team-mate, but accepted Johnny Dumfries because, the cynics said, he was worried about Warwick's competition. (Senna's reasoning was that Lotus couldn't field two equally competitive cars.) Certain of his peers joined in the disparagement: Mansell attacked him physically after one on-track encounter, Piquet did it verbally, and the word along the pit lane was that Senna was dangerous and not to be trusted in close racing situations. More recently there was the trouble with his McLaren team-mate Prost, which caused Prost to leave the team.

These conflicts have contributed to what for Senna is the worst part of his profession. "The most difficult time is when you have to put up with people that you don't really enjoy. When you have to live with people that you cannot trust, or people who you know by previous experience are just waiting for a small mistake from you, to beat you. That is the worst, that is the most difficult time."

Here, Senna is not speaking just of those drivers with whom he has had much publicized feuds, but of others within the Formula 1 environment with whom he finds himself at odds. When his public criticism of FISA and Jean-Marie Balestre in late 1989 led to a demand for an apology, or the governing body would take away his licence, it caused him to come within a phone call of retiring from the sport. He returned out of a sense of loyalty to his team, particularly his mechanics, and those at McLaren who depend on Senna to earn their living.

"If I had pushed for what I think was right, and what I thought was true, I would have created a major problem with everybody on the team. I practically gave up racing. Then I had to face up to it and give in, not for myself, but in the interest of a whole group of people, particularly those who really work, day after day. They need their work, so I gave in. But for no other reason than the responsibility I felt to those people who gave me the chance to win races. It was the least I could do for them."

Though he has never had to work for a living he feels his privileged upbringing in Brazil provides him with a special perspective. "I think I am in a very fortunate position. First of all, I had the opportunity to be in a healthy family environment. It was very positive. I had love at home, which is important for later development. I had the opportunity of being well educated. I grew up doing all kinds of activities, sports and intellectual things. So I had what I consider a perfect environment to create the basis for when you are an adult.

"On top of that, on the material side, I had anything I wanted. My father is a self-made man who was always able to give me and my sister and my brother whatever we wanted. And I came to racing because it was my desire, my dream. I made it my profession, but it was always first my hobby. Money has never been my motivating factor. I don't need racing for any material reason.

"I only need Formula 1 for the pleasure it gives me. Once you have that self-confidence, to throw it all away at any time, you are in a much stronger position. I am not the only one, but few have that situation. It is very unique, generally speaking, in terms of drivers, engineers, mechanics, team owners, managers, sponsors. Perhaps that makes me a little bit different in being able to stick to my principles and not compromise them in my profession.

"I think Formula 1 is very superficial, generally speaking. Formula 1 is today a very strong business, a way of promoting names and products . . . and people. Of course, there are a few special people here, but as much as I try to find those few special people, and to get through to them, I find it very difficult. Because consistently I find problems and troubles that I go through which tend to drive me away from personalities. So it is a very difficult environment to be part of. It is almost impossible.

"The competition naturally already makes life difficult for everybody, not only drivers but team managers, press people, sponsors. Anybody that is in here, somehow he is competing, and the nature of this competition means the ego is always being tested. When you have your ego being tested all the time, it tends to bring out lots of problems in terms of relationships among these people. And as a direct link to the ego fights, you can naturally find difficulties."

When those difficulties are chronicled in the motor racing press Senna feels he is too often made the villain of the piece. After confiding in certain journalists he felt his trust was betrayed, the truth distorted. He became suspicious of interviews and retreated into a shell of silence.

"I got hurt badly, and the only way I could continue, and remain healthy, was to stay away from interviews. You may pay an expensive price on some occasions by not answering some criticism, not giving your version of factors. Then people write only what they are told. But I am of the opinion that if you have principles in your mind, if you have good character and you have a clean mind, a positive and constructive mind, time will bring things to reality by itself. On the other hand, it is no good for me just to be nice to people and keep smiling if I don't feel like it. Because if I don't feel like it, I will not do it properly. I must be true to myself, to my beliefs, to be at peace.

"So it is very difficult to find someone in this environment with whom you can have a constructive conversation. And that is frustrating in a way because I have always a desire, it is in my nature again, to share with people that I like some of the special feelings I have, that I get from doing what I am doing here. It is the only thing I can give that has some value, at least for me. And I find it frustrating not to be able to share those things with the public in general, with the fans.

"After all, the public are interested in the people. OK, they follow the racing and the fighting on the circuit, but the racing and the fighting are done by people: the drivers. They are the ones that by their personality, by their character, by their instinct, end up making the show boring or exciting. That is what gives the show some shine or some darkness. People are interested all about the driver that is in the car. The way he looks, not only physically, but the way he looks through his eyes, the way he speaks, by his voice being soft, sharp. The way he makes his answers, the contents of his answers, the enthusiasm he passes on, the instincts of fighting, all those things.

"And we are all different. Therefore what holds people, what gets people and holds them in admiring you, is what you are. Not just because you win. They are after winners, of course, and there are several winners in a season. But there are maybe one or two that really shine and the rest are just winners. There is a difference between a true champion and just another champion, The true champion who shines is one who people love to see, love to know, love to think about and to be with in their minds."

As Senna was speaking his mind during this interview a fan broke through the circle of onlookers which perpetually surrounds him. The man shyly presented the superstar with several gifts, among them a piece of ceramic sculpture with Senna's name on it. Speaking in Portugese, the fan respectfully explained that the Brazilian was his hero. Senna was deeply moved.

"I think to have lots of people after you and showing that they admire you and they like you, it is super. I have never seen the guy before and he comes with a piece of art, something that he made himself. And his wife has baked a cake for me. It . . . it makes me feel embarrassed and humble. It does, because it shows how much you can touch people without knowing, without ever talking to them, just by your behaviour publicly. What they see on TV, what they hear you saying personally in some interviews, what they read about you.

"In many ways we are a dream for people, not a reality. That counts in your mind. It shows how much you can touch people. And as much as you can try to give those people something, it is nothing compared to what they live in their own mind, in their dreams, for you. And that is something really special. Something, really, really special for me."

PETER WINDSOR

"I have strong feelings about certain people and things in this sport and have total disinterest in the rest of it."

It's unlikely that anyone along the pit lane feels more passionately about the sport than Peter Windsor, a man who once wrote about the likes of Ayrton Senna, then moved to the other side of the fence. Windsor is now General Manager of the British-based Ferrari GTO development centre where the chassis and suspension for the Ferrari Formula 1 cars are built.

Formerly the Sports Editor of *Autocar*, Windsor then became an executive with the Williams team. He was a passenger with Frank Williams when the team leader had the car accident which left him paralyzed. Then, when Windsor became part owner of the Brabham team, a dispute with his Swiss partner resulted in a protracted court case which sapped all of Windsor's resources. The case was eventually decided in his favour and Windsor was given a cash settlement, but his romantic view of racing has survived.

Born in England, Windsor then went to Australia, where he witnessed his first race as a spectator. "That was the first and last. I had such a dreadful feeling on Monday morning, that I didn't know what all those guys were doing on Monday morning and I had to go to school again. It was the worst feeling I'd ever had in my life. And I said to myself then, I'm never ever going to have this feeling when I leave school. I'm going to have a job where I feel great on Mondays. Not terrible. I still have a job where I feel great on Mondays, and I feel lucky and privileged that I'm like that."

To get closer to the sport the 15-year-old Windsor became a flag marshal and worked for the club in Sydney which organized the local race in the Tasman Series. His hero was Jimmy Clark, and Windsor was enthralled at a chance meeting with the great Scot. It was at the Sydney airport and Clark's plane was delayed. He invited Windsor to sit down with him over a cup of coffee.

"I remember actually saying then that I wanted to be a racing driver and nothing else. And he said, 'Well, if you want to be one bad enough you'll make it. If you want to do anything in life badly enough you'll get it.' That inspired me enormously, and after I went back to England at the age of 20, not knowing what to do, and with no friends, and my job wasn't going well or whatever, I always used to remember what he said. I always felt almost as if I had some sort of obligation never to give up. I still feel that now.

"You've got to believe in yourself. You can't just get out of bed in the morning because you love motorsport. You've got to get out of bed because you believe in what you're doing. That's what got me through the court hearings. I just couldn't look myself in the face if I hadn't taken them to court and gone as far as I could. I'm not saying I had a lot left in me, I was just about up against the ropes when everything got settled. But it never entered my head that I would not do what I did – spend every cent I had and risk my whole livelihood in order to prove that I was right."

When Jimmy Clark was killed, about three months after their meeting in Australia, Windsor was devastated and "physically ill for some time". He was equally shattered by the death of Gilles Villeneuve in 1982. "Gilles means a great deal to me and I still drive along the road now and remember the things that we used to talk about. And the enthusiasm he had for racing is identical to my enthusiasm for racing. And that's something that will never be lost. If I was a racing driver I'd like to think Gilles was the guy that I would have been like, that I would have behaved like him and I would have been the person that he was.

"You do meet a lot of very, very good people in Formula 1. It's very stimulating in that way. About all the wheeling and dealing that goes on, well, I love it at a certain level. I love it at the Bernie Ecclestone level. I think Bernie is absolutely fantastic in the way he's run his life, and the money he's made, and the way he does his deals, and the intrigue he's created. Everybody is scared witless the minute they walk into his motorhome. And I think that's unbelievable that somebody's managed to create that aura. And I really admire that, I have to say. And I enjoy that part of Formula 1.

"I have strong feelings about certain people and things in this sport and have total disinterest in the rest of it. I'm very, very up and down about my racing. I only enjoy talking to the people I like, I only enjoy watching the drivers that I'm interested in. To me, Jim Clark is still the greatest driver that the world has ever seen, and nothing will ever change that. But I'm sure a lot of people, born later than I, would say something different. But other people have driven me, that's always been what's kept my interest up.

"Right now, I think racing is going through an enormous change. In the 1980s the money and the power and the motorhomes created an atmosphere akin to war; everyone was trying to stab everyone else in the back. People who should know better – drivers like Senna and Piquet – were saying the most absurdly destructive things about their peers. I mean, how can any so-called sportsman, no matter how conceited he is, sink so low that he makes disparaging remarks about another driver's wife? That's just sick. And it makes you realize that the racing world is a very small world. Hopefully, things are now getting better. One senses a new appreciation of values.

"Many drivers are over-rated, of course. The drivers that attract my attention are the ones who are individualists, who naturally do not adopt the classic textbook lines. Mansell is one of those – and Ross Cheever is the best driver around currently not in a Grand Prix car. Senna is a classic stylist – good in the Jackie Stewart sense. But he is not a Clark. Clark was imaginative and innovative, yet the statistics will now rank him behind Senna. That just shows that statistics, in Formula 1, are meaningless.

"There's a lot of people that can drive a racing car well. There's very, very few who can do it exceptionally well. What it comes down to is that racing is the cruellest, most unfair sport you could possibly have. Because you have guys that potentially could be as good as anybody, but never get the chance. And that's the greatest tragedy in life, I think, never to be given the opportunity. And racing is more guilty of that than any other sport I can think of. Because you need so much in order to go racing. You need the right car, you know. In tennis all you need is the racquet. And golf is the same. And it's very frustrating that you see a lot of people in there who are only in there because they've got a rich daddy, or they've got connections with whatever sponsor. And really they're not that good, they're average.

"I don't understand why some of the sponsors do the things they do. I'd love to talk to some of the people that actually write the cheques to see how they justify spending the money they do on some of the teams they spend it on. I wouldn't say that unless I felt that I could genuinely do a better job. But I really think I could spend their money considerably better.

"I feel that I'm ready to do all I can to try to get my own Formula 1 team, and to run things as I want to run them. I've got enough experience and I know enough about racing, I feel, to do the job. I'd love to be out there. Having a go. I'm going to do all I can to get into that position, that's my goal. Whether it takes me another 20 years, I don't know. I'm never going to give up.

"My goal doesn't seem to be as unreachable as when I was starting as a journalist. When I came to England from Australia I didn't know a soul. I thought it would take me 50 years to become Sports Editor of *Autocar* and go regularly to Grands Prix. I never imagined that I would ever achieve that. And I was never that happy with anything I ever wrote. And yet, probably because I did enjoy what I was writing about, and I was enthusiastic about what I was writing, things luckily worked out for me.

"I feel very lucky to have been a part of it, to be honest. I think the greatest thing in life is to be able to do for a living what you would do as a hobby. And I've been doing that since I was 15 years old. I feel privileged to be able to have done that, and I feel grateful to motor racing for it."

CESARE FIORIO

"Everyone is watching you and they're listening and they're talking, and everybody wants to say that maybe you could do it better."

"As Race Team Director for Ferrari I don't feel special, but there is a lot of expectation, probably from many more people than for all the other teams put together. Therefore, you cannot really make many mistakes. Everyone is watching you and they're listening and they're talking, and everybody wants to say that maybe you could do it better. So there is a lot of pressure.

"But I am in motor racing now since 30 years, and for nearly all the time I've been doing this I was hoping one day that somebody would call me here to Ferrari. And so when it happened I was very,

very happy. I was in rallying, sport prototypes, touring car races, everything. I've been working in motorsport all my life.

"Because it's Ferrari, many people that work here are top engineers or top people and top drivers. We have many stars, and you have to keep the people together and make them work together, and it's part of my job to do that. You have to deal with more personalities here.

"But Formula 1 is very similar to other racing in terms of running a team. The approach to the problem, what you must do to be competitive, that's the same everywhere. The only big difference here is the pressure you get and the audience and the big space in the media. It's part of the work, but of course I have to give priority to getting the cars fast and the drivers good and everything. I am more a team man, not a PR man. We have no PR man at Ferrari. Normally you have a PR man if you have to sell something to the people!

"Our motorhome here is not a hospitality unit. It's a technical office where the engineers and the drivers meet, and the tent here is for the mechanics to eat. We have a very good Italian cook. And we eat very simple, but very genuine. And the boys like that because they eat here like they eat at home. People say we have the best food in the paddock and I think that is true."

SHERIDAN THYNNE

"I think that what a sponsor should want is that his team win the World Championship by one point in the last race of the year."

"My job is to provide the money that we need to spend during the year, the £15 million to run the Williams team. I began with Williams in 1979, but I've known Frank since 1962. I met him when we were both club racing. I raced touring cars and my enthusiasm for racing goes back to 1949 when the father of a school friend of mine won Le Mans.

"My experience of talking to people in big business when I was a stockbroker is helpful here. I think that people in Formula 1 tend to be people who, if they hadn't worked in racing, might have worked in the motor trade, or electronics, in small companies of 100 to 200 people. While understanding small companies, which I hope I do, I am at the same time able to talk to big companies. I am a sort of interpreter.

"For major sponsors, the teams toward the front of the Formula 1 grid provide a unique media coverage throughout the world and throughout the year. The two sporting events which are comparable to Formula 1 in size are the World Cup and the Olympics. They are finite for time and only occur every four years, whereas the Formula 1 season operates for eight months and with previews and other information, it really is a year-long event. And it has worldwide TV and media coverage which, especially for a company which is growing internationally, can be very profitable. For instance, one of our newer sponsors, Labatt's, is expanding its activities and becoming a world brand name and we believe we offer a great appeal where worldwide media coverage is of importance.

"I think the Formula 1 audience consists of two levels of people: a smallish core of really passionate enthusiasts who know intimate details about the drivers and the teams and the technology of Formula 1, and a much larger group of people who quite like racing and usually watch it on television, but aren't particularly partial to it. If they have a theme running through them, they are young rather than old (or they may be young at heart), they are pretty keen about life, they are competitive people about life in general. They are people who are not necessarily interested in all sports, but see perhaps Formula 1 as I do: a fascinating blend of sport and commerce and technology. And they are quite big spenders most of them – a very attractive audience to sponsors.

"We spend a great deal of time thinking about how we can help our sponsors and work with them, and we have a very close relationship with them. It's not simply a question of doing a deal and then returning a year later and asking for more money. Myself and two assistants in my department are speaking to our sponsors pretty much every day during the season, discussing future projects, how we should work together at a particular event and so on. Because their success and their achievements through us are so important to us, as well as them.

"For the sponsors, the Paddock Club at a Grand Prix is a very comfortable area with nice surroundings where they can eat and drink in a degree of privacy away from the great mass of the public. They have a grandstand seat as well and we like to believe that it makes it of greater interest to them because they are actively associated with the Williams team and therefore have somebody to support during the event.

"I often ask sponsors how many races they would like us to win, and sometimes they say they would like us to win all of them. I ask that question because if they do say that I want to correct them, because I think they are wrong. I think that part of what they are being associated with is an ultra-competitive activity and if one team won all 16 races, it is not ultra-competitive. So I think that what a sponsor should want is that his team win the World Championship by one point in the last race of the year.

"I take a very active interest in each race, not just because it is related to the success which is part of our income, but because it is what I believe in. During the actual race, I am maybe talking to one or two very senior sponsors, or I have a radio as part of the radio contact that the team has with the drivers. So if I am not actually talking to sponsors I am on one or the other of the drivers' radio nets which gives me the opportunity to worry if they have problems during the race or to worry about how they are performing.

"Formula 1 is an extremely competitive business and so is the competition for sponsors. But I have never made a competitive pitch to another team's sponsor. That is not what life is all about for me. I think that the expression 'nice guys finish last' is silly. I like to think that I am a nice guy and I hate finishing last."

CREIGHTON BROWN

"It's publicity, it's a promotional exercise, it's a spectacle, it's a technical exercise. It's ritualized more, but it's still a sport."

Creighton Brown's specialties are in marketing and liaison with commercial sponsors and the press for the McLaren team. He also heads the new McLaren road car venture with Gordon Murray, duties that will eventually require more and more of his time. But Brown's McLaren involvement, and his motor racing expertise, extends into the many other facets of the sport he's experienced in nearly 30 years. And Creighton Brown is not about to give up what he loves best.

"I thoroughly enjoy the Grand Prix scene still. I enjoy the excitement, I enjoy the strategic side, I even enjoy the politics to a certain extent. I don't envisage turning my back on it and both Gordon and I will still be sitting on the board of McLaren International, and therefore we do have some responsibility ultimately for the wellbeing of the Grand Prix team. And the two companies, McLaren Cars and McLaren International, are going to be running in parallel, very close together. I would never give up being around racing.

"The first time I ever saw a motor race was when I was about nine years old and my father took me to a race at Goodwood. From that moment on I was hooked, and I subsequently built my first car, a sports car, when I was 21 years old. I raced it for a couple of years, ran out of money, then had a few years in 250cc international karting. I raced with my brother and we built our own chassis. I then went back into sports cars, Mallock Clubmans cars, and in 1974 I won a couple of championships.

"Arthur Mallock's younger son, Ray, was at that stage quite a promising young professional driver and he'd run out of money. He'd lost sponsorship rather late in the day, and I'd just had a very good year in my farming business, so I offered to buy a chassis and put a little team together around him if he was prepared to provide the engines to keep them going. We actually won 94 races in sports cars, in a short period of time.

"Later on we went into Formula Atlantic and latterly into Formula 2, because the prize money and starting money was better there. After some success, and in conjunction with a friend of mine, Guy Edwards, we gained sponsorship to run two cars in the European Formula 2 Championship from ICI and *Newsweek* magazine. ICI, of course, is still in Grand Prix racing with the Williams team, many years on, but they started with us.

"In 1978 I had Derek Daly, Elio de Angelis, Patrick Tambay and Jochen Mass alternating in the cars. And at that stage I'd already got to know Ron Dennis very well. He was an arch rival running another team, Project Four. We became friends and I bought a chunk of equity in an expanded Project Four and we started off again. In 1979 we won the British Formula 3 Championship, the World BMW Procar Series, we were the most successful team in Formula 2, and we built around 30 BMW M1s for the BMW factory. We also, at the end of that year, contacted John Barnard, because we decided to build a Formula 1 car. We founded McLaren International when we joined up with Teddy Mayer and Tyler Alexander and formed a new company at the end of 1980. And the rest is recent history.

"I actually raced for nearly 25 years and only stopped at the end of 1985. But I never did it purely for fun. Although I did it as an amateur in a relatively modest way, I always ran with commercial sponsorship and I always did it to try and win. So I took it seriously. I think anything you do in life, whether it's a sport or a pastime, you should still do it to the best of your ability. While I was racing myself, and running my teams, I also had two other farming businesses, and ran a garage at the same time. Until recently, I've been living abroad, in Brazil, where I had quite a large farming business. Now I've got a vast new array of opportunities and challenges at McLaren.

"There are four companies now, beginning with McLaren International, which is the Grand Prix team. McLaren Cars is the new company, which involves Gordon on the technical side and myself on the commercial side. Another company is TAG McLaren Marketing Services, which is very much run almost as an in-house advertising agency, and their function is to bring in sponsorship money and provide services assisting commercial sponsors. We can do anything from tailoring complete programmes, to graphics design work, to organizing travel and hotel bookings, the whole lot. And then we have TAG Electronic

Systems, which is another new company which specializes in advanced automotive electronics, engine management systems and everything else.

"It's all evolved from racing and it's the racing aspect that creates the motivation. Everybody is motivated in this sport, you have to be. To win, I think you just have to be utterly and totally single-minded. You have to put everything else behind you, particularly as a driver. The racing has to come first. It comes above your family, your wife, your girlfriend, any other interests you have. It's all-consuming if you're going to get to the ultimate point.

"Team success, I would say, really all starts back in the factory. The basis on which you go racing, and the opportunities you have to be *able* to win, are definitely a result of the hard work that goes in right back at base. And however hard you try to do a good job at the circuit itself, there's no way you can win these days unless you've got the basic product right, the organization right behind it, and everything very well planned. Formula 1 is many, many things, of course. It's publicity, it's a promotional exercise, it's a spectacle, it's a technical exercise. It's ritualized more, but it's still a sport."

RON DENNIS

"We all have an intense desire to win, and these desires tend to put people in a sort of personality showcase."

"When the One Great Scorer comes to write against your name, He marks – not that you won or lost – but how you played the game." That was an idealistic vision of the game of American football penned by sportswriter Grantland Rice. But Vince Lombardi, ultra-successful coach of the Green Bay Packers team, had another point of view: "Winning isn't everything, it's the *only* thing."

It would be hard to find a serious player of the modern Formula 1 game who didn't agree with Lombardi's sentiments, certainly they are shared by Ron Dennis. And when the scores of the last decade are tallied his McLaren team is by far the most successful. But his winning ways are often at odds with the Rice-like perceptions of fair play that persist among some Grand Prix people, particularly in the pressroom: "Anybody could win with the kind of budget McLaren has; Honda gives McLaren an unfair advantage; McLaren's supremacy makes Formula 1 boring."

Says Dennis: "Most people like a winner, but they don't like consistent winners. If I walk around with a grin on my face people say I'm smug. If I walk around with my normal scowl people say I'm miserable. It is so disheartening to try so hard to do a job well, then achieve success and feel it should logically attract positive recognition of a job well done, then not get that recognition. When people perceive you as an underdog, they are very supportive. Then when you're on top, they turn you from a David into a Goliath and immediately try to tear you down. But I say to the guys that work in the company, you should be proud to be part of any success and never feel ashamed, no matter what you read.

"It is very easy to say we have the best of everything: the perceived best drivers, the perceived best budget, the perceived best engines. It might appear to be very simple, but it isn't. I think the thing that makes McLaren successful is that it is very much a successful *team*. My role in the team is to put it together, making sure that all the political, promotional and organizational considerations marry. I have to package the elements and make it a team effort. It's a knitting together of egos, likes, dislikes, motivational forces, things that destabilize, things that harmonize. Having the ability to try and dissect all these things and then getting them to mesh together, I'd like to feel that is what I'm reasonably competent at.

"The secret is attention to detail, *everything* is important. You break the whole Grand Prix scenario down into the tiniest details. Individually, you might barely perceive them, hardly measure them. But you look at each of these facets and try to improve them. Those little improvements add up to considerable improvement. Attention to detail – that is the key.

"You have to start with the really fundamental basics. When someone walks into a room I notice straightaway such details as fingernails, whether they are cleaned and manicured; how the person is dressed, whether they're scruffy, or neat and tidy. If you don't have any respect for your own body, then I think you tend to have a lack of personal discipline."

Ron Dennis began in racing by getting his fingernails dirty, though his personal discipline, and ambition, soon came to the fore. When he was 18 he left school and became an apprentice mechanic at a garage near the old Brooklands track in Surrey. Previously, he had puttered around in a go-kart, but he was more interested in taking it apart and putting it together again than driving it. When the garage where he worked became home to the Cooper Formula 1 team, Dennis joined it as a mechanic on Jochen Rindt's Cooper-Maserati. Two years later he went with Rindt to Brabham where he became Chief Mechanic. In 1971, after "putting a lot of blood, sweat and tears into Brabham", Dennis persuaded Ron Tauranac (who owned the production side of Brabham) to loan him two Formula 2 cars and, together with Neil Trundel (from the Brabham Indycar division), he set up Rondel Racing.

His dedication to success caused him to suffer a serious road accident in 1972, but Dennis sees that setback as a blessing in disguise. After working all night to prepare his cars for a Formula 2 race he fell asleep at the wheel and crashed. He received severe facial lacerations (repaired by plastic surgery) and an eye injury that put him out of commission for two months. Typically, Dennis turned this negative into a positive. "In fact, it was probably the most positive thing that ever happened to me, because it pulled me into management. We employed another mechanic to do my job and I ran the team. That was the big starting point."

Rondel Racing began building their own cars and the Dennis-run team gained a reputation for immaculate mechanical preparation, smart turnout of team personnel and the employment of top drivers (Graham Hill, Bob Wollek, Carlos Reutemann). Next, Dennis formed his Project Three and Project Four teams which were successful in Formula 2 and Formula 3 with such drivers as Eddie Cheever and Stefan Johansson (who was British Formula 3 Champion in 1980).

"But the real turning point came when we won a contract to build BMW Procars. The contract was split with Osella, but by the time we'd built 15, they'd built two and we took over the whole contract. I devised a structure and got the people to build the cars 24 hours a day. We built something like 30 cars in a month. It was so lucrative that it kicked up enough money to build a Formula 1 car, which took place with John Barnard. That car was the leverage that gave me the opportunity to obtain 50 per cent of the equity in McLaren in 1981."

Since then the team has won nearly 50 per cent of the races, with a variety of drivers (Watson, de Cesaris, Lauda, Prost, Rosberg, Johansson, Senna, Berger), three brands of engines (Ford-Cosworth, TAG Porsche, Honda) and chassis designed by several people (Barnard, Murray, Nichols, Oatley). The one common denominator has been Ron Dennis. Now, his 'Star Wars' factory in Woking houses an empire that extends far beyond just fielding a Formula 1 team (the new McLaren road car is a major effort) and his role has changed. Dennis is now called Team Principal and retains overall control of McLaren's commercial and sporting interests. He maintains that he comes to Grands Prix now "to relax" but he seldom does that, for "to stand still in Formula 1 is to go backwards".

A major part of Dennis' role is handling the drivers in his team, a task that might be described as ego management, particularly when he was the employer of the feuding Senna and Prost. "The relationship between any two human beings is a very complicated thing, like in a marriage, and the drivers' relationship is very, very complicated. But the negative aspects of having two such drivers can be turned to produce a motivating force. However, as in any finely tuned situation, you walk a tightrope between falling off it into failure and successfully getting to the other side. That's the challenge. The challenge is to try to understand their negative differences, try to isolate them, then turn them into positives. I'm not a marriage counsellor, but I think guidance and support are the words to use when it comes to handling the drivers. I have to support and guide them through racing problems and human problems.

"We all have an intense desire to win, and these desires tend to put people in a sort of personality showcase, and therefore you get a complex situation. It brings out both weakness and strength of character. And if you can identify the weaknesses in individuals, you can provide the support structure to compensate. And that's what I believe good personnel management's about. It's about giving the support structure to the individual, from the mechanics through to the drivers.

"A team by its nature is a group of human beings, and human beings make mistakes. No-one's perfect. But if you are in a position of 'this is where the buck stops', then you have to take responsibility for all the actions of all the people in the team. So if something goes wrong, a driver makes an ill-conceived comment, or a team member does something wrong, or makes a mistake that is careless, then in taking the responsibility, you take the pain with it.

"The only way I measure my own performance is by my own values. It's very similar to the methods Ayrton Senna uses to get his performance. Ayrton is tremendously demanding, both on himself and his team. You really have to keep your mind focussed and watch that everything functions in an optimum way. It's damned hard. Very wearing, and very fatiguing, and not made any easier when it's criticized.

"I sympathize with the job the press have to do. And I think very often the truth accurately portrayed can be quite boring, so the role of the press is to colour the truth. And I think how well or badly it's coloured depends on the quality of the journalist and their medium. If you go from one end of the spectrum in the tabloid press to the other, in a quality sense, then down to the bottom end, you see almost pure fiction being portrayed as the truth. Which is understandable because those types of journalists tend to be focussing their attention on sensationalism, and the eye-catching headline that sells the paper.

"I think the journalists have a very difficult job. I think they are a little unfair sometimes, and don't go to the trouble of understanding the sport of motor racing. So many of them think they understand, when in reality they have virtually no understanding. But generally, I recognize that it's not an easy thing. They've got deadlines, they're given word quotas that they have to adhere to, and sometimes they're required to over-colour, or under-colour a situation. What I do feel is that for so many of them, the shade of the picture they portray reflects their current relationship with the particular people they're writing about."

TYLER ALEXANDER

"I think this thing's like an overbred cocker spaniel, and most of it's created by the journalists."

Tyler Alexander first became involved in Formula 1 racing over a quarter of a century ago. What does he think about the sport and the people who shove tape recorders into his face when he's trying to work?

"I think this thing's like an overbred cocker spaniel, and most of it's created by the journalists, because it isn't anything any different than it's ever been. You come here, you fuck around with a car, it's got four wheels and a motor in it, you start it up, and you're on. But the journalists pump it up into something else. I mean, there's all those people crowding around in the garages. There must be 50 million pictures of Ayrton Senna, sitting in there picking his nose!"

Well then, what about all the prestige, glamour and mystique that you hear about in Formula 1?

"Bullshit! Racing is just a plain old bunch of very difficult, complicated, hard work that's a pain in the arse. Sure, it's an exciting big deal thing. And the drivers are very important. The good ones are very good and certainly deserve a lot of credit. But to be successful you have to have a lot of good people. It takes a whole bunch of people. It takes a design team, engineering team, the backup people at the factory, the driver, the race team itself."

After studying aircraft engineering in Boston, Alexander helped a friend prepare a Formula 3 car which they raced successfully. He became friends with Teddy Mayer and his brother Tim, Roger Penske and Jim Hall, all of whom went on to become deeply involved in racing, though Tim Mayer later suffered a fatal racing accident. In 1964 Alexander and Teddy Mayer came over to England and teamed up with Bruce McLaren's new organization. Now, in the hierarchy of approximately 200 McLaren International personnel Tyler Alexander is listed as Special Projects Manager, responsible for the management of all development programmes.

Over the years Alexander has also spent some time in Indycar racing in his native America. Where, then, would he prefer to be?

"In Mexico, scuba diving."

According to Alexander, racing takes up too much time, too much of the time. He might also rather be sailing or even taking photos of Ayrton Senna picking his nose. In fact, Alexander is an accomplished photographer. Some of his work has been published in American magazines and there have been exhibitions of pictures he took during his early days in racing. His preferred subject matter is not cars, but people. His technique for getting candid shots is to "basically, hide in the crowd".

Speaking of people, how would he compare the pit lane people of Formula 1 with those in Indycar racing?

"They all put their pants on one leg at a time."

But aren't the CART people more relaxed and casual? They actually talk to each other, while in Formula 1 there seems to be a lot of animosity.

"I guess if people have their head up their arse, they have their head up their arse, you know. I don't think there's anything here that breeds the animosity except the people themselves, and if they choose to be like that, well that's their own problem."

He must have noted big changes in the Grand Prix people over the years . . .

"Well, if you look around, you'll find that a lot of the people here are exactly the same ones."

"One of the big changes since those days is the money, the sponsorship aspect of the sport. Some people, the purists, say that it was better in the old days.

"Well I've never really been able to understand what a purist is. That sounds like a phoney load of bullshit for somebody to call something a sport when it's really a business. Once upon a time it was a sport, yes, but that was an awful long time ago. It was a business to us when we started. I mean that's what we were doing for a living. That's it, that's all we did."

Nowadays, when he walks down the pit lane, is it possible to describe what goes on in his mind?

"Not that you'd want to hear, No!"

GORDON MURRAY

"You've got to be absolutely mad keen about the sport to work in it."

"I found him standing under a dust sheet," was how Bernie Ecclestone once explained where Gordon Murray came from. Actually Murray, who had come to England from South Africa, was working in the drawing office at Brabham when Ecclestone bought the team and eventually he became one of the most successful designers in Formula 1. His cars have won more than 50 Grands Prix and four World Championships.

From Brabham, Murray moved to McLaren, where he is now Technical Director of the new road car project at McLaren Cars. That position means Murray will spend less time along the pit lanes of the world's Grand Prix circuits, but he intends to return as often as possible.

"I don't think I can actually go 'cold turkey' after 20 years. I still get excited about it after God knows how many Grand Prix starts . . . still get the butterflies at the start and everything else. It's still a huge part of my life. I mean it's been *half* of my life. On the other hand, there's the other side people don't normally know about. And that, from a creative point of view, as Formula 1's progressed, it's been absolutely mind-boggling. In the last 20 years I've gone from being the only person in a design office to one of 23. And the role I play now, although it is technical, it involves a lot of management and administration.

"I actually do almost nothing from the point of view of creating bits and pieces. And I'm one of those people who *have* to be creative, whether it's a house or whatever. When I'm 80, if I'm alive at 80, I'll still be creating things. So I've actually got to the point where I'm sort of over-qualified to design Formula 1 cars. I've done so many Formula 1 cars, there's nothing I can see in the office that looks like a challenge. And doing the road car at the level that we have to do it at is about as big a challenge as I can have. But I am going to miss certain aspects of the racing, and I'm not going away from it completely.

"I was *passionately* in love with motor racing as a boy in the South of Africa. My father was a motor mechanic and he helped me build several small racing cars, on Fiat 500 chassis, when I was quite young. I've always liked speed and cars and motorbikes. In the summer I still ride motorcycles, several different 1,000cc racing bikes. In cars, I drive a 911 Carrera Super Sports and I recently acquired a 1968 Lotus Elan.

"So as I went through school, and subsequently college, doing mechanical engineering, I wanted to race cars. But racing cars were so expensive I decided the only way I was ever going to race was to design and build my own. So I borrowed what then seemed like a lot of money from various aunts and uncles and set about designing and building a sports car, which took me two years to build. My father taught me how to weld, but I literally did everything. I also designed and built the engine based on some bits from Peugeot, some bits from Jaguar, some bits from Ford. The pistons were handmade and I built everything, apart from the gearbox and the rear axle. I raced that in '66 and '67 with a limited amount of success and lots of accidents.

"But as I got into suspension geometry and steering geometry and the engine side, the engineering aspect built up very quickly. I had nearly completed my five-year engineering course and if I wanted to go any further, in the driving, or the engineering, or in any kind of career, I'd have to go to Europe, mainly England, which was sort of the centre of the universe for racing.

"Going to England combined with my other love in life, rock 'n roll music. I kept seeing these black and white British movies on the news, with The Rolling Stones and people like that, so I thought I've got to get a bit of that. I sold everything up in '69, the racing car and everything I had, and scratched together enough money to get on a ship over to England. I arrived and was without a job for six months. I think I was down to 15 quid before I got that job at Brabham.

"Today, I certainly think people in motor racing are reasonably well paid, but in the early days it was actually the opposite. You accepted a fraction of what you could earn in normal industry for the benefits you got from going motor racing. But then, as now, you did it for the love of it. I don't think I've ever met anybody on a race team that isn't passionate about racing cars and motor racing. And they're also, I think, a special breed because they do have to work fairly long hours at race meetings, and they're under a lot of pressure in really hostile environments with regard to noise and extremes of chaos.

"In the early days at Brabham, we had a chap in the workshop who was doing some regular nine to five manufacturing job and he wanted to go racing, become an active mechanic on the team. Eventually I took him to a race and, with the pressure the guy had to work under for the first time in his life, with all the noise and trying to get the car out and all that, he actually had a mental collapse. We had to get a doctor and shoot him home. So you've got to be absolutely mad keen about the sport to work in it.

"From a personal point of view, the technical innovation bit still excites me. But still, what excites me more, is standing at the start and watching several thousand horsepower disappearing and everybody trying to win the race, which is where I started from. And fundamentally, though Formula 1 has grown into lots of things, the racing is still there at the end. And when you see a *really* exciting race, it's still all worthwhile. I mean, I still get *so* fired up watching a great race!"

HARVEY POSTLETHWAITE

"All this sort of business about drivers being good test drivers or bad test drivers is a load of absolute bollocks. A load of codswallop!"

Dr Harvey Postlethwaite, PhD, might have been a pilot, which was a boyhood ambition, except he discovered that he was colour-blind. He might have pursued a conventional career in science, the subject he studied at Birmingham University, except he found that prospect boring. He might have been a racing driver, in fact he was, competing in a Mallock in club events, but he ran out of money. So, he became a racing car designer with March in 1970. Next he worked for Lord Alexander Hesketh, then Walter Wolf, then Enzo Ferrari. Now he is the Engineering Director for Ken Tyrrell's team.

"What I like about Formula 1 is the immediacy. The fact that it's real engineering. Most engineers don't do real engineering.

Because the consequences of their decisions are not seen, normally not for years, sometimes never. The consequences of our decisions are seen sometimes within seconds, usually within hours, and always within weeks.

"There is a negative side to it, though. If you get close to the top, it requires personal sacrifices which are very difficult to balance between your professional life and private life. When you spend 16 weekends a year away racing, and many, many days on top of that involved in testing or travel associated with racing, it's not very conducive to a stable family background. But I happen to be extremely fortunate in that my wife has always put up with this. And I think one only actually achieves that delicate balance by being able to switch off 100 per cent. I can go away from this and I will switch off completely from it. For 48 hours I might not think at all about racing. I'll go and do something completely different.

"I go and play around with my motor cars at home. A couple of Ferraris and a Jaguar, which are my hobby. I've got a 250 GT Lusso and a Daytona, and I've got a Jaguar XK 120. All of which I find a great deal of fun, tinkering with them and just playing around and driving them. They're interesting because all three are from different decades. They all have different characters and it's just like talking to three different old friends.

"Formula 1 cars are something else again. These cars are technically so superior to anything we built 10, even five years ago. Those are like Noah's Ark compared with what we're building here and now. I think that the understanding and the knowledge that goes into building these cars is so much more than it was, than even last year. And that's what makes it fascinating. Of course it's the money that's made this happen. And I think the money wouldn't be there if it didn't want to be. I mean, nobody's holding a gun to anybody's head to put that money into the sport. It's all coming in because sponsors want to be there. They want to associate with it. I think that's terrific. I think the sport has never been better.

"One of the things that fascinated me about Enzo Ferrari, despite his age, was his ability to look forward, always. He never looked backwards. And if there was anyone who could have looked backwards, it was him. I think that's a very interesting lesson. Don't fight old battles, and you should never look back upon any period as being the good old days. Because the good old days are here and now. It's what makes Formula 1 interesting, that it's happening here, it's happening now, and this is the best that it's ever been.

"To understand a modern Formula 1 race, when you know what's going on, is fascinating. And I think it is a shame that there are technical aspects to the sport which make it fascinating, which perhaps the public never get to see or hear about. That's partly because teams don't necessarily let on what they're doing. And it's partly because the people who are covering the racing perhaps wouldn't understand, or be able to absorb and put across the information.

"I think that sort of information would also make the race tactics a lot more interesting for the public. For instance, it'll make a great deal of difference at many tracks knowing whether a car is running a lot, or little, downforce. Pointing out a few of those little details, and you can see them on the television as clear as anything, would make it much more fascinating for the fans, rather than just to see the cars droning round and round and round.

"For the press, I suspect that if the racing isn't very good, you have to invent something else to make it interesting. When there was a total dominance by McLaren, it meant that you had to try and develop a situation out of nothing. Now we have a much more varied, competitive situation. So probably we haven't had to invent conflicts between drivers, or their wives, or their boyfriends, or whatever.

"I have a great deal of admiration for the drivers, for what they do. But the drivers are part of the moving background, aren't they. They come and they go. And all this sort of business about drivers being good test drivers or bad test drivers is a load of absolute bollocks. A load of codswallop!

"A driver is a driver. The driver cannot tell you how to set up the car. If he tries to, then he's wrong. The driver can only report to you on what the car is doing, and it's up to the engineers to be able to set up the car to make it go quickly. Alain Prost can tell you what the car is doing. But Alain Prost can't tell you what springs, or cambers, or castors, or ride heights to run. That's us. The car has to be 90 per cent right and then, with the driver, you can achieve the other 9 per cent, or even 10 per cent, to get it completely right.

But if the car isn't nearly there, the driver's input is wasted. When you get the car balanced and going quickly for that driver, then whether the driver is absolutely quick, or not, is a measure of his ability. And a very few of them have exceptional ability.

"And there are probably as few good engineers in Formula 1 as there are good drivers.

JOHN BARNARD

"I never think of this business in terms of pleasure any more.
I think of it in terms of the amount of aggravation!"

One of the most successful Formula 1 designers is John Barnard, whose first major drawing board achievments were Indycars, the Chaparrals which won the Indy 500 and the CART title in 1980. Back in England he masterminded the all-conquering McLarens of the mid-'80s, then switched to Ferrari in 1987 where his chassis became winners and his automatic gearbox enhanced his reputation as an innovator. Now Technical Director of Benetton, Barnard recalls how his quest for new challenges first brought him into racing, and have kept him there.

"I was at college until I was 23, taking mechanical engineering, then worked for a while in a company outside racing. I suddenly thought, God, I can't see myself doing nine-to-five like this until I'm 65. There must be something more. And I literally started writing round to racing car companies. I got a break with Eric Broadley at Lola, and I thought, well, let's go and do it for real, see what it involves. And I was away. It was just obviously right for me. I was happy to work all hours, they basically had to throw me out at the end of the day.

"At the end of the McLaren thing, where I was losing motivation, it was a bit like sticking a pin in myself, taking on the Ferrari thing that everybody said, 'It's impossible, you can't survive, don't do that, it won't work'. Certainly, in Formula 1 it's very easy for somebody who's done it for a long time to slip down into something where perhaps the competition is a bit less and it's a bit easier. And if you take some Formula 1 technology with you, you're going to be looking good for a few years. It's very easy to do that.

"But, you know, one of the most difficult things is staying at the top. I think you've always got to be faced with a target. If the target is simply staying there, that's for me a very difficult thing to cope with. I'd much rather be aiming at something which is higher and further on. The stimulation is coming up with a new idea, a new direction, and facing all the usual critics, the finger-pointing and the sniggering, and the political battles that very often follow these things. And then, eventually, to see it work and to see everybody else forced to turn round and say, 'Shit, I suppose that is the new way, we'd better start looking at it'.

"Before the gearbox it was the first flat-bottom cars with the coke-bottle shape. Everybody said, 'Why doesn't it look like a dart?, Why isn't it rocket-shaped?' And the gearbox offended some of the purists. Looking at it from my side, as a purist engineer if you like, the need for a driver to thrash around changing gear seems a bit stupid in this day and age of superfast hydraulics and electronic controls. I think what's happening is the driver's input's changing. We're past those days when a guy had to go out there and wrestle with this enormous steering wheel, and if he had bigger biceps than the other guy, he'd go faster. Now a driver's input is one of absolutely super fine feeling for the car.

"As a general performance package, from the point of view of lap times, 25 per cent is probably still up to the driver, 25 per cent is probably tyres, 25 to 35 is the engine, and the rest is the chassis aerodynamics and so on. A new-spec engine can give you a second a lap and you can bolt on a set of tyres and get another second. With chassis, aerodynamics, stuff like that, it's much more difficult to find those jumps in time. And there are some drivers who are quicker than others. I think it's not disputed any more that Senna's the quickest guy here. But I think the real driver input is generally keeping the sorting of the car, the set-up of the car, going in the proper way. Prost is one of the best at this. Because I know him quite well, I know how he works. He's so methodical, so sensitive and he's so analytical in everything that's done to the car, step by step, that he will get more from the car than other drivers.

"I certainly don't feel bitter about the money they get. I'm amazed at the money they get and I keep asking myself, is it really fundamentally bad for motor racing, that they're getting up to that level? But, other than that, it's just a kind of grading system. You can argue that we're all over-paid. I'm not lowly paid, though I'm not even in the same universe as the drivers. You look at the designers, I think generally speaking we probably earn more than we would be earning if we were in ordinary industry.

"I never think of this business in terms of pleasure any more. I think of it in terms of the amount of aggravation! There tends to be an enormous amount of aggravation from journalists and photographers and people like that. That's a bit of a nuisance. Everybody tells me it's what makes Formula 1 tick and all the rest of it, but in a lot of ways I would prefer to walk down the pit lane and nobody knows who the heck I am.

"Formula 1 is well served by a few journalists but, I hate to say it, I think the majority are serving it badly. My recent experiences with the Italian press, for example. I mean, probably 80 per cent of them, if they can stir up trouble somewhere, that's all they're interested in. That will sell papers. They're not really interested in the sport, in the finer elements of the thing. They just want to get the story where one driver stepped on another one's toe and pushed him down the stairs, or some other rubbish!

"There's a great deal of winding up here. I mean, a lot of it is done specifically to wind up a situation, or a person, or a team. No question about that. And if you're a bit green, it can wind you up, and it can really get you going. But if you've been in it for a while, you have to smile and just sort of see the funny side of it, really."

PATRICK HEAD

"Sometimes if things go badly now it does occur to me every now and again, why am I doing this?"

As a schoolboy Patrick Head's attention sometimes wandered from the lessons of the day and he sketched racing car suspension systems in his exercise books. He looked forward to the weekends when his father, Colonel Michael Head, would race his Jaguar in

British club events. A short spell in the Royal Navy proved to Patrick that life on the high seas was less interesting than the racing world and he parlayed his schoolboy sketches into a career.

In 1970 he passed his engineering exams and joined Lola Cars and by the mid-'70s had worked on a wide variety of single-seater designs up to Formula 5000. His first Formula 1 venture was with the Trojan project, and he spent two years in Walter Wolf's team before being recruited by Frank Williams in 1977. "Mainly because I think he'd got totally desperate for an engineer!" And there he remains, a director of the company and one of the most respected designers in the sport.

On the surface Head seems a pillar of calm strength, yet he admits to being prone to volatility when under fire. "Fairly early on I realized that when things were going at their worst, that's when you have to be calmest and try and keep the brain working hard, and I have great difficulty doing that when things are going badly. I suppose, once you've realized that that's the only way you're going to get yourself out of a problem, you have to force yourself to do it."

His racing experiences, particularly prior to coming to Williams, were not always happy ones for Head and there were times when even getting seasick in the Royal Navy began to look attractive again. "I began to think that it was a bit of a mug's game and was looking for other work. I mean, there are awful times when one's either very uncompetitive or having reliability problems. Sometimes if things go badly now it does occur to me every now and again, why am I doing this? But then I think of other things I might do, and think, well I know why I'm doing it."

So far the pros have outnumbered the cons for Head, and he can quantify his job satisfaction in terms of scholastic achievement. "In a way it's a very simple job. There is a competition and you finish first, second, third, fourth, fifth or sixth. It's rather like being at school where you're being marked out of 10, you know, and if you get three out of 10, it's the equivalent of finishing seventh, if you like, and it's not so good. And if you get 10 out of 10 it's like finishing at the top of the class. You get direct affirmation of how well you're doing, whereas in a lot of jobs that people do, they don't get that. So from that point of view I think it's quite good."

Patrick Head thinks that the Formula 1 press could benefit from more competition and if he was a schoolmaster issuing report cards for journalists there would be a few failures. "I'm not a great believer in the quality of what I see in the written word about motor racing, really. Sometimes I'm amazed by what I read in the name of race reports, particularly in some sections of the national press. It seems that the facts are not allowed to get in the way of a good story. It would be helpful if some of these people took the trouble to actually come and find out exactly what did happen instead of bursting into print with their own conclusions, which are often far removed from the truth. In the sport itself, if you don't perform you're out, but this doesn't seem to happen amongst the journalists.

"My impression is that too many of them seem to spend their time speculating about the money that's involved with names and sponsors and teams instead of concentrating on what I would regard as good journalism, which is being a reporter of facts."

FRANK DERNIE

"It's not as challenging when the rules get more restrictive . . .
the opportunity to be a bit clever on the opposition isn't there."

"If things are going well the driver's a star, and if things are going badly the designer's a wanker," says Frank Dernie, Technical Director of Team Lotus. Because the cars he has been associated with have generally tended to be successful, Dernie hasn't often been able to read about himself. He thinks the credit or blame for any success or failure should be more evenly distributed, perhaps in the proportions once mentioned by the founder of his team. "Colin Chapman was quoted many years ago as saying it's 25 per cent organization, 25 per cent tyres, 25 per cent car and 25 per cent driver. And who am I to contradict him?"

Frank Dernie was never interested in anything other than the technical side of racing, certainly not driving. "I'm too much of a coward!" But before he applied himself to solving racing problems he tested his degree in mechanical engineering from Imperial College, in London, in other pursuits. There was a sojourn working with gears at David Brown Industries, mainly because that company also owned Aston Martin. Then he had a go at record players with Garrards, in Swindon. Nowadays, he describes listening to music as his only other interest, but it was the technical side that appealed then. "People think all you've got to do is make the record spin at 33 and a third rpm. The problem is to stop it doing lots of other things as well. And I found that interesting."

Still, the concept of harnessing a racing chassis to a motor spinning at innumerably higher rpms was even more fascinating to him and he geared himself up for a Formula 1 career. After some consultancy work with Hesketh and Williams, he joined his friend Patrick Head at Williams in 1979, staying there for 10 years and becoming an aerodynamics specialist.

"My original reason for coming into motor racing was to try to calculate what were the important forces necessary to make the car go quicker. And it was very obvious as soon as you sit down and do a few sums that a thing like suspension geometry makes a minute amount of difference and things like aerodynamic forces make *huge* differences."

So Dernie applied himself to wind-tunnel testing, playing with toy cars, in search of the right package to contain the engine, fuel and driver. He is well pleased when one of his creations is produced in full-size, but thinks it would be a foolish exercise to try test-driving it himself. He wouldn't even be able to get the tyres warm. "In aircraft terms, for example, it would be like comparing a Cessna with the Space Shuttle."

With the whole business of Formula 1 design having taken on a 'Star Wars' aspect, Dernie notes the need to be secretive and suggests that a certain amount of industrial espionage takes place along the pit lane. "I try to look at it objectively all the time and say, 'I wonder why that team's doing that?' Because sometimes you say, 'We wouldn't do that'. Which means either they've discovered something we don't know yet, or they've discovered something we already know, and you're trying to suss that all the time."

Dernie has a bone to pick with the rulemakers, whose legislation he feels cramps his style. "Over the last 15 years the regulations limiting what you can do to the chassis have become more and more strict. The tyres have been limited a little, but basically the engine has been allowed fairly free reign. So whilst the governing body say they want to make the cars slower, the means by which they've chosen to do it is by limiting the chassis. The areas where you can make technical breakthroughs in the car have been enormously limited. It's not as challenging when the rules get more restrictive, when everyone has to do the same. When all cars have to be like this or that from here to there, the opportunity to be a bit clever on the opposition isn't there."

Despite the relentless competition, Dernie finds his rivals a decent bunch. "I'm very friendly with the teams. In fact the thing that I will always remember about motor racing when I stop is the wonderful people that are in it. And I'm not talking only about the people I've worked with in my own team, but the other teams as well. They're a very special bunch of people.

"Because they work hard. A hell of a lot of people round the world think that it's very, very clever to get a large amount of money for doing bugger-all. I don't. Nobody in motor racing does, or they wouldn't do it for more than about one week, because they'd be sacked. They work incredibly hard. The hours that are worked, typically by mechanics, that sort of thing, are very hard. And they're all very good at what they do. It's nice to work with talented people. They have a good sense of humour – maybe it's just that there's a large number of like-minded people together. You know, everyone's full of admiration for the effort that people put in, and the success they get, and everything else. And they're just a whole lot of people who are highly motivated and go for it. Whereas you meet some pretty wet people outside – at least I do!"

Dernie has always admired racing people, particularly those who ply his trade. "When I was a student and schoolboy, people like Colin Chapman and Tony Southgate impressed me a lot with their general approach, and Gordon Murray with his detailed approach, though I often thought Gordon didn't actually understand the physics of what he was doing, but the detail – like the use of materials – was very tasty.

"Motor racing's much bigger now and you need organizational skills and political skills as well as design skills in order to get together a team of people to get the job done. You've got to get the budget and all the rest of it. You have to say that John Barnard's done a good job, but on the other hand *nobody* has ever had as much time or as much money to get the job done as he did. It took him three years, and maybe $100 million, to turn Ferrari around, when Ferrari was already the biggest and potentially the best team anyway. And that was without going to any races. So you know, you could say that he's had the luxury of the easiest job to do. But he did indeed do the job. Patrick Head I know well, of course, and I've got a lot of admiration for his capabilities and strengths."

While he appreciates the talents of his rivals, it's Frank Dernie's job to out-think them, a task that once resulted in insomnia. "I used to be in a high state of panic, I couldn't sleep. But I've been doing it so long now that I wouldn't say it's routine, but I'm not frightened by it: trying to beat the other bastards!"

BOB DANCE

"People will be saying that the '90s were the good old days when we get into the 21st century."

Bob Dance began working with Team Lotus about 10 years after Frank Dernie was born. Officially he's Test and Build Co-ordinator, but Dance is also the longest-serving man on the team, having joined Colin Chapman's organization in 1960.

"I'm still enthusiastic about it all. If I wasn't I wouldn't be here today. I don't have to come to the races any more, because I'm involved with the testing. But this is where it all happens. It's where you see the results of all your testing and development work. And I just enjoy the atmosphere of racing."

As a youth Dance was fascinated by all things mechanical, though his only method of transport was a bicycle. Real cars were beyond his means, but he managed to scrape together enough money to buy motorized model racing cars in kit form and became adept at making them go faster than their makers intended. He had never seen a proper race, but thought working on full-size racing machines would be an interesting career. He decided to approach Lotus, because the company was at that time within cycling distance of his home in north London, and was hired as a mechanic to work on transmissions.

"In those days we were a lot closer to the drivers because they were about more than they are now. Graham Hill even used to do some work when he was driving for the company. Aside from that, I suppose the biggest change I've seen is the amount of money which is directed at racing in the way of outside sponsorship. Before it was mainly wealthy enthusiasts. But the money is obviously a good thing. It keeps a lot of people employed. The number of people now involved doesn't bear any resemblance whatsoever to when I first started.

"People often say those were the good old days, and maybe they were. But people will be saying that the '90s were the good old days when we get into the 21st century. You can enjoy your thoughts and conversations about the past, but one also has to look ahead. I wonder what it will be like in another 10 years' time. But I shall be retired, officially, by then . . . I think."

CHRIS DINNAGE

"It becomes a bit like a drug. You couldn't go back to work in a garage, on road cars or whatever."

During his time at Lotus, Bob Dance has seen a lot of people come and go. One of his current young work mates, Chris Dinnage, thinks he'll be around for a while.

"I'm one of the senior mechanics at Lotus, responsible for one of the racing cars. I started with the team eight years ago, at the bottom in the factory, working in the sub-assembly department. In the first couple of years, you think, 'Jesus, I'm working all sorts of ridiculous hours that I never used to in my old job'. But once you've done it a while, that's just how your whole system operates. When you're at home, you take off the hours you can and work the ones you have to. And we get paid well enough for it.

"The thing I enjoy most at the races is when the green light comes on and 26 cars, all with screaming engines, disappear down the race track. That's the best bit, that's the biggest buzz. But there's one or two bad bits about this job. I think when you have a normal job, you go to work in the morning and go home at night and you have good days and bad days. I feel that in Formula 1, if you have a good day, it's very, very good, and you're very, very high. If you have a bad day, you're at the other end of the scale, you're right down the bottom. Another bad time is when you have to work a lot of hours, like all night, to get the thing ready if it's been off the track and crashed or something. Then in the race there's a big disappointment if the car doesn't finish, especially if it disappears at the start and you don't even see it come around for one lap.

"We're all very competitive, and we even have that amongst ourselves. It's not fierce, but all the mechanics within the team like to think that they can do it better than the next guy. Which I think's good, keeps you on your toes. And we get along with the other teams, mechanic-wise. From our position you don't really see much of the higher management. But the mechanics mix and there's a certain degree of respect for everybody and all the rest of it, whether you're having a good season or bad. If you're out in a bar somewhere in the world, then yeah, sure, we'll have a drink with them. There's always something to chat about.

"From our point of view, Grand Prix racing is not a glamorous thing. The glamour is all generated by the photographers and the press. On race day itself, the main batch of glamour is when you see the girls in the pit lane and on the race track, everything like that. But it's put there for about an hour, to make it look that way. For us, this is not a glamorous job. At times it gets a little bit samey because we only see airports and pit lanes and they're all very much alike.

"I suppose the reason I'm doing this is because I had a friend who worked here before myself, and I thought, that looks like a good job, I want to have a go at that. And I was lucky enough to get involved, and it becomes a bit like a drug. You couldn't go back to work in a garage, on road cars or whatever. Because here you're working with top people and in Formula 1 you know that everything you've got is the best there is, the latest materials, the latest bits and pieces, though they're almost too high-tech at the moment, with everything electronically controlled and all the rest of it. But when you're working with the absolute best of everything, for me it's not good to go back and work on something which is not to the standard that we have here."

ALAN CHALLIS

"There's a lot of things we read in the press or see on television about the nastiness between the teams. But in reality, when you get close to it, there isn't any."

Alan Challis is the longest serving of the mechanically concerned men on the pit lane. And after over 30 years of experience Challis knows that when he leaves home to go to yet another Grand Prix there's a possibility he won't get any sleep until he gets home again. Yet he loves his job as Chief Mechanic for the Williams team, and the passage of time has seen no waning of his enthusiasm. "I've always said the second I stop enjoying it is the second I'll get out. I personally really enjoy having to hit the deadlines. Because you know when practice starts, when qualifying starts, when the race starts, you've got to hit it. If you don't hit it, this business doesn't happen."

Meeting those deadlines means Challis has no time to savour any of the varied ambience or atmosphere along the pit lane that might impress casual interlopers. Mexico, Montreal, Monaco or Monza represent only another job to be done. But the people going about their business in the garages are kindred spirits and Challis enjoys the camaraderie of the sport, not just within his own team. "Amongst most of the teams there's a very close relationship. There's a lot of things we read in the press or see on television about the nastiness between the teams. But in reality, when you get close to it, there isn't any."

Challis has been involved in the reality, the nuts and bolts of Formula 1, since 1958 when he went to work for BRM as an engineering apprentice. It seemed a natural thing to do since he lived in Bourne, Lincolnshire, where British Racing Motors was located. He later worked for Lotus, Shadow and Ensign before joining Frank Williams in 1980.

While he was with BRM Challis learned another reality of racing. He became very close to Mike Spence, and his death in 1968, during practice for the Indianapolis 500, affected Challis deeply. "After he was killed I said I'd never get really close to a driver again. Because I think you can get too attached. You have to stand back a little bit."

From where he stands now, Challis finds his perspective has changed over the years, as has the sport. "When you start, you're looking at it through rose-coloured glasses. I'm certainly not looking at it through rose-coloured glasses today. I can see the realism of it. It's a business now. It may be classified as a sport, and to the spectators it's a sport, but inside, there's no sport about it at all. It's all business."

Challis doesn't consider himself as a businessman, though he doesn't often get his hands dirty any more. He supervises those who do and describes his Chief Mechanic's role as providing the liaison between the mechanics and the engineers. His main job satisfaction comes from seeing two Williams cars take the chequered flag on Sunday afternoon. "From my side of the operation, I feel we've achieved our aim if both cars start the race and both finish the race without any mechanical problems. If we finish ninth or tenth it's not necessarily down to us."

PHILIP HAWKE

"You're in the pit lane, you stay in one position for up to two hours . . . You don't get to see the race until you fly back home and watch it the next day on the TV."

In 1990, Philip Hawke found himself in a similar position to that of Alan Challis 32 years earlier: in his first season as a Formula 1 mechanic. Now working under the supervision of Challis, Hawke served his apprenticeship in Sports 2000 and Formula 3 before working in sub-assembly at the Williams factory for three years.

"I'm really a fan of the sport. I don't know what it is about it, perhaps it's just the razzmatazz, or the noise. And Williams is one of the best teams to work for. I think it's a very professionally run team. We've got a good bunch of boys who seem to work well together. You have to get along because you spend a lot of time away together. I don't mind the travel, yet, though the long hauls are a bit of a bind.

"I look after the gearbox side and the brakes, mainly. The most exciting part of my work is during a pit stop. I put the wheel on the right front side. I'm a 'putteroner'. It's a matter of concentration, really. You've got the adrenalin going, but you must make sure you get it on the first time.

"Other than a pit stop, I suppose the race itself is one of the low points for us. Because we don't actually get to see a lot of the race. You're in the pit lane, you stay in one position for up to two hours. You're waiting because you never know when a car is going to come in. Maybe a nose to be changed or something, you don't know. You stand there, you can't move. But you have to be there. That's probably the worst bit. You don't get to see the race until you fly back home and watch it the next day on the TV."

GUSTAV BRUNNER

"These people are a little bit temperamental, a bit like artists in their own way. Stubborn, as well."

"Because we have the same travel agent, most of the teams fly together. And the competition starts in the airport, to see who gets the first seats on the plane: the front row, seats 1A and 1B."

Since he began in Formula 1 in 1978 Gustav Brunner's thirst for competition saw him travel to several different teams before he landed at Leyton House Racing, where he is now Race Operations Engineer. As an Austrian, from Graz, he was motivated by the exploits of Jochen Rindt to seek a career in racing. After graduating as a mechanical engineer he found employment in Germany as a junior designer with the McNamara company, which specialized in Formula Vee chassis.

"In those days, in the late '60s, it was more of a hobby sport. At that time motor racing, even in Formula 1, was less about design than it is today. In the last few years the design dreams have grown bigger with all this modern technology. I think it is for sure better now. It is not the driver alone any more these days. It is the teamwork that is important. Even on the engineering side, it is not one designer any more. One designer can achieve nothing without all the people and the team around him.

"With all the teams I have been with I think it is very good experience to see what is happening on the other side of the fence. The English teams still mainly lead the field because of their approach. The English are more cool, less emotional. This is important because I think the solutions are really more for technicians these days, less for the emotional and temperamental politicians.

"Of course, all racing people are ambitious people because even the man who swings the broom, or the last truck driver or mechanic, they are not only in there for the money. They are in love with what they are doing and I think they all have the ambition to do better. The name of the game is to do better and it is the same feeling for everybody. And these people are a little bit temperamental, a bit like artists in their own way. Stubborn, as well. I think you need these qualities. If they are not like this they would be in the wrong place. So they are not easy, for sure, but maybe that is what makes them special.

"Formula 1 has become very difficult for success. Really, if you look at the last few years it has been limited to a handful of drivers who won anything. The others haven't achieved anything. But, still, I think most of them, they haven't given up. They are still trying to beat the others. It maybe looks impossible at the moment, but everyday we improve and solve something and think it is an achievement. I think this is more satisfying. Because at the top you only can go down. At the moment I think this way. Maybe once I am with a team who wins everything, maybe that is also enjoyable, I don't know.

"It is so competitive, you have to be on the ball every day. I am as enthusiastic as I was in the beginning. But the thing is it is a stressful job. I don't think you can do it forever. And maybe once you are well over the 50s, you might have to look for something more quiet, or just stay at home."

TOMMASO CARLETTI

"At the finish of three days you are really tired. And during the race you are too nervous to be happy."

Now Race Operations Engineer for Minardi, Tommaso Carletti began in Formula 1 with Ferrari in 1981. He had studied engineering at the Polytechnic of Torino and the University of Pisa and decided that it was probably wiser for him to use this training along the pit lane than to compete out on the circuit. This was after racing many types of cars himself, none of them very fast, he says, though he managed to attain enough speed to have several accidents. But Carletti kept his competitive ambitions active by tackling the Paris–Dakar Rally three times, and he finished the London-to-Sydney Marathon.

Carletti finds the environment at Minardi rather less intimidating than at Maranello. "Here it has been easier than Ferrari because we are a little team. Ferrari is big. When I arrived at Ferrari I was without experience in Formula 1, so for me everything was new and difficult to understand. The first time I remember I was so frightened about the rapidity of the things.

"Still, for me, during the race is the most difficult time because you don't know what will happen. The car runs by the pits once, you don't know if the second time the car arrives. You wait, you know nothing. Sometimes it is slower, so maybe the car has trouble. You know nothing. You wait. Without the possibility to do anything.

"And every time that you see a driver start, you don't know if he will come back or not. I was with Villeneuve and Pironi at Ferrari. A very bad time. Now it is also difficult, especially when you have new cars and it is impossible to be reassured everything is good. Generally it is safe, but it is impossible to know. Sometimes the pilot does not arrive, maybe because he has broken the engine. But before you know if it is his engine, or other things, you are afraid.

"Yes, Minardi is more relaxed than Ferrari, but everybody is nervous during the race for the dangers, the problems. You have to be every time fast. And you try to be every moment better than before. Everybody's nervous. At the finish of three days you are really tired. And during the race you are too nervous to be happy."

STEVE NICHOLS

"If you screw up you know about it, if you do it right you know about it, immediately."

There are only a handful of Americans along the pit lane, among them Steve Nichols, who is in charge of the Ferrari technical operation at the races, as well as being involved in the team's research and development. He came to Ferrari after several successful years at McLaren. Nichols was born in Salt Lake City, Utah, and first became interested in Formula 1 in 1962 when he read about that season in *Car and Driver* magazine. Though he raced karts as a teenager, he was more interested in the technical side of the sport and resolved to somehow become involved in it. In 1972, after graduating in mechanical engineering from the University of Utah, he worked for Hercules, the aerospace company which later supplied carbon fibre for the McLaren chassis. Then he went to Gabriel, designing dampers for Indycars.

"I still remember sometimes being at Indy races on some weekends when there would be a Formula 1 race and it would be on television at the hotel, and I would be looking at it and thinking, that is where I have got to be. It has always held a huge fascination for me.

"I was attracted from the point of view that I was racing karts, so I liked the driving aspect, but also I liked the devices. I have always liked competition, and car racing to me was the best combination of interesting devices and sport. Many of the other sports, the classic stick and ball games, were too simplistic in terms of the equipment, whereas these cars that we have now are probably the most sophisticated sporting devices in the world. And I like this combination of the athleticism of the drivers and the sophistication of the devices that we use.

"In the early days Formula 1 always seemed the ultimate to me. The cars turned right and left and went up and down hills and this sort of thing. However, after I was involved in Indy for awhile, I gained a much greater respect for that type of racing. You hear Europeans say all they do at Indy is turn left and it is one type of corner, and so forth. Of course, when you are there you realize that there are subtle variations in all four corners, but there is a very high speed to the thing and with the wall there you have to get it absolutely right. You can't afford to have anything other than virtual perfection, and this is in some ways more difficult to do than what we do in Formula 1. We come to a different circuit every couple of weeks and encounter a lot of variations in corners. We have to do the best we can in a few hours of practice and we never get so close to perfection as they do at Indy. However, I still prefer the wider variety of problems and solutions we have here.

"Sometimes the political things in this sport become wearisome, but political astuteness is a big part of the job. There is a lot of money involved, there is a lot of manoeuvring going on and people with political skills do well. There is a lot of organization required and people with organizational skills do well. And people with entrepreneurial skills do well because of the amount of money that is required.

"It's a very competitive environment, but I don't think it is 100 per cent true about nice guys finishing last. You take Alain Prost, for example, he is about as nice a guy as you would want to meet. In addition to that he is one of the most competitive and one of the most skilled in his profession and he is very successful. He is just a hell of a nice guy, one of the least affected people that you can imagine. He doesn't act like a superstar at all, and yet he would have every right to be tainted by the superstar syndrome. I think you can be quite determined and quite skilful and do exactly the right job without actually being mean and nasty. You don't have to be a son of a bitch to succeed.

"I have said on many occasions that I can't really think of anything bad to say about Ayrton Senna. He is actually one of my truly favourite people in the world. Although they are very different people, I could say the same about Alain. Alain has a better press image, where he is perceived as quite a nice guy, whereas Ayrton isn't perceived so.

"Sometimes I think the press places too much emphasis on the personalities here. Most times I am more interested in the performance of the people, as opposed to their personalities. With a driver, for example, I don't care so much about his personality as long as he can do the job well, as long as he can drive quickly, as long as he can communicate with the engineers and so forth.

For many people, though, the *Dallas* syndrome exists and they want to know all about the soap opera sort of thing.

"I get along quite well with most of the journalists that I know. They have a job to do and many of them do their job quite well. It is, after all, a sort of entertainment business and they are the ones that are the communication link between what is going on here, for the few thousand who actually attend, and the rest of the millions who follow it in the press. In that respect it is a very important function. Generally I think they do quite a good job.

"Formula 1 is a continuous difficult challenge and I quite like that. I quite like a job where it matters if you do it right. If you screw up you know about it, if you do it right you know about it, immediately, which doesn't happen in many other jobs. This is the sort of job where if you make a mistake it can be extremely bad, but it is very stimulating and interesting when you get it right. I quite enjoy having the pressure on, as opposed to just sitting in an office and thinking, well, maybe I will finish this tomorrow. In that respect I quite like the activity in the pit lane, the tremendous pressure to get it right in the next hour and a half, or less.

"It is a bit like walking along the edge of a cliff, I suppose. I am a little bit afraid of heights, yet it is exciting and stimulating to look over the edge. And in the pit lane it is a little bit like walking along a cliff, with a great feeling of satisfaction at the end of the session when you have done well and you haven't fallen off the edge. Quite a high state of awareness and nervous energy are necessary to elevate your performance, tempered with a calm, rational approach. It is a good feeling.

"When I grew up in Utah I got used to seeing road signs that said, 'Salt Lake City – 20 miles', or something like that. Now it is fascinating for me to think, my God, London is just down the road, or Milan, or Monaco. I quite like Europe, where there are so many different cultures. It is very stimulating, though I tend to feel like a foreigner wherever I go. I have been away from America long enough that I tend to feel a little bit of a foreigner when I go back there, and I haven't been in England or Italy long enough to feel completely at home there. But I don't mind that, I like the feeling of being a foreigner. I have always liked travelling. It is a big world and there are a lot of interesting things in it."

ENRIQUE SCALABRONI

"The only theory I ever follow is to put myself always in a difficult situation, to prove to myself if I can solve the problem, or not. And until today, I am still alive from the fight."

Many Grand Prix people have overcome considerable obstacles and made sacrifices to be a part of the sport, among them Enrique Scalabroni. An Argentinian, he came first to Italy where he worked with Dallara on Formula 3 and Lancia Group C cars, then went into Formula 1 with Williams in 1985. When he was Chief Chassis Designer at Ferrari in 1990, he hadn't been home to see his family in eight years.

"I would like to go back every year, but the problem is it's too hard work and no time to go back. To go for a week is impossible. I need a minimum of one month. One month is impossible, there is too much work. And I am leaving it for the next year, next year, next year, and never come back. And I have no time to stop for thinking about old friends. So it is possible if I come back now nobody understands me and I understand no-one. When my father died in '86, my economic situation was very bad. I could not go and it was really bad for myself for three or four months. But I continued on. I dedicate my life to one thing, only one thing.

"When I came to Williams it was very difficult because my English, now is bad, before was worse. I was always completely alone, living in an old hotel in England. And it was very difficult to understand the engineer meetings. The same thing when I came to Italy for first time and I was not speaking Italian. I was learning every day, with a small dictionary, and trying to translate what was going on.

"I don't drive a car. I have no licence. I test for it two or three times, but never was interested to drive a car. Because I am not concentrating enough on all the problems in the traffic and all the other cars and things. I concentrate, every day, thinking about design solutions. When, if the car is winning races, that is better. But this is only for 24 hours. Tomorrow I am thinking about the next race. It's only for that day that you enjoy it.

"But I enjoy this life because it's mine and I am fighting to do what I want and that's the main thing to me. When I was very young I thought that it was possible to change all the world. But now I change only the things that are related with me. And I try to forget all the other things, because now I know it is not possible to be so theoretical about all problems in life. I solve problems in Formula 1, where you must solve problems to stay. The only theory I ever follow is to put myself always in a difficult situation, to prove to myself if I can solve the problem, or not. And until today, I am still alive from the fight."

BERNARD DUDOT

"It's very exciting in qualifying, and in the race, because you see exactly the picture of your work."

The sound of a Formula 1 engine is music to the ears of Bernard Dudot. As Chief Designer of the Renault V10 (and Field Manager of Renault Sport) he is partial to its sounds, but his music appreciation extends to competitors' melodies.

"The Lamborghini, for example, it's a typical 12-cylinder noise, like a Ferrari, but it's different. I like the '10' because it's more concentrated, a lower frequency. I prefer it and I believe I can hear the difference between the Honda and our engine, because the Honda is a lower frequency. From the beginning we can hear the difference. Now we are very close in noise."

Bernard Dudot was born in Nancy, France, and graduated from the highly respected CESTI Industrial Engineering College there. His mechanical engineering degree brought him work at Citroen for a year, but there was no competition involved and he grew restless. The siren song of racing engines had beckoned since he first heard them, at Reims, as a teenager. In 1967 he went to Dieppe, where he worked on the exceedingly raucous engines of the Renault Alpine sports cars.

By the end of his eight-year Alpine tenure Dudot was in charge of the engine department, where he was particularly proud of an experimental turbo motor. His interest in turbocharging took him to Garrett Research, in California, for a few months. He returned to France to work on Renault's Le Mans effort, which they won in 1978. But Dudot's first foray into Formula 1 was a year earlier, at the British Grand Prix, where the Renault turbo engine made its debut. It expired in a cloud of smoke and was ridiculed by many in its early days.

"But it was all new technology and we had to race to test. Everybody saw that we had some problems, and for Renault it took a lot of courage to do that. Soon it began to work and we did well (15 wins and 31 pole positions) before we stopped in 1986. In 1979 I was technical manager for the engines, but in 1980 I was technical manager for all the team. And I made the chassis, gearbox and engine when Renault had its own team. But, really, I am an engine engineer, and this is what I like best.

"At the races now I try to concentrate only on the engine. Because now we have all the information about how the engine is during the race, with the telemetry. And I have the possibility to check both engines and compare them. My race is before the computer monitor, but I also have a screen there to watch the race on television.

"Before that, I believe the most interesting time for me is just before practice. Because then we know exactly what we shall do and we shall work like real engineers. And we shall check that all our work is good, or not, and it's really an engineering time. It's very exciting in qualifying, and in the race, because you see exactly the picture of your work."

DICK SCAMMELL

"I think most people in Grand Prix racing have the attitude that very few things are impossible, so they always have a go at it."

Now Director of Racing at Cosworth Engineering, engine suppliers to many of the Formula 1 teams, Dick Scammell came into Grand Prix racing as a mechanic for Lotus over 30 years ago. "I saw it as a challenge and it offered all sorts of interesting things to do.

And for somebody who is young and hasn't made his mind up what he wants to do, it's a good introduction into the field of life.

"Racing forces you to do all sorts of things, though when you compare it to the racing now, it really was a sort of kindergarten then. We all struggled along as best we could and we didn't have the amenities of today. Now, it's far more professional and people tend to be far better organized and take everything they need to a race meeting. Whereas back in the beginning you took what you had, and then you went around to see if somebody else had what you hadn't got. The thing I liked about it then, and still do, is that you get instant success or failure for your work. It's not a long-term thing. You work hard, you get either a reward or a poke in the eye!

"I looked after Jimmy Clark's car for quite a few years and that was very rewarding because the man had a lot of talent, and it was nice to work with somebody like that. It gave you the urge to do the job well, because you knew he was always going to do *his* job well. You always had faith that when he went out there to race, he'd drive hard. And he obviously drove some cars in a state which it was totally unreasonable to still be driving them. But, still, he used to bring home the goods.

"Of course, the big day as far as Cosworth was concerned was June 4, 1967, when the Ford DFV engine made its debut. I was Chief Mechanic then for Lotus and looked after building the 49s, putting the engine in the cars, and so on. That was a big breakthrough because the engine was obviously in a different class. Graham Hill put one of our cars on pole, but didn't last because some teeth came off the timing gears, but Jimmy got the other one home and we won.

"It had been a real panic to even get there, to Zandvoort. I mean, we arrived late for it and it was a scrabble all the way because, in fact, we weren't ready, and it was all very fraught up to the time of racing. It was a sort of wonderful surprise. I don't think anybody thought it would happen, to race it the first time and win. Those are the moments in motor racing that you remember best.

"It had started when Colin Chapman asked Keith Duckworth at Cosworth to develop the engine, and then he went to Ford and got the funding. Colin was the man in the middle, and it cost Ford $100,000. For three years of racing with that engine. Imagine that compared to now. I can't even add the noughts. It must be several noughts plus a very big number in front of them. I mean, it's millions and millions these days to develop an engine.

"The Japanese are spending money that is just beyond total imagination for the rest of us. The last figure I heard was $450 million since they started their current Formula 1 programme. And Honda have in their racing department more people than we've got on our entire site at Cosworth in Northampton. They've got 400 people or something like it, while we've got about 350. And that's for all our racing activities, Formula 1, Indycars, Formula 3000 and so on.

"I think our DFR fundamentally is still quite a good engine. The only trouble is its concept is 25 years old and everybody *looks* at it a little as if it's 25 years old. But if you compare the engine now with the original, it looks approximately the same, but I don't think there's anything that's interchangeable. And with engines, it's not all to do with the ultimate power or anything like that. It's to do with all the systems and everything else that goes with it.

"And of course to win, it's not just the engine. This is the trouble. Even the best engine can't make a bad car into a good one. And the drivers, the good ones, might be worth a second, even two seconds, a lap. Because, for instance, Senna's nearly always a second quicker than anybody else in qualifying. In terms of overall performance, between driver, chassis and tyres, and engine, it's probably a third each.

"Though I'm not really a designer, what I can say is that along the way I've picked up quite a bit of the practical commonsense side of engineering from having worked for a long time with cars and engines. At the races I try to make sure we are approaching it in the right way, because at a race meeting you are not into the details. So, it's more to see if our people are operating in a fashion that I think is good and meticulous, so that they will not be making mistakes. I try to be observant, and when I walk down the pit lane I always look at what the other people are doing because there's always something there which you can learn. I think you should look closely because there might be something there that triggers off some idea in your mind. Then you go home and think about it. You're always trying to improve.

"I think most people in Grand Prix racing have the attitude that very few things are impossible, so they always have a go at it. There's a single-minded sort of drive towards it and they really do want to get things done and try and get them done well. They apply themselves to it and have great enthusiasm for it. That single-mindedness can have a bit of a downside on occasions when some of them get too blinkered, and therefore become fairly uninteresting people because they really only have one thing in their life."

LEE CARDUCCI

"You read a lot about the big egos in Formula 1. But a lot of that's just drummed up because everybody hates someone who wins a lot."

According to FISA, approximately half the world's population sees Formula 1 racing on television. While Lee Carducci considers himself extremely fortunate to be able to attend the races in person, he too is glued to the small screen, monitoring the performance of the Lamborghini engines in the Lotus and Larrousse teams. A mechanical engineer from the USA, Carducci has fulfilled a boyhood dream to work for 'Engineer Forgery'.

His parents were born in Italy, and when the family visited there in the summer of 1970, little Lee Carducci was so impressed with the new Ferrari Boxer road car that he decided he just had to someday work for Mauro Forghieri, the man who designed it. "I called him Engineer Forgery at the time. Then, when I was working for the Chrysler-Maserati programme, Chrysler bought Lamborghini and Mauro Forghieri came to me in 1988 and asked me if I wanted to be part of his team. I was one of the first seven people at Lamborghini Engineering. Now I'm responsible for all the electronics in the Lamborghini Formula 1 race programme and all the telemetry acquisition at the race tracks.

"It's tremendously exhilarating. You get a real rise, especially when you go to places like Italy or Brazil. And you come out to the circuit at 6 o'clock in the morning and you open the garage front door and you start the engine, and there's 60,000 people going wild! That's what you're doing it for. The other thing is, when you're an engineer, you can make changes and see it right away. And you're working with the forefront of technology. When you're doing something else like a production car or a sports car, you don't see that movement for three to five years. Here, you get immediate feedback.

"We have our own little society here. You know everybody up and down the pit lane, and you get to know the drivers, the managers, the engineers, the designers. And you look at someone like Derek Warwick, who's had a lot of experience. He's basically a clown out there. But all the drivers are great guys, and it's fun to work with them. And everybody's after the same goal. Everybody's out there to win, to put on the show, to do everything to their best.

"The atmosphere of competition is just incredible up and down the pit lane. And the thing about it is, everybody talks about how secretive things are, but I can walk up to the Ferrari pit and talk to my friends there, and talk to my friends at Benetton, and everybody's saying: 'We tried this new programme, or we tried this or that'. Sure there are secrets, but it's open to a point. Not like you'd see in CART racing. There, they come into the box and they throw blankets over the car. You don't see that here, everybody's talking to everybody, the cars are open.

"You read a lot about the big egos in Formula 1. But a lot of that's just drummed up because everybody hates someone who wins a lot. The press writes about prima donnas – but inside here you don't really have prima donnas. People complain Dennis is too into himself, and things like that, but the first time we raced with our engine, Ron Dennis came down and congratulated us on finishing. That's just an example. You read what's written about them and you hear what's written about them, and you see them in the pits and they're entirely different."

Carducci also finds 'Forgery' somewhat different than he imagined. "You see, he's very charming on TV, very charismatic, but when he gets you into his office working he's really tough on you. But he tries to drive the best out of you and I think that's what's fantastic about him. It's amazing what he can do. One weekend he went out and did a rough sketch of a gearbox because he didn't like the gearboxes that were available on the market, and the guy is just incredible!"

MAURO FORGHIERI

"We are forced to have a quicker life. We don't choose the life, the life chooses us. It is upside-down."

"A madman, but also a genius," was how Niki Lauda described Mauro Forghieri, who designed the cars and engines and ran the Ferrari team when Lauda was there. Forghieri was born in 1935 and went to Ferrari shortly after getting his engineering degree from the University of Bologna. He took over the Prancing Horse racing department in 1961 and stayed there nearly 30 years. Now the designer of Lamborghini's Formula 1 engines, Mauro Forghieri has a love-hate relationship with his life's work.

"Yes, I was fighting sometimes with Niki Lauda. I was his boss, so he had to follow what I am saying to him. Usually, it's difficult that a boss be loved by the people who work for him. But Niki is also a friend now. And he can tell you that he had a lot of results with us. Because he won two World Championships and almost a third one. He learned to race in Ferrari, he learned to work on a car in Ferrari. Maybe I was learning from him also.

"I put 28 years of my life in Ferrari, you know. I think there is a little bit of it still inside myself. I was involved in 55 of the victories they had. But, for me, Ferrari's the past already. It is a nice story, a nice memory. Me with Ferrari. Sometimes bitter, sometimes sweet.

"After 30 years in this sport, it's much too long. Yes, I am enthusiastic about the work, but not about the environment. Too much business I don't like. We are always fighting to have enough passes for the mechanics. Can you imagine this? We don't have enough passes to come to work. I buy the other day a pass to come here, to park the car in the paddock! Yes, me! But when I travel around the paddock I see everywhere there's cars and people that have nothing to do with racing. I don't know how they get them. I don't want to know. But I am disgusted about that. My voice doesn't count. It's like a voice in the desert. But I think that something is going very wrong with racing. Especially Formula 1.

"When you are working in Formula 1 you work because of enthusiasm, not because of money. You work for the racing. Now I am manager of the engine and gearboxes, not all the car. We are less involved with the racing, unfortunately. We cannot influence the team. It is less stressing today, but, of course, I would prefer to have our own team. I miss the racing. But maybe it's time also for me to miss some races.

"I design not only engines. Sometimes for my wife I design jewellery. I design many other things, for furniture, for houses. I like to make drawings of many kinds of things. Even when I was young I was designing and making projects of different things, not only of racing cars. The furniture I design is modern. Today you cannot design traditional. Nobody is interested in it. I like the traditional. My house is a 17th century villa close to Modena. I restored my house completely with much original art.

"I like very much indeed paintings. When I travel around the world I try to visit all the museums I can. I collect some paintings, of course not Raphael or Michelangelo, but some good paintings of the 16th century. I like the Italian painters, and others too. Rembrandt is a favourite, and Breugels. Also I like very much the impressionists. I have a good painting by an impressionist that cost a lot of money.

"But when I am picking something for my house it is not because it cost a lot of money. I take it in my house because I like art. Anything can be art, a photo, a Lamborghini engine. Everything that is born with mathematics and human hands usually can be art. When I say artists use mathematics it doesn't mean they have been at university. When they are choosing a certain sequence of colour, or writing in music, they are using a skill. And this is mathematical order. So, sometimes, the natural feeling of a man is much higher than what you can find from study. Don't forget, Einstein, he didn't find his intelligence because he was studying in the school. He was a genius, by himself.

"Art and engineering are very close. Michelangelo was an engineer. When you paint the Chapela Sistina, you can't be only a painter. You must have knowledge of everything. Chemistry, engineering, and so on. And when you study the composition of a painting, you must have a deep feeling of what is construction.

"Anyway, in racing, when I tell you that I am preferring the olden days it is because I was very young then. Now I'm old. I honestly have to say that the present days are better, especially because mechanics work less. The life is easier now. But from a human point of view, for human relationships, and human feeling, the past days were much better. It was much easier to be in contact with the other people. Today you see motorhomes, closed sections, closed pits. Everybody has his own life without any contact with the other. That's bad in my opinion. But sponsorship and the kind of racing that you have today, which is much too expensive in my opinion, forces people to be like that.

"The people are accustomed to have different lives. They are forced into a different life. In the past we have seven, 10 Grands Prix per year. And maybe a few tests. Now we have a race or test every weekend, at least every weekend. And so we are forced to have a quicker life. We don't choose the life, the life chooses us. It is upside-down.

"People in racing, often they have family problems, because they travel too much. They have no time for human relationships, they cannot have a normal life. They don't know what it means Sunday, Saturday and Friday. Some people, inside and outside Formula 1, come here because what television and newspapers are saying about racing. Inside is nothing special. There's a lot of work to do. But the people of today enjoy to believe it is possible for everybody to win. To be like the star. Like Prost. Or like the star in the movies, or the star in golf, or in tennis. Everybody sees himself in the place of the star. I believe this is so. The fans believe it too. Otherwise, I cannot explain why people are staying outside of the fence watching three hours inside the paddock.

"Honestly, sometimes I don't have much pleasure to be here. I told you that the life takes us. We are not in charge. All my life I was involved more deeper and deeper in racing. And, you know, I have tried twice in my life to say, 'Stop'. When I say, 'No more Ferrari', I go away. I try to change my life. Because I have my own life, I have three sons and a family and I need money to live. And then the people come to me again and want to pay me for what

I am able to do. And so I've been forced to be back again. And sometimes, when I was away from it, I missed racing. So I enjoyed to be back. It's the same story, always up and down."

IAN PHILLIPS

"As a journalist I quickly got bored with racing drivers and their bullshit answers."

There is a body of opinion within the pit area of Formula 1 which views the representatives of the media as little more than an irritant, whose presence becomes a time-wasting intrusion on their own preoccupation with trying to win races.

For the people in the pressroom, therefore, there is considerable sense of satisfaction when one of their number is invited to abandon the pen, typewriter or word processor in order to take up a senior position with one of the teams. It is a recognition that those whose job is primarily to observe, question and report may even actually understand what it is all about. Yet for those who do make the transition, and over the years there have been several of them, life on the inside of a team can be full of surprises.

Ian Phillips, who left the pressroom to become Managing Director of the Leyton House Racing team, now realizes that journalists, who often think they get the inside news as quickly as it happens, are instead something like a month behind the times. In fact, Phillips has discovered a whole new world along the pit lane and in the paddock that he never knew existed, despite being intimately involved with the sport from a very early age.

"The thing that was very, very different for me is the emotion that's involved. Because as a journalist you go to a race and it doesn't bother you when someone loses. You may have friends amongst the people there, but at the end of the day you just write your race report – and so and so won – and that's all. To suddenly be pitched into an area where you only care about two cars, two drivers, and the highs and lows of that, I found to be an incredible emotional strain because you feel so deeply for the guys involved in doing the job, everybody on the team as well as the drivers themselves.

"When I was four I was taken to Silverstone by my father, who was an avid fan and chief flag marshal at one of the corners. That was in 1955, and I don't suppose I really knew what was going on. I do know that I saw Stirling Moss and Fangio, and then I was taken to every race weekend up to the age of about 11 or 12. I thought football was much more fun, or cricket, and all sorts of things that I could actually compete in. But when it came around to thinking about a career I suppose I was thinking about motorsport. In school, where I was supposedly studying for my Classics A Level but reading 'the bible' – *Autosport* – instead, I saw a little advert in there asking for a motorcycle messenger boy. I applied for the job and somehow I got it. I was 18 and I started three days after I left school in July 1969. That's how it all began.

"At the magazine one day there was nobody to cover a little MG Car Club meeting. 'Right, I'll go.' From that moment on, until I started at March (now Leyton House) in January 1987, there can't have been many weekends when I wasn't actually at a race, writing a race report. I had no aspirations then to become involved with a team. And to be honest, I never even really thought about being a journalist. I just went off and did all the race reports and nobody at *Autosport* ever said anything, whether it was good or bad. By mid-1973 I was editor of the thing. To this day, I don't know why. I stayed at that until the middle of 1976.

"Then I was feeling a bit deskbound and at the age of 25 I didn't think I wanted to be at a desk for the rest of my life. So I went to help Tom Wheatcroft finish building and opening the Donington circuit. I was Managing Director there for 18 months, then realized that I missed the buzz of London. So I went back to London and was a freelance journalist from then on, doing a lot of writing, but I also got involved in other things to do with motorsport.

"I ran the Gunnar Nilsson Cancer Campaign. Most of 1978 was spent with Gunnar, who was a good friend and lived at my house in London earlier in his racing career. I was taking him to and from hospital for his treatments, two and three times a day sometimes, just being at his beck and call. And then, when he died, I was asked to run the campaign to raise funds for research, which went on for about 18 months.

"But I missed the racing side a lot and went back to reporting on a regular basis, mainly on Formula 3000 racing. At the same time I was doing a lot of below-the-belt promotions, like press releases and so on, for financial reasons. Nobody was paying enough money for straight journalism and it was the only way to live.

"One of the companies that I was involved with was March. I did brochures and press releases for them. And in 1986 I spent about seven months in Japan, working for Philip Morris, who were sponsoring a car in the Japanese Formula 2 Championship. Obviously I had got to know Ivan Capelli when he was winning the European 3000 Championship and then he came over to Japan to drive for Leyton House. I was with him the weekend when he got the money from Leyton House to go into Formula 1.

"Then March turned around to me and said, 'Can you help us put a Formula 1 team together?' And, you know, the risk was theirs, not mine, to be honest. In the space of a year, I could lose everything they had got, whereas I could pick up a typewriter and carry on where I had left off. Anyway, it worked out, and very soon I was aware that I didn't know anywhere near as much as I thought I did as a journalist.

"Formula 1 is sometimes a frighteningly competitive arena. It requires complete application seven days a week, 24 hours a day. I mean, you can forget being involved in anything else in life, having any other interests whatsoever. You have got to be just totally geared to this task. The will to win, the absolute need for it. We are not interested in racking up the numbers. We don't want to go Grand Prix racing just to be there. We're all driven on by an incredibly competitive spirit. We want to win. Nothing else will do. When it doesn't happen, the bitter disappointment felt by everybody is enormous. But on the other hand, it's the spur to get it right.

"Then there are the journalists. I find the approach of the majority of the English journalists a little bit strange in that if you're not doing well you never see them. They are only interested in the top half of the grid, the people who are actually fighting for the lead. These days, the facts don't seem to come into it too much, either. I was brought up as a journalist to go to a club meeting at Castle Combe or somewhere at a weekend, where there might be 190 competitors. Well, you almost had to come back with a quote from every single one. It's the principle that people like to see their name in print and therefore, as a club reporter, you would mention as many people as you possibly could. Well, I carried that through with me as a journalist, all the time. Whatever it was I was reporting, I would want to talk to every single person involved. And I find it very strange that in Formula 1 that doesn't exist at all.

"These days I find it absolutely astonishing that at the end of every session we have to put out a press release saying what we have done. If you don't, there's a chance you would get no mention at all. And, really, there's only 30 cars and they've got three days in which to talk to everybody. But the journalists are totally spoiled. Everything has to be done for them. It's fine that we write the press release and they don't even bother to rewrite it half the time. But it offends me to think that people don't want to know what the real story behind it is. Because what we put in there is often complete and utter bullshit!

"I think I would love to have been served by the PR industry as a journalist. It makes life so easy. But they are not getting the real story. There is a lot more in what's going on behind the scenes with the bottom 10 teams than there is with the top six. Okay, everybody wants to read about Ferrari and Nigel Mansell and McLaren and Senna. But where do all the stars come from – the drivers, the engineers, the team personnel – where do they find their feet? They don't go straight into the top jobs. There's a lot of talent down there which is going to emerge over a period of five years or so, and that was always my interest. As a journalist I found that stimulating. It was nice to know these people in their infancy, to see them make their mark.

"I don't think any journalist, unless they have worked within a team environment, can ever appreciate the level of effort that is required. And how widespread the industry is. All they see is a team along the pit lane and they are probably only interested in the two drivers who are sitting in the cars and maybe one or two key personnel. But behind that, there are anything from 60 to 160 people or more directly involved, and then a massive industry backing them. It's fascinating and very stimulating, yet no-one writes about it.

"As a journalist I quickly got bored with racing drivers and their bullshit answers. Quite early on in the game I found I would get a far better understanding and perspective of the sport by talking to engineers, race mechanics, people involved with the teams who would always give you the true story. I don't say I had a disregard for drivers, but I would be very careful in believing what they actually said.

"Yet they can play a very significant role. And the successful ones do so because they integrate into the entire operation. At the end of the day they are the ones to whom everybody is looking to produce the success. Their attitude to everybody in the factory, everybody that works on the cars, is so very important. They have to relate to people as well as performing their full duty in the car. This includes being able to relate correctly what's happening to the engineers and then getting out and racing the thing as hard as they damn well can.

"So their job, to my mind, is an awful lot more than just bolting them in their car. I think they can contribute enormously. These days, obviously, none of us would be on the grid without the sponsorship that we get. It is a very important aspect of it, because without those people's support we can't go racing. It's as simple as that. You cannot go motor racing now just as an engineering company, because that's what you want to do. And the drivers have to respect and co-operate in the commercial areas. They've got to do it, go and shake people's hands or stand like a stuffed dummy in front of 200 disinterested guests on a Sunday morning.

"There is so much more to this job than just the racing. We've got 130 people. We've got mouths to feed, mortgages to pay, and so on. And that has to be my prime responsibility, making sure the company itself is run correctly. The pressure to produce and to be successful is intense, and there are so many areas that need careful attention that more than one person is required in each of those key areas. Otherwise, an individual, working alone and lacking the time and the space in which to operate efficiently and develop his own particular skills can get burned out very quickly. It's part of my job to keep everyone motivated. And that means having the right people to feed off each other. By working together, they reduce the individual pressure. Deep in my heart I would love to say this is still a sport, but the commercial pressures are such that it is very, very difficult to give any kind of priority to the sporting aspect of it.

"At the race there is a satisfaction in seeing the team at work and achieving something, because it probably means that you've got most of the elements back at base correct. It's an inner satisfaction, obviously, and you're very pleased for everybody that's involved. On a personal level, I get an intense attack of butterflies and I'm very nervous at the start of a race. Because, you know, there are two guys who you are very, very close to strapped into your cars. I guess I haven't really 'seen' a race since the start of the 1987 season. I can't relax enough to be able to take an overview on what's happening in the rest of the race.

"If our guys drop out or something happens to them, the feeling of disappointment both for them and everybody else involved is, to me, very intense and I'm not really interested in anything else. It probably takes me an hour or so to actually be bothered to find out what's happened to everybody else. Right now I can't envisage the sort of high that an actual race win will bring and I know that I can't wait for it to happen. But I certainly know the depths of despair you can get into as far as failures is concerned. Every time our cars go out onto the grid, for me it's very much an elementary lump in the throat feeling."

TONY RUDD

"You must be able to see yourself and laugh at yourself as well. Otherwise you get pompous, and there's nothing quite like motor racing for deflating egos."

A.C. 'Tony' Rudd, Executive Chairman of Team Lotus during much of 1990, looks to be in perfect health, but thinks his obsession with racing is like an incurable ailment. "It's a disease, really. You have some flaw in your makeup that attracts you to it. Once you've got it, you can never be cured. You have this thrill, or feeling for speed, and in my case this desire for the ultimate."

Obviously his affliction is not terribly debilitating since Rudd was first infected by it in 1936. It was then that he announced to his parents his intention of becoming an RAF pilot. They were horrified, and in order to distract him they introduced him to a family friend, the Siamese, Prince Chula, whose White Mouse Stable team ran the ERA racing cars for Prince Bira. The young Rudd spent his summer holidays with the royal racers and very soon decided the more earthly pursuits embodied in racing cars would be an entirely adequate substitute for flying.

But fate, in the form of World War Two, intervened to give Rudd his chance in the air. He became an RAF pilot after all, serving in Bomber Command and surviving no less than 27 missions over Europe. From the cockpit of his Lancaster bomber Rudd got a bird's-eye view of much of the world where he would later engage in Grand Prix conflicts.

He became an engineering apprentice with Rolls-Royce, earned his BSc Eng, and worked on the development of aircraft engines for civil airlines. During this time Rudd kept his hand in motor racing by competing in British club races in his Aston Martin. When his employer proposed that Rudd go to BRM to oversee the installation of Rolls-Royce superchargers on the racing team's engines Rudd was only too happy to oblige. That was in 1951, and by 1962 he was Chief Engineer and Team Manager at BRM.

In 1969, Rudd was hired by Colin Chapman to make Lotus an engine manufacturer, though his duties quickly expanded to encompass work in all facets of the Lotus racing and production car divisions. Twenty years on, Tony Rudd had become Technical Director of Group Lotus, Deputy Chairman of Lotus Engineering and Director of Lotus Cars and Millbrook Proving Ground, sitting happily in boardrooms as these responsibilities required, but really coming to life on Grand Prix weekends.

For some time he didn't go to the races, but when he returned during 1989 it was soon clear he was glad to be back. "People say I look 10 years younger. I suppose I'm as enthusiastic as I ever was. Either that or I'm particularly mad because I still enjoy it. I'm past retiring age, so I don't have to do it if I don't want to.

"I enjoy the competition of qualifying, getting the car to go a bit faster than somebody else's, yes. But there's really no sensation to beat your car winning the race. It doesn't happen very often, but you know, it's a wonderful sensation when it does.

"The low point of the weekend for me is just before the race, the half hour after the pit road opens. The car's ready, you give it to the driver, and it's his. There isn't any more you can do to it. It's out of your control. But he hasn't taken over yet. It's all in limbo. I hate that bit."

Being intimately acquainted with the realities of war, Rudd doesn't see many parallels between them and the hostilities along the pit lane. "In my version of the war you never saw the enemy. You knew who they were, but you never saw them. You'd look over the side of the aeroplane sometimes and see a few flashes, rock a bit, and you'd realize that they weren't very keen on what you were doing to them, and they were shooting at you, but it's not like racing.

"Of course, in motor racing in my early days, you were really quite good friends with your rivals. I got on very well with Colin Chapman in my BRM days. Jack Brabham is often at the races now and we reminisce about the old days. But I made a sort of little promise to myself years ago that I'd never say it's not as good now as it was in my day. I heard people say in the '50s and '60s that it wasn't as good as it was prewar, when it was a sport for gentlemen amateurs. And I vowed I'd never say that. But sometimes I have a bit of a job not to do it!

"Nowadays, there's a bit of he who has the most money has the best chance. But it's quite surprising that some of the principles that worked 50 years ago, 25 years ago, still work now. There's no such thing as luck, and if you start getting it a bit wrong, you're vulnerable, then it all goes wrong on you. If you make one mistake, then the heavens fall in on you. And it's not bad luck, it's because your organization is not quite strong enough.

"In this business you've got to have a good knowledge of human nature and understand people, what makes drivers tick, what makes engineers tick, and so on. For me, anyway, you need to have an engineering instinct as distinct from an engineering knowledge. It's a case of making quick, split-second decisions that are going to be with you for months. And having the nerve to make them, rather than agonize over it. Because no decision is the wrong decision. Sometimes it may be wrong, but it's better to have made it, and live with it, than not make one. I suppose a sense of humour helps. You must be able to see yourself and laugh at yourself as well. Otherwise you get pompous, and there's nothing quite like motor racing for deflating egos.

"I think if you've been on top, and sunk, and come back again, you come back with a lot of humility and so on. Ferrari have been up and down. I can't say that humility applied to Old Man Ferrari, but he did at least understand what it was like to be down and how to fight back up again. It does deflate people, and eventually it comes to everybody. Things go wrong, you have a bad spell. I can think of some people here who are getting a bit pompous who will eventually get deflated."

When that happens Tony Rudd will probably read about it and smile wryly as he lounges on the desk of his boat in the Mediterranean, or perhaps the Caribbean. The water has long been his other great passion in life, and late in 1990, after deciding that perhaps it was time to enjoy rather more of it, he planned his withdrawal from motor racing for the second time. Had he finally been cured? Don't bank on it!

RUPERT MANWARING

"If you're not winning at the moment, you can't give up. You just duck and dive and scheme and wheel and deal until you do win."

Rupert Manwaring, Team Manager of Lotus, explains what it takes to build a winning team . . .

"If you go to a team and it's a shambles, the first thing you have to do is whip it into shape and get it operating properly. And once you've done that, the next thing you have to do is to win. And as soon as you've won one race, the next goal can only be to win the World Championship. It's as simple as that. And then, when you've won a World Championship, the driving force is to do it again immediately, to show that you're the best and that it wasn't a fluke. So the driving force is just to be better than anybody else.

"And if you're not winning at the moment, you can't give up. You just duck and dive and scheme and wheel and deal until you do win. The only way you can win is by having the best sponsor, the best engine, the best car, the best driver and the best engineers, all at the same time. And they all have to come together. Then you have a good team."

Manwaring, always "mad keen" on motor racing, once had racing driver aspirations himself. He showed a fair turn of speed, but also a propensity for shunts, so he decided to investigate other ways of being close to racing cars.

"I started off with Team Surtees. I was studying engineering at university and worked there during my holidays, just because I lived near the factory. And when I left university I didn't know what I wanted to do, so I ended up working at Surtees as a draughtsman. I thought I'd do it for a year, just for some fun, and then I'd get a proper job.

"After about three months the guy who was organizing the spares and equipment left. It was a chance to travel, and I was only 21, so of course you go for it. Did that for the rest of the year, thoroughly enjoyed it. Did that for a second year and I was made Assistant Team Manager. Just organized all sorts of things – hotels, cars, customs things, spares and equipment, by which time I was well and truly hooked.

"One of our drivers was Vittorio Brambilla, the 'Monza Gorilla'. A fantastic bloke, really. But you did need lots of spares! The team wasn't doing so well, didn't really have any money, and John Surtees was a difficult guy to work for. But I learned a lot, I learned how to go motor racing with no money, which was good training.

"Anyway, I was approached by Brabham and went to work for them in '79, about the same time that Piquet started, so the team's drivers when I started were Lauda and Piquet. I was a sort of spares co-ordinator, which really meant organizing all the spares and equipment. Did that for about three years, then I also did all the buying, kept track of production in the factory, that sort of thing. All the things linked with procuring parts, organizing things. Then, after another year or so there, I was made Assistant Team Manager, which just meant I did even more things and got a bit more recognition.

"Eventually, in 1984, I was made Team Manager, but there was still Herbie Blash and Bernie Ecclestone above me, whom I found very good to work for. When you work for Bernie you are really one of 'Bernie's Boys' and he always treated us very well. He's a very hard man, very difficult to negotiate with, but he's very shrewd and commands a lot of respect. Also, it was a pleasure to work for Gordon Murray. He was brilliant, very calm, very logical. I learned a lot from Bernie Ecclestone, Gordon Murray and Herbie Blash. And working with Nelson through his great years was a privilege, really.

"I left Brabham at the end of '84 because I had been there seven years and thought I really needed to do something else. I went to work for Kraco, the Indycar team. We set up a workshop in Surrey, though the team was based in California. I did five or six Indy races that year, then realized quickly that I needed to get back into Formula 1.

"I was frustrated by the way that Indy teams operate. By that I mean they basically buy a works March or Lola, and I just couldn't handle running a car that you hadn't designed and constantly developed. And it wasn't really run like a Formula 1 team. It was run a bit more like a club team, and I just could not handle not doing things properly. I'm more practical and quite good at getting the priorities right, but I just didn't like the way the teams operated. Also, I found dealing with the American team manager particularly difficult. Basically I didn't agree with lots of things.

"So after nine months of that I managed to get a job with the newly formed FORCE, the Beatrice Haas team, as Assistant Team Manager to Tyler Alexander, another American, whom I got along with very well. I have a lot of time for Tyler Alexander. He's very, very experienced and very capable. And it was a big project, a whole new factory and new people. The people needed the experience I had, which was nice, and it was coming along OK. It just unfortunately got a bit political at the very top, then Beatrice pulled out and the whole thing collapsed. It was coming good, we had some very good people, fantastic facilities, and that was a crying shame. I spent a month closing the factory down and it was most unpleasant. I think I wished I'd left straight away. It was all very sad.

"When the writing was on the wall for the last couple of races at Haas I did the usual thing of hunting around and trying to sort out the best place to go. For someone like myself there are only about six jobs down the pit lane and you have to find a job available and then decide whether the team is on the way up or on the way down.

"I contacted Peter Warr and got a job at Lotus as his assistant. The team was expanding, they'd just changed from JPS to Camel sponsorship, and they had Ayrton Senna and Honda engines. So I started there and basically did all the things that Peter didn't want to do, didn't have the time to do. All the nitty gritty organizing, and it was good. I learned a lot from Peter Warr, he has fantastic experience. And working with Senna was definitely special.

"If you've worked with Senna and you're not involved with the press or whatever he's fine. I guess I have stronger feelings towards Piquet, because at Brabham we won two World Championships and I worked with him for seven years. We always got on particularly well together. But also, working with Senna was a pleasure. He's a complete professional, totally dedicated, and you know that nobody can drive faster in your car than he can, and that makes the team feel that all the effort is not wasted.

"When Peter Warr left I became Lotus Team Manager. My duties are mainly concerned with the business of going racing and operating the racing team. The company is split into two main parts: the people that travel, and all that goes along with that, and the people who are permanently based in the factory and manufacture the cars. My job, primarily, is to choose and look after the drivers, keep them and the team motivated, look after all the testing and decide where we go. I look after the business side of the actual motor racing. I don't do it alone, of course; I talk to Frank Dernie, the Technical Director, the engineers and our commercial people, and it's always sort of a joint effort, leading to a commonsense decision based on the facts that lay before you.

"I realize Lotus does have a very special history, and it's something that you should never throw away. But having said that it's also not something you can rely on. And I think Lotus are very vulnerable to be criticized heavily when they do badly because of their great past. So it's a mixed blessing, but the past is always there and we need to make sure that we do it all justice.

"Part of my job is to keep team morale high. My background is comprehensive and I spent a lot of years working with the mechanics so I can relate very closely to what they have to do. And I think I can judge when somebody's slacking and when they're not. Sometimes you have to be hard, and sometimes you can have a laugh and a joke. So it's sort of a commonsense combination. I try to lead by example and not by dictating.

"A lot of the jobs that I tell people to do I've done myself before, and they know that. I'm quite good at listening and I'm prepared to listen and give people quite a bit of rope and see how they get on. I don't believe you can't have a good time and still be a complete professional and do the job properly. But whenever anybody here oversteps the mark I let them know straight away – too jokey, not enough sleep, too much drink the night before, late, slack, anything like that. There's a line. You can do what you do in the evening, you know, as long as you turn up on time, you're smart, you're clearly not tired and do the job properly. If anybody goes too far you just let them do it once and then: crap all over the place!

"Speaking to the press, I adopt a policy whereby I'll be more or less completely straight with them until they prove that they can't be trusted. So far the relationships I have with some of the journalists are very good. And so far they've played it straight with me, so I'm prepared to give them some time. I understand the importance of their job and I try and work with them. So far I haven't come unstuck.

"In this business, in Formula 1 in general, you do get people who by some miracle got themselves in a position that they really shouldn't be in, but they don't last very long. I guess a lot of people want to get into the sport, but it spits the poseurs out the side quite quickly. Basically, there's no room in Formula 1 for incompetence. But on the whole, I have a lot of good friends here, team people that I can trust, and call on for favours, and they can do the same with me. It's quite a healthy situation.

"The attractions for me in Formula 1 are that I'm doing something which is interesting, it's demanding, it's quite good fun, there's a lot of travelling involved, and you meet hundreds of people. Once you start travelling it does become a drug, even if you don't realize it; it's just a nice thing to do and a nice way to earn a living.

"I suppose the worst thing is the amount of time you spend working, and the amount of time you don't spend at home. I have a wife and a four-year-old son. Fortunately, my wife has only ever known me whilst I've been travelling, so she has got used to it. And the important thing is that when you're back, you give them the fullest attention. So your life, your relationship, goes through a series of highs and lows. You're away for a long time, you come back, everything's fantastic, then you leave again. So you don't get bored with each other. It wouldn't work for everybody, but it does for us.

"This is a job that you get completely involved in, and that's always got to be the healthiest thing. Plus there's this massive challenge that you're always chipping away at."

HERBIE BLASH

"A lot of teams are very unhappy. But happy teams can win."

His real name is Michael, but no-one has called Herbie Blash any such thing since he was a schoolboy. "I used to do very silly things, and Herbert, in those days, was used as a term for people like that: 'Oh, he's a right Herbert!' And of course the worst thing I could have said was, 'Don't ever call me that'. So that was it, the nickname Herbie stuck."

Now listed as the Commercial and Marketing Director of Brabham, Herbie has been in Formula 1 all his working life, beginning with a job as an apprentice mechanic for Rob Walker. His first duties were to wash the Walker team's Lotus cars for the likes of Jo Siffert and Jo Bonnier. Meanwhile, Herbie attended college and studied mechanical engineering, cramming a seven-year course into four and a half years. He must have been a brilliant student.

"No, I was desperate! With Rob Walker, you bought a car and you just ran it. I wanted to become more involved in the building of cars and to understand it a lot more. I was very fortunate that I went straight on to the Lotus Formula 1 team as a mechanic, with Jochen Rindt and Graham Hill in '69 and '70."

At Lotus, Herbie came to know Rindt's manager Bernie Ecclestone. "After the death of Jochen, Bernie did an awful lot of work to sort it out and I helped him in some ways and we became close. When Bernie wanted to buy Brabham I checked out the quality of the bits and pieces for him beforehand. Then I started on the Monday morning when Bernie took over, had a disagreement with Ron Tauranac, and I left after four hours!"

Blash worked with Frank Williams for a while, returned to Brabham when Tauranac left and, apart from a sojourn with FOCA when Brabham wasn't racing, he's been a Brabham man ever since. Part of the attraction is the special atmosphere of the team.

"Every team has a different character to it. Very different. I think our team has always been very hard-working, which every team has to be, and it's very dedicated. But it's also a very happy team. I just hope it remains that way, because a lot of teams are very unhappy. But happy teams can win. We've won two World Championships. Part of my job is to make sure that we keep on as we've always done, which is in a lighthearted but very serious manner."

In keeping with that philosophy, Blash describes the most exciting part of his Grand Prix weekend as, "When I go home! But seriously, the start of the race is to me still the most exciting. And the most frightening as well. But apart from that, to me, because I've been doing it all my life, it's the same as going to any other office and doing any other job."

At the races Blash's office is in the team motorhome, but he discounts the oft-repeated theory that all the wheeling and dealing in the paddock is where the real Formula 1 racing takes place. "Basically, a World Championship is won back in the factory, not at the race circuit. And the motorhome is the link between the factory and the race circuit. Still, all these motorhomes are not just purely for socializing, there's also a lot of business done here.

"This is much more of a business now than when I started. You only have to see how much money everybody was earning in those days. Then, you only went motor racing because you wanted to go motor racing. But now, a lot of the mechanics, even, are making a very, very good living out of it. I suppose I prefer the old days, when it was more fun. A lot of this is just serious work now . . . unfortunately."

JOAN VILLADELPRAT

"Because they are in a job where the intensity is so high and the tension and pressure so big, everybody needs to be really nice to each other."

Barcelona, Spain, is the birthplace of the Tyrrell Team Manager, and witnessing a Spanish Grand Prix there was responsible for Joan Villadelprat choosing his way of life.

"Since that day it was something natural for me to work with cars. My family used to have some transport business, four or five trucks, and I was always involved with the guys who worked around the trucks. I was interested in what the mechanics did and my Mum used to hate me for that. Always my clothes were dirty. When I was 16 I decided, with my dad, not to carry on with the family business. I started to work in a garage.

"I have been in motor racing nearly 20 years now, in Formula 1 since '79–'80, when Project Four joined McLaren. After McLaren I worked in Ferrari, and now I try to put into Tyrrell what I have learned, what I think is the right way to do things. We've been putting a lot of effort in trying to change a bit the image of the team. We put a lot of effort in the way we set up the garage, to make sure that everything is nice and clean.

"Also the way we are dressed is something that's been thought about, though on some other teams this is a second priority thing. For us it was one of the first priorities. It creates an atmosphere that makes people feel a lot more comfortable. It's a lot easier to work in nice clean clothes, and in a well-organized and clean garage, than when everything is untidy and dirty. Plus, I think one of the most important reasons is it represents an image of the team as having a professional approach. And that's something the sponsors can always see. Obviously, none of the sponsors wants to have their name full of grease and oil, or be dirty or badly presented.

"The duties of the team manger are basically to organize the team. And to drive the team in the right direction, in the way we work and present the team. Then, there's the logistics side, the travelling, booking hotels and things. At the race there are decisions on how to approach the race, in the sense of how to attack the race. What tyres to use, and if there's going to be a pit stop or not, that kind of thing. The team manager talks with the engineers and the technicians, and he's the one who puts the peace in if there's a disagreement between two technical decisions, he's the one to find the middle ground.

"And for all the people around here, apart from obviously making a living with your job, the most important thing for everybody here is to win. This is a very hard job and you can only do it if you like it. Everybody has the same objective and because they are in a job where the intensity is so high and the tension and pressure so big, everybody needs to be really nice to each other.

"The best time of all is after the races, when everything comes down totally. You've been fighting for several days, and you've constantly been working and thinking and having some nights without sleep. Then it's all over and you have a bit of relaxing. You have a couple of cigarettes, you calm down yourself, and then you start thinking for the following Grand Prix.

"My job is my hobby, and that's one of the more important things in life. If you can combine your professional side with your hobby it takes up a good percentage of your capacity in life. Though I am Spanish and working in a British team, as long as you speak the language and can communicate, it is not a problem. You put all that to one side. Here, your nationality is your team."

KEN TYRRELL

"The easy thing to do is go out and sell the team, but why would I want to do that?"

Only the teams founded by Enzo Ferrari, Colin Chapman, Jack Brabham and Bruce McLaren have contested more Grands Prix than the Tyrrell Racing Organization. After over three decades at the cutting edge of the sport, 'Uncle' Ken Tyrrell still flourishes as head of his own team. And with all those racing miles under his belt, all the triumph and tragedy he has seen, his enthusiasm remains undimmed, his sense of humour intact.

His craggy features are frequently creased in a snaggle-toothed grin, a smile that once required a certain amount of reconstruction. Back in the days when 'Chopper' Tyrrell performed in the cockpit himself, and used a woodsman's axe as his personal insignia on his 500cc Formula 3 Cooper, he came a cropper at Goodwood. He remembers his shunt was not in vain, however, since he was leading a certain Stirling Moss at the time.

"I was going down the Lavant Straight and a brake pipe failed and I went straight on, hit a bank, got some broken teeth, a split lip and all that sort of thing. In the daily paper the next day, there was the picture of me and the caption said, 'Tyrrell leads Moss through the chicane at Goodwood'. And I read it in Chichester Hospital!"

Goodwood was Tyrrell's 'home' circuit, though it was Silverstone where the racing bug first bit, and it was another sport that brought him there in 1951. "I played football, halfback, for the local village club, Ockham, and they got up a coach party to go and see a race at Silverstone and that was my first involvement or interest of any kind in motorsport.

"I was sitting in the grandstand and watching the race and looking through the programme and there was a driver from Guildford taking part, Alan Brown. And so I sort of went and knocked on his door afterwards and said could I have a look at his car? And so Alan, being the salesman he was, got me involved and I bought his car from him at the end of the year.

"It was a Mark V Cooper with a single-knocker Norton engine in it. After I'd paid him the money, which I seem to remember was about £500, Alan said to me, 'Take it down to Brands and if you can't get round in a minute, sell it.' It was something which I *just* achieved, after spinning off several times in the attempt. But I thought it was wonderful, I thought it was fantastic! The nearness to the ground is what I remember most of all – sitting so close to the ground, being able to put your hand out and touch the front and rear wheel. I loved it!"

Consumed by racing euphoria (he admits to yelling "Yippee!" in his helmet), Tyrrell quickly became addicted to the sport, though it was a habit he was ill-equipped to finance. His father had been a gamekeeper, labourer and gardener and young Ken left school when he was 14. He had aspirations about going to technical college, but failed the entrance exam. He joined the RAF and was trained as a flight mechanic, then became a flight engineer on heavy bombers near the end of the war. After a couple of missions over Europe, Tyrrell spent his last six months in the service flying bombers out to Singapore and Ceylon.

"My brother was in a reserve occupation as a tree feller during the war, and when I came out of the RAF in '46 he suggested that we work together, and, in fact, we did a sort of tree-lopping and topping in people's gardens and things like that. We never had any money; the only money I had when I came out of the RAF was, I think, a £30 gratuity for five and a half years of service, and a new suit."

Tyrrell changed his driving suit for the civilian clothing of a team manager after becoming disenchanted with his own performances behind the wheel, though he always showed a fair turn of speed and won a Formula 3 race in Sweden. The move to the organizational side also made some financial sense.

"I seem to recall it was a combined Formula 1/Formula 2 race, probably the Aintree 200, and Michael Taylor drove my car. The opportunity arose probably because we could get more starting money if Michael drove. And he drove so much better than I did that I realized this was the slot that I ought to be in.

"I'd fallen in love with motor racing, you see, and I'd been driving from '52 until '58, and so by now I knew a bit about it. I obviously wanted to take part and wasn't satisfied with my own driving performance. I found I got as much pleasure, more really, from running a team. I just enjoyed doing it, I mean, we never made any money doing it – it *cost* us money to do it, you know. I just enjoyed doing it."

Tyrrell showed considerable aptitude for wheeling and dealing, and for finding drivers. In 1960 John Cooper loaned him some chassis, BMC loaned him engines, and the Tyrrell Formula Junior team began. Three years later Formula Junior became an international Formula 3 category and Ken Tyrrell found a new driver that established his reputation as a talent-spotter *par excellence*.

"One day, Robin Mackay, the Circuit Manager at Goodwood, called me up and said, 'Ken you're always looking for new young talent and this Scotsman does knock around here quick in an old Cooper Monaco.' I respected Robin's opinion and I had met

Jimmy Stewart, so I called him up and asked him about his younger brother. I asked him, 'Does your brother want to become a racing driver, or is he just having fun?' Jimmy said, 'No, I think he wants to take part seriously.'

"So he gave me Jackie's number and I called him and I invited him down to try this new Cooper Formula 3 car which Bruce McLaren had been testing for us. He'd been a Cooper Formula 1 driver. So Bruce had been doing some laps around Goodwood and then Jackie got in the car and on his third or fourth lap he was quicker than Bruce. It was his first ever time in a single-seater car, so this was quite outstanding. And in fact we called him in and I gave him a bit of a chat, you know, and said we'd got all day, we don't have to rush this thing.

"So then Bruce, being the nice chap that he was, said, 'This is ridiculous, let me get back in that thing again'. So Bruce got in and of course he went quicker. And then later on in the day Jackie got in again and he went quicker still. And John Cooper, who'd been watching on the first corner at Goodwood, came rushing up and said, 'You want to get that boy signed up quickly, he's bloody good!' So we did. Incidentally, Jackie and I never did have a contract – ever. He drove for me on a handshake."

Thus began the illustrious Tyrrell/Stewart partnership that made so much racing history. The team swept through Formula 3 like a whirlwind, with Stewart winning 16 of 18 races, then they tackled Formula 2. An introduction to Matra, the French missile company, by the French journalist Jabby Crombac, resulted in Matra Formula 2 chassis for Tyrrell and another championship win for the team. The title went to Tyrrell's other driver Jacky Ickx, since Stewart was simultaneously racing in Formula 1 for BRM and thus not allowed to score Formula 2 points.

This was in 1967, and in June of that year the famed Ford-Cosworth Formula 1 engine made its debut in the Dutch Grand Prix at Zandvoort. Jimmy Clark had one in the back of his Lotus and he made the motor a winner first time out, an achievement which was witnessed by Ken Tyrrell. "I took a flight over on the morning of the race. It was a day trip and as soon as I got back I sent a telegram to Cosworth ordering three engines.

"They replied saying they didn't know whether they were going to be selling engines. But then I got talking to Walter Hayes at

Ford and he said they might be making engines available to other teams. So then I talked to Matra and said, 'Look, if we get the Ford engine, why don't you build a chassis?' And they agreed to that, and then we had to find some money, because the arrangement was that Matra loaned the car and we had to supply the gearboxes, the engines, and all the preparation. We had no money at that time.

"We had to buy engines and they were going to cost £7,500 each, and I didn't have 7,500 pence, let alone pounds. I had already asked Jackie, if I put it all together, would he race for me? And he said, 'Yes, but what about some money?' I asked him how much he wanted, and he said '£20,000'. I said I didn't have £20,000. But I had already gone to Walter Hayes and told him, 'Look, this is what we're trying to do, and if we don't do it Jackie's going to go to Ferrari, and you don't want Jackie to go to Ferrari, do you? I think I can get the money together, but Jackie wants 20,000. Will you guarantee me 20,000 so I can get Jackie sorted out, in case I can't find enough money?' Walter didn't hesitate, he said 'Yes' straight away and so I did the deal with Jackie.

"Then Jackie and I went to see Dunlop. Dunlop were a bit pissed-off because Firestone and Goodyear were winning the races that were traditionally won by Dunlop-shod cars. And they said, 'We're going to get out but we don't want to get out being beaten. So we will sponsor you.' And they paid us £80,000. I was able to call Walter and say, 'Thank you very much, I don't need the 20,000.' And I gave Jackie 20 of the 80 and we went racing. So we took part in Formula 1 for the first time in '68."

Driving Tyrrell's Matra-Ford, Stewart was World Champion in 1969, then Matra, who had made their own Formula 1 engine, told Tyrrell he would have to use it if he wished to continue using Matra chassis. The 12-cylinder device made a terrific noise, but it produced little else when Tyrrell tested it. "So then we had to go and find a car and that proved much more difficult than I had thought. I went to McLaren, to Brabham, to Lotus and none of them would sell us a car.

"As it happened, this group called March set themselves up and said they were going to make Formula 1, Formula 2 and Formula 3 cars, so we did a deal with them. But it wasn't a very good car at all. It was too heavy, it was like a truck. And so the writing was on the wall that if we wanted to continue in Formula 1 we were going to have to build our own car. Early in 1970 I approached Derek Gardner and asked him if he would like to join us and design a Formula 1 car. We wanted to keep it quiet because there was no reason making a fuss about it until something really happened."

This project established another hallmark of Ken Tyrrell's character: a penchant for secrecy and springing surprises on the Formula 1 world. The first car bearing his name, built under cover in a shed at his Ockham premises, emerged fully formed and very quickly became a world beater. Stewart was World Champion in a Tyrrell-Ford in 1971, finished second the next year, won his third title in 1973, then retired at the end of that season.

But what should have been a time of celebration for the team turned out to be the worst time of Ken Tyrrell's racing life. "We lost Francois Cevert in practice for the very last race that Jackie was going to drive in, at Watkins Glen. It was absolutely terrible. Unbelievable. Of all the drivers that drove for me, the relationship between Francois and Jackie and ourselves was fantastic. Francois, for example, worshipped Jackie and Jackie helped him tremendously, and Francois of course was going to lead the team the following year.

"And when he got in the car to go out for that last time, he said, 'I'm going to get on pole'. He was very confident that he was going to put the car on pole. And it wasn't to be. He just lost it. He lost it on that part of the circuit where the track went over the entrance road and the guardrail was right up close to the track. The car went between two guardrails and forced them apart. Obviously it was a terrible shock to us all and we came home in a very depressed state.

"But I can't say that I gave serious thought to giving it up because of it. I thought that we should be able to contribute to making the cars more safe so that they could survive such an accident, and just leaving and going away wasn't going to help. And I think, almost certainly, today's car would have survived the accident.

"We lost so many drivers in the era when Jackie was driving, and it's still always a possibility. And when you know that your car's gone off the road, you've always got those terrible few minutes of wondering, first of all, if the driver is OK. It's become much less so in the last few years because the cars have become so much safer; the drivers walk away from accidents so often now."

Stewart, Cevert, Scheckter, Cheever, Peterson, Pironi, Depailler, Brundle, Palmer, Alesi . . . Tyrrell has a reputation for being very close to those who drive for him, often having what has been described as a father-son relationship. "Well, I don't go for the father-son bit, but certainly, I suppose because I once drove myself, you know, I've got a great deal of sympathy for the problems of a racing driver. But I'd agree, generally speaking, we were always friends. And the team-mates always had a good relationship."

Entering the '90s, the Tyrrell Racing Organization had won 23 Grand Prix races, though the last one had been in 1983, when Alboreto was victorious in Detroit. Yet the team has never been disgracefully uncompetitive and, in fact, it is the most successful of the smaller-budgeted teams. The head of the team places the blame for any lack of resources firmly at his own feet.

"We've had some bad cars in the last few years and I can't say that the design team was solely responsible for it. It was really my failure to attract the right sort of sponsorship to enable them to do the research that was necessary. You see, the first responsibility of a team owner, such as myself, is to go out and find the money to do the job – and if you don't find the money to do the job you can't expect your design team to be able to produce competitive cars. And if you can't produce competitive cars then it's difficult to get the major sponsors. It's the chicken-and-egg thing, you know. We started to look quite good again when Harvey Postlethwaite designed a very good car for us for 1989. Alesi drove it well and our good results attracted sponsors and also helped us to get Honda engines for 1991. So success breeds success, which encourages sponsors, which enables you to have more success."

Still, several times in the past, the red ink on Tyrrell's financial statement had him waking up in the middle of the night with his hair standing on end. "It was quite frightening, actually. But this sport has always been a business. When we got into Formula 1 I sold my interest in the timber company because it was obviously going to be a full-time business and it's been a full-time business really since '68. But it's all been worth it. Because I know it *can* be done. Ron Dennis has shown everyone how to do it, and Frank Williams. It's up to us to get on with it and I think we're on our way to doing that now."

Tyrrell could have solved his financial problems some time ago had he sold his team, as others have done. But he refused to relinquish control, "for several reasons. First of all, I like the business. It's true that I'm getting on now and I'm going to be playing a lesser role in the future. I'm 66 years of age and my youngest son Bob, who has been very much involved with the team, has recently taken over from me as Managing Director, although I am still Chairman. One day I would like to be able to hand it all over to him. That would give me a lot of pleasure, being able to do that. The easy thing to do is go out and sell the team, but why would I want to do that?"

Ken Tyrrell's staunchest backer is a member of his own household. Norah married him 40 years ago and has been coming to the races with him ever since. Their eldest son is a captain with British Airways and one of their two young grandchildren wants to become a racing car designer. Should that happen, the chances are his grandfather will still be in a position to give him a job.

Formula 1 racing is Ken Tyrrell's fountain of youth, though his sporting blood is also raised by cricket and football. "I follow football quite closely and I'm a fan of Tottenham Hotspur and England. I go to watch as many of those games as motor racing allows me and then in the summer I follow cricket. England has come through a difficult time recently, but test match cricket is something special for me. I could sit in front of a television set watching all five days of it, without any trouble at all."

Another Tyrrell interest is reading about his main passion and he is something of a connoisseur of motorsport writing. "I think it's very much better now than it used to be. I always remember Francois Guiter of Elf saying to me years ago, a long time ago, that the quality of the motor racing press was very poor. The writers were paid so little that it didn't attract the right sort. But we've got wonderful writers now. I think all the lead writers are good. Nigel Roebuck, and David Tremayne of *Motoring News*, Alan Henry, and what's his name, the Irishman . . . Hamilton! Maurice – a *wonderful* writer."

INNES IRELAND and ROB WALKER spent much of their motor racing life in the pit road as driver and entrant respectively, although now they spend more time in the pressroom.

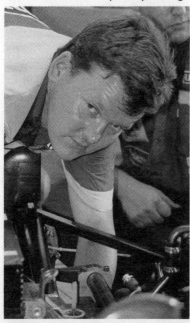

PHILIP HAWKE loves the noise and razzmatazz of Formula 1, especially pit stops, when he becomes a Williams wheel 'putteroner'.

For BERNARD DUDOT the sound of a Renault engine at maximum revs is music in his ears.

Once Jimmy Clark's mechanic, DICK SCAMMELL now directs the racing division of Cosworth Engineering.

LEE CARDUCCI, Lamborghini's electronics man, thinks a lot of the animosity in Formula 1 is dreamed up by journalists.

MAURO FORGHIERI's love/hate relationship with Formula 1 has lasted 30 years with Ferrari and Lamborghini.

Team manager RUPERT MANWARING finds himself on the same wavelength as his Team Lotus boss TONY RUDD, who has been "afflicted with the motor racing disease" since 1936.

ENRIQUE SCALABRONI suffered much hardship en route to becoming a top designer, whose skill has served Williams and Ferrari.

Where every second counts. Ferrari mechanics rush to clear the pit road of NIGEL MANSELL's Ferrari after a qualifying run.

The problem with doing something special is that everyone wants to know about it, as ALESSANDRO NANNINI discovered in 1990 when he finished third at Imola between BERGER and PROST.

Autograph-hunters are not confined to the grandstands and terraces as NIGEL MANSELL found when he tried to walk from Monaco paddock to pit road.

All smiles from ALAIN PROST and NIGEL MANSELL as they prepared for their first race together a Ferrari team partners.

Formula 1's most experienced driver, RICCARDO PATRESE explains what it feels like to have 200 Grands Prix under his belt.

A knowledgeable Formula 1 crowd always appreciates a 110 per cent trier, which is why DEREK WARWICK invariably receives a cheer as he strides towards his car.

JEAN ALESI gave some outstanding performances in his first full season of Formula 1 racing, but found contractual negotiations a more difficult art to master.

He knew it would be a demanding job, and perhaps a lonely job, but when CESARE FIORIO was appointed Ferrari's team manager it was a life's ambition fulfilled.

AYRTON SENNA is not only the fastest driver of his time and a worthy World Champion, he has a way with words – in several languages – which testify to an outstanding intellect and depth of feeling.

The bond between McLaren's CREIGHTON BROWN and Marlboro's JOHN HOGAN is based on more than their long and successful business relationship; they are both incurable racing enthusiasts.

JAMES HUNT's pithy remarks delight BBC television viewers of Formula 1 racing. They are inspired by his experience as a McLaren-driving World Champion long before RON DENNIS took control of the team.

KEN TYRRELL and RON DENNIS have more in common than the use of Honda engines in 1991; Dennis' McLaren Marketing Services division is responsible for sponsorship negotiations on behalf of the Tyrrell team.

After years of innovative design in Formula 1, GORDON MURRAY has accepted a new challenge masterminding the development of McLaren's supercar, though he still visits the paddock whenever possible.

Aerodynamics has long been a speciality of Dr. HARVEY POSTLETHWAITE, and his work for Tyrrell has been largely responsible for the re-emergence of the team as a leading contender.

Having introduced carbon-fibre mono-coques at McLaren and 'hands off' gear-changing at Ferrari, JOHN BARNARD is exploring other new avenues of innovation as technical director of Benetton Formula.

After the high-pressure environment of Ferrari, TOMMASO CARLETTI feels more comfortable guiding the fortunes of the smaller Minardi team, but the tension during the race remains.

HERBIE BLASH is back doing the job he likes most, running the Brabham team, after a spell away on race administration, and can always be relied upon for a good quote.

Formula 1 demands people with staying power, and ALAN CHALLIS has stayed longest of all: Williams' chief mechanic joined BRM in 1958 and has been part of the scene ever since, with undiminished enthusiasm.

Tyrrell's team manager JOAN VILLADELPRAT is Spanish, but he says that in Formula I your nationality becomes that of your team.

EOIN YOUNG, dispensing hospitality to INNES IRELAND and ROB WALKER, was to be found at the ELF motorhome for many years before he was head-hunted to perform a similar role for Ford.

Grand Prix people tend to be versatile. TONY JARDINE tried art, journalism and truck driving long before he secured the Camel account for his public relations company; JEFF HUTCHINSON teaches Formula 1 drivers to fly when he is not writing race reports; and GIORGIO PIOLA, seated, combines journalism with technical drawings of Formula 1 cars which are the envy of some of their designers.

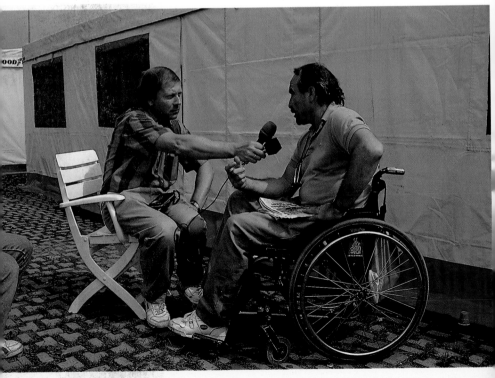

CLAY REGAZZONI has done a lot of television reportage since a Formula 1 accident confined him to a wheelchair, but on this occasion he finds himself on the receiving end of HEINZ PRULLER's microphone.

DENIS JENKINSON and JABBY CROMBAC have more than a flat cap in common. Their Formula 1 involvement dates back to the '50s and neither of them is overjoyed by all the changes that have taken place.

A pair of presidents. JEAN-MARIE BALESTRE of the FIA and FISA has reason to be grateful for the financial support which Formula 1 has received from Philip Morris Marlboro, thanks to ALEARDO BUZZI's enthusiasm and guidance.

There are times when paddock people would like to tell everyone else where to go, but in ALAN WOOLLARD's case it happens to be his job.

Grand Prix racing is all about timing and the man at the technological end of the Olivetti Longines service is LUIGI SARTORIS.

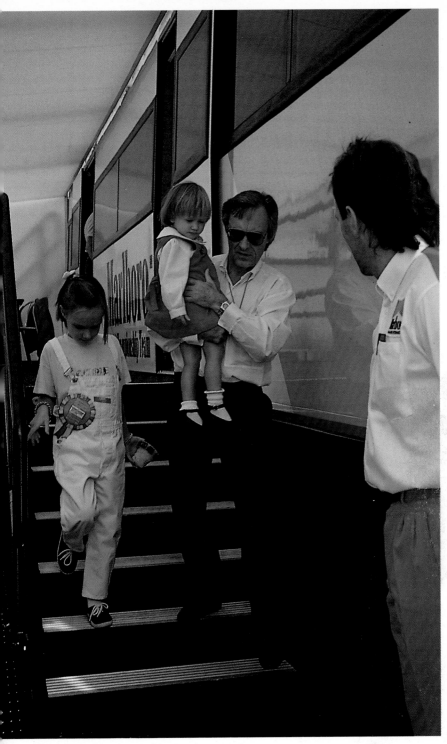

BERNIE ECCLESTONE has been described as the godfather of the Formula 1 family, but he is also a devoted family man in his own right. Here he accompanies two of his three daughters, Tamara and ...tra, after their rare visit to the Marlboro motorhome.

The pit road and paddock would become hopelessly congested with 1,500 Formula 1 journalists roaming loose, which is why monitors have been installed to bring more of the action and information into the pressroom.

The paddock, however, remains the focal point for dialogue, the part of the Grand Prix working area where all the elements come together, many of the stories are discovered and quite a few of them are created.

2
VIEWS
FROM THE PRESSROOM

MAURICE HAMILTON is nothing if not creative and to prove it he forged his first press pass.

EOIN YOUNG's specialities are racing history and humorous observation of the present.

MAURICE HAMILTON

"Just doing your job, be it a journalist, be it a mechanic, be it a PR person, is so competitive that you have to do it better than the next man. Because that's what Grand Prix racing is all about – it's about winning."

Suspended from a cord around his neck is Maurice Hamilton's FIA Formula 1 World Championship press pass, issued to him by the *Fédération Internationale du Sport Automobile*. On the back of the piece of laminated plastic, beside a photo of him grinning through his neatly trimmed beard, is an inscription: 'The holder of this credential must be given free access into the circuit and its confines at all times during the season.' Hamilton, now a highly esteemed journalist writing for several prestigious publications, was once so desperate to gain access to the pit lane that he forged his own press pass.

Maurice Hamilton, who was selling plastic underground drainage systems at the time, had the bogus credential made up at a booth in Victoria Station in London for 50p. Beside his photo was the inscription: 'Maurice Hamilton, Motor Racing Features'. On the back was a list of magazines he was supposedly writing for, the last one being *Cart & Track*. The cart in question was the donkey-powered variety, as found in his native Northern Ireland. Hamilton's theory was that if his credential was called into question he could point to *Cart & Track* and say the whole thing was a joke. But his ruse worked and gained him entry to the Monaco Grand Prix.

"It's all my father's fault. He'd been a motor racing freak and got me started when he took me to the Tourist Trophy race at Dundrod when I was seven. This was in the early '50s, and we went up there, north of Belfast, where an uncle of mine got me a pit pass. And I got into the pits at that age, which was really something. The noise, the smell, all the things that still hit you today, the sensual things. The speed, but particularly the noise and the excitement and the smell. The drama. And I came home thinking this is just wonderful – absolutely incredible!

"Later on my Dad bought me an autograph book. I still have it, with Fangio's, Hawthorn's, Collins' – all their autographs.

Everybody. Jimmy Clark, Graham Hill, Phil Hill, Jackie Stewart, right through the '60s. I kept it then and took it with me right up to when I became a professional writer, and then I felt guilty about it. It wasn't the same, anyway. When you have access to these people it doesn't seem the same thrill.

"But I'll never, ever forget going to get Clark's autograph, because it was the one I wanted most. And I chose the perfect moment. The '66 Gold Cup, Oulton Park. On the Thursday or the Friday there was an unofficial practice session. Clark was there and the car wasn't ready and he was hanging about. My mate Tim got the camera ready and I went up with my autograph book and asked him for his autograph. Perfect. Yes, certainly. And he started to write it, and my pen ran out of ink!

"Can you believe that? And the point about it was, *he* was more embarrassed than I was. And he sort of did it hard on the paper, and then – I was nearly in tears – Tim and I went and got another pen and filled in the indentations. You can see it in the book."

Hamilton's passion for the sport was still being diluted by occasional bouts of "hooliganism", usually involving girls and drinking. "But the major turning point was when four of us took a Volkswagen Beetle from Northern Ireland and we went to the 1966 British Grand Prix at Brands Hatch, with a tent in the back of the Beetle. And we just hung about, camped in a field nearby, and really got deeply involved in it. I thought: This is it, this is phenomenal! All these big star names – Graham Hill, Jackie Stewart, Jim Clark, John Surtees, BRMs – the whole business – a Grand Prix with all the pizazz and the trumpets and the whole show. I'd never seen anything quite like that before. This was suddenly big time, and I was aware of it. It really just swept me off my feet, and from that moment on I was looking at ways of somehow getting involved."

Hamilton was being groomed to take over the family building company when his father retired. On leaving school, where he "hadn't been a particular success", his father got him a position with an accounting firm in Belfast. Young Maurice worked there for two years and "hated every minute of it". Next came an attempt to be a quantity surveyor. Four times he failed to pass the examinations for the first stage of this occupation. "Whereupon, my father said, 'Well what are you going to do? You're hopeless, your heart's not in it'. And I said, 'Well, I want to get involved in motor racing'. And he said, 'Don't be so stupid. How can you do that?' And I literally didn't know.

"Then Tim and I bought a 14-day coach tour to the Nurburgring 1,000 kilometres and the Monaco Grand Prix. This was the first time I'd ever been abroad outside the UK and you can imagine the effect those two races had on me. Mind-blowing, just absolutely and *utterly* mind-blowing! More determined than ever now, there had to be a job for me in there somewhere."

On that trip Hamilton stopped in London to seek career advice from a vocational guidance concern. His capabilities were assessed, and Hamilton came away with a document proving he was entirely unsuited to deal with mathematics. Instead, he was an ideal candidate to work with people and, much to his surprise, he learned he had an affinity for writing.

He had never written anything for public consumption, though English was a favourite subject at school, and the only literature he was interested in at the time was contained in *Autosport*, *Motoring News* and *Motor Sport*. His favourite author was 'DSJ'. "I remember Tim and I saw Jenks at Oulton Park in his left-hand-drive E-Type leaving the circuit. Must have been '66 or '67. And we debated whether to rush up to him – he was stuck in a queue of traffic, as we were. And the debate was, do we go up and sort of speak to him and say 'Hello', and we decided against it. We were too shy to think we could go and intrude on the great man's presence."

Nowadays Jenks and Maurice are good friends, but on the day of that Oulton Park sighting his young admirer went back across the Irish Sea to Belfast where he sold Volvos for three years, spending every spare penny on ferrying himself back over to England to watch the races. He answered the ads in *Autosport*, offering his services as a 'gofer', team manager in Formula 3, willing to fill any motor racing vacancies that existed. But no-one was interested in him. He decided he had to be on the spot, in England.

"The turning point came after I went to the 1969 Oulton Park Gold Cup. I came back across on the Monday morning, drove off the ferry in Belfast and tried to drive up the Falls Road to where the car showroom was. I couldn't, because there were soldiers blocking the bottom of it. And I'd never seen soldiers in Belfast before. It had been that weekend of the first rioting. And I drove around the back streets and got in to where the showroom was and it had been blown up. And I remember saying to myself, 'This is it. This isn't going to end tomorrow. The trouble will get worse and worse', and I immediately began making plans to get out."

He packed all his worldly possessions, boarded the ferry, and set sail on a voyage which he hoped would lead to a career in motorsport. But he was to be blown off course several times, beginning with a stint selling Olivetti typewriters, door-to-door in London.

"It was cold-calling. It taught me a lot about myself and it brought me out of myself, and it did me the world of good. And funnily enough, going back to the vocational guidance thing, they had said that because I'd failed in so many different ways, I was introspective and lacked confidence. They said if you could get something which you're quite good at, you'll change. And they were right. I did.

"Meanwhile, I'm still looking at motorsport and I can't think of a way into it at all. I didn't want to be a driver, I knew I wasn't good enough. Couldn't be a mechanic, I'm hopeless with anything like that. I'm not interested in that side, anyway. So, what do I do? Then I remembered the guidance report said maybe I should try writing.

"I went to the 1973 Monaco Grand Prix with my Dad and I thought the secret has to be to write a piece that nobody else has written. There's no point in trying to write a report because there are guys out there writing reports and I wouldn't know where to start and I haven't got access to the drivers. So I decided on a piece about the Monaco Grand Prix from a spectator's point of view, what it's like going there and what it's like being there – what you see and what you don't see."

So Maurice took copious notes, borrowed a typewriter, and pecked out a story about his adventures at the Monaco Grand Prix. He sent it to *Motor Sport*, and when they failed to respond he visited the magazine's office. "And I got as far as the secretary, who told me to go away. She came up with the immortal line, 'Mr Jenkinson never comes in'. I said, 'OK. Is Mr Boddy in?' 'Well, he is, but he's busy. Anyway, he gets a lot of letters, you know, and a lot of correspondence, and some of it isn't very nice!'"

Hamilton was similarly discouraged by several other publications, then tried *Competition Car*, which was edited by Nigel Roebuck. "So I took the manuscript in. Nobody about. The secretary took it, she said she'd show it to Mr Roebuck. I thought, Here we go again. I told her, 'Tell him I'll come back next week to see what he thinks'. She said, 'Alright, yes he will read it, don't worry'. She must have seen the despair in my face!

"Later, I came back to the office, and I thought, I'm going to sort something out here, come hell or high water. I went in, and there's this little fellow in a leather coat wandering about. I said, 'Can I speak to the editor please, Mr Nigel Roebuck?' And he said, 'Yes, it's me.' He wasn't what I expected at all. And I introduced myself. 'Oh', he said, 'Yes. I read it. We like it. We're going to publish it!'

"And we became very firm friends from that point on. I held on to him because, suddenly, here was the first person who I'd met in the business who I could sort of cling on to, and I did. I started to go to races with him, he fiddled me a press pass, and one thing and another. He encouraged me to write other features and articles. He then gave me a monthly column in the magazine and then it went bust!"

Before that happened the budding journalist had several Grands Prix under his belt, though he was still employed in the workaday world. His tenure selling houses for Wimpey had little impact on the London real estate market because Hamilton tended to be abroad during weekends, the prime selling time. When he switched to selling plastic underground drainage pipes his company car became a vehicle to escape to the races. "I actually did very well at that. I was my own boss, worked from home, they gave me a company car, so what I used to do was work like *mad* Monday to Thursday, fake Friday's report, take the company car, fill it with fuel and go to Zolder or somewhere to the Grand Prix. This was when I made up my own credential and used it to get myself an armband at Monaco."

An introduction by Roebuck to fellow writer Eoin Young provided Hamilton with his next breakthrough. "It was at the Nurburgring in '76 where, again, I'd bummed my way there and fiddled my way in. Eoin asked me if I would like to take a ride around the circuit with Jackie Stewart in a BMW, then write about it. I did that, it was magic that ride, wrote a piece and showed it to Eoin. He said, 'Right, I'm going to syndicate this for you to all my magazines.' I thought, what's the catch? Why is he doing this? And I said, 'Alright, do you want to take a percentage of whatever it earns?' 'He said, 'No, you just seem a likely lad.' He was just giving me a leg up. So he sent it to magazines worldwide with a covering letter from him saying this is a bloke I know, this is what he's written. And five magazines published it worldwide, which was phenomenal! To me that was a *big* step forward."

Eoin Young then invited Hamilton to work for him. At that time Young was heavily involved in public relations for Elf and First National City Travellers Cheques, the Tyrrell sponsor, and Hamilton would write press releases for him. "Eoin said, 'If you're keen you can come and work for me, but I really can't afford to pay'. I said, 'Well, I can't afford not to have an income.' And I turned it down, that was in November '76.

"Christmas of that year, I went home and father said, 'Right. Crunch time. I'm standing down, I'm going to retire shortly. If you're going to come into the company, you're to come in now. You'll have a directorship, house, company car, everything, but you have to decide now, because once I stand down, you can't come in, for obvious reasons, over people who have worked there a long time. What are you going to do?'

"So I spent three or four days thinking about it, and I thought I've got to give it one shot, I've got to try. I said to Dad, 'Look, I've got to go back, I'm going to resign from my job, I'm going to try to become a full-time writer. I'm going to go and work for Eoin Young and I'll see how it goes.' So I went straight back to Eoin, and on New Year's Eve, '76–77, we shook hands and I became a full-time freelance motorsport journalist.

"It was very slow the first year, made no money whatsoever. He paid me, I think, a nominal sum, but he took me to about five or six races abroad and he paid the expenses. He took me right up into the top level of Grand Prix racing and introduced me around and said, 'This is Maurice Hamilton'. And that was my passport, Eoin bringing me in under his wing, It was tremendous because I wasn't coming in as a junior and hanging about. He was introducing me to all the right people, which was *just priceless!* Fantastic."

In 1978 Hamilton was nominated by Eric Dymock to replace him as the motorsport correspondent for *The Guardian*. Shortly after that he was appointed editor of the annual, *Autocourse*, and Hamilton held both positions until recently. Now writing for *The Independent* and several magazines, he still marvels at his good fortune and is somewhat bemused that his scribbling (he is one of the few in the pressroom to write in longhand) is so highly rated. "After all these years I still can't believe that I can do it. I still can't believe that I can sit down and produce a piece that's actually quite good. It's a gift and it's one of those things that you're ever so grateful for."

Humour is a Hamilton hallmark, and his tongue is never far from his cheek. He believes this is partly an ancestral legacy ("Coming from Ireland, you can't help it because life is a laugh over there.") and partly to make light of some of the disappointment he found in the reality of Grand Prix racing.

"It came as quite a shock when it became a business for me. Your outlook changes dramatically when suddenly it's not a hobby any more and you've got to make it pay. Sounds terrible, but you do. And you look upon things slightly differently. You look upon it from a more commercial viewpoint. It tends to lose that lovely sort of glossy image which you had when you looked at it from the outside.

"The romance doesn't disappear, it's still there, but it's different because a large part of the romance is wiped out by the sheer commercial side of it. I tended to believe that *everyone* involved was a 100 per cent enthusiast like I was. Of course, when you get on the inside you realize there *are* some great people involved who are super enthusiasts, but there's a hell of a lot who just treat it as a business, and it's a very hard, cut-throat, occasionally nasty business. No point in crying about it or being upset. My attitude now is that I will never see it the same way again. But I don't want to do anything else, so I accept it.

"Just doing your job, be it a journalist, be it a mechanic, be it a PR person, is so competitive that you have to do it better than the next man. Because that's what Grand Prix racing is all about – it's about winning. And it filters right down through everything in Formula 1. Everybody likes to do a better job. I want to write a piece that is considered to be the best, it's as simple as that.

"The whole business is so competitive. It always amuses me that some people have to be off the airplane first, and first in the car hire queue. They've got to have a better car than you. And if there are any freebees in the paddock, they've got to make sure that they get them, they don't want to be seen without. It's very competitive in *every* respect.

"From the minute I arrive at the circuit, or even at the airport when you start to meet Formula 1 people, I'm always conscious of not knowing everything that's going on, and I want to know. But you never do know everything that's going on. That's the frustrating part. You never do get to the bottom of everything. The first thing everybody asks when they meet you is, 'What's new, what's happening?'. It's not just curiosity, it's competitiveness. Because you don't want to be caught out, not knowing something.

"But there's no point in being totally competitive and spoiling friendships just because you're not going to share a secret. Because you need to trade off each other. You need help from each other. Also, I don't think it's worth being totally secretive and alienating yourself. You've got to live together. So you do tell each other things. Alan Henry, for instance, of *The Guardian*, and myself, from *The Independent* – we're very close friends, but we're rivals. I will help Alan if he's in trouble, and he will help me. But if I find out a little thing, I won't necessarily tell him. And I would not expect him to tell me. But I wouldn't send him the wrong way, chasing after the wrong story, and I wouldn't lie to him.

"Inside the world of journalism you tend to find the guys on the specialist magazines are disparaging about the tabloid press. But once you've become a newspaper writer you respect the job they're doing, because it's different. It's quite hard. You have to have a very racy style. You have to chase after drivers more and get quotes. It is more difficult than I had ever imagined watching from the outside, being a tabloid writer. That's what I like about writing for a quality paper. I can sit down and write a reflective piece, whereas they can't. They've got to have quotes, saying Nigel Mansell said this, Nigel Mansell said that.

"I've talked to a lot of drivers and I've learned that they're human beings, just like the rest of us, and that they've got their foibles and phobias, and what have you. But, what hasn't changed is my view that when they get into a car they are somebody special. That hasn't changed. In fact, if anything, that has been magnified. Some guys I like, some guys I don't, but when they're in the car I think they're all up there, on a plateau.

"Out of the car the physical, and emotional, and mental draining they have to go through is phenomenal. All the PR stuff and the debriefs and the dealing with the press. And the pressure they're under all the time to succeed, and the mental pressure if they're not doing so well. I'm more aware of that now than I ever was before.

"When I walk down the pit lane I'm just observing the scene generally. If I have one failing it's that I'm not a very good news hound. Never have been. Sounds a strange thing for a newspaper man to say. Working for a quality it's not quite so vital that you get every last bit of tittle tattle in there. Some journalists thrive on the gossip and the latest piece of news, and who's doing what. I don't particularly, and I find all that a little bit tedious and a bit boring.

"I like to just breathe in the whole atmosphere, take it all in. I watch the way the teams work. The mechanics never cease to amaze me, just how they do their job. The drivers, just to see how they're dressed or what they're saying, or how relaxed they are, or otherwise. I'm always looking for insights into the drivers. I like to talk to them, not of anything in particular, just to chat.

"Senna is the one driver who won't talk to me, and I'm very sad about that. Because it's mainly due, I think, to a misunderstanding over something he thought I wrote. It was during the time of the Senna/Warwick signing controversy at Lotus for the 1986 season. I wrote my tongue-in-cheek Old Mo's Almanac thing in *Autosport* and Senna confused that with something else that appeared in *Motoring News*. That piece Senna interpreted as being insulting to his mother, though I didn't write it. I explained it all to him, but from that day to this he still has it in his head that I might kick him sooner or later. It's not true, and I'm very distressed about that. So we hardly communicate, which is a shame. And I think that's indicative of him, that he's got this thing in his head, so that's sad. But then, it's a reflection of what you have to deal with, with Grand Prix drivers.

"We also have to deal with the public relations aspect. I see sponsorship and PR as a necessary part of Formula 1, but not the vital part, and I take exception to the PR people who try to ram it down your throat. I think that most of the PR people generally know what to do, and they do provide a service. I think, though, some of them, and some of the sponsors, tend to have an inflated idea of their station in life in the Formula 1 paddock. About the motorhome syndrome, I have no objection to it. I think it's part of Grand Prix racing today, and you have to accept it as such. Besides, without it we wouldn't get a decent lunch!"

EOIN YOUNG

"I never have been and never will be technically minded. And I've always thought that the majority of readers are like me, so why bore them?"

Besides bringing Maurice Hamilton into Grand Prix racing, Eoin Young was for many years also the unofficial *maître de* at Hamilton's favourite paddock luncheon spot, the ELF motorhome. There, where the hospitality and gossip flows freely, Young found much material for the journalistic side of his life.

Eoin Young's 'Diary', featured in *Autocar & Motor* and syndicated internationally, is an idiosyncratic look at the sporting aspects of the world of motoring. Young also runs a thriving enterprise called Motormedia Limited, which caters to collectors of rare motoring books and motoring and racing memorabilia. His treasures are housed in the Vintage Gallery, premises which are so well hidden in the wilds of Surrey that Young's catalogues contain directions for finding it ('Turn right at the Lord Howard pub'). In the catalogues Young also mentions that he is away at the Grand Prix races during the season. When he is not thus engaged he can often be found holding court in another nearby pub, The Barley Mow, which premises he has made famous in his columns.

He began his working life as a teller in a bank ("because my mother told me it was a very reliable field of work") in his village near the town of Timaru, on the South Island of New Zealand. His father was a rabbit trapper and drove a horse and cart, and Eoin's own transport was a bicycle. But he was entranced by cars, especially sporting ones that were raced. He bluffed his way into

race reporting for the local paper, using the *nom de plume*
'Dipstick'. After five years of banking Young managed to syphon
off enough wherewithall to fund a pilgrimage to England in 1961.

Young knew Bruce McLaren, whose sister lived in Timaru, and
in England he met another racing Kiwi, Denny Hulme. "One day,
Denny asked me if I wanted to come around Europe with him to
help him run his Formula Junior Cooper. So we headed off, towing
the Cooper behind his Mark 1 Zodiac. In one of the first races he
blew up a piston. He said, 'I'll change the piston, you change the
gear ratios'. I said, 'No problem'. It was easy: drop the box off,
change all the bits, box on again – we'll go and have a beer. Then
he said, 'Are you finished already?' I said, 'Well there are a few
bits left over, but you can use them as spares'.

"He said, 'What the hell are you doing?'. I said, 'I've never
done this in my life before'. He said, 'For Christ's sake I thought
you were going to help me. You helped me by getting in the way!'.
I did myself a real good turn there. I was never asked to do
anything again. But I stayed with him the whole 1961 season and
had a real good time.

"I was doing the Formula Junior races for *Motoring News* and
at one of them I first met Jenks and began chatting away with
him. I was never aware that people thought he was God. I knew
he was a well-known journalist, but I thought he was just another
bloke. Out in the Colonies you don't tend to have Gods. Anyway,
like all Colonials, I soon went broke and headed back home,
where I had arranged to be the night editor of the Hobart Mercury,
in Tasmania.

"First, I had to do the Tasman Series for *Motoring News*, and
Bruce was there. He asked if I would like to be his secretary back
in Europe. I asked him what a secretary did. He said, 'I'm not
quite sure, but everyone else seems to have one so I should too'.
He said he would pay my ticket back to England and take it out of
my wages. So that year, 1962, I worked for 12 quid a week and
really had a ball. I used to look after his correspondence and wrote
a column for him. We did it with a tape recorder and I slavishly
wrote down every word he said. Then, later on, I used to write
down what he meant!

"In those days I knew practically everything that was going on
because Jimmy Clark and Graham Hill and all that crew were just

mates of McLaren's. And because I was at all the races as a mate of McLaren's I knew them all just as mates, and we all used to go out to dinner together. It was never a question of, well, we're not going to ask him because he's a journalist. Then, in 1963, McLaren Racing started and the directors were Bruce and his wife and me. I still have the share certificates somewhere."

Young stayed with McLaren for three more years, then married Sandra, John Surtees' secretary, and became a full-time journalist, beginning in 1967 when his first column appeared in *Autocar* during January. "My stuff was always the comment on the news, rather than the news itself. I always think that when you see a news release, methinks that I know what it says, what does it mean? I say, read between the lines and then write between the lines. But I always think I am fortunate because I can write about whatever I want to write about.

"And I like to think I write the way I talk. I always use the parallel that when I turn into The Barley Mow after a Grand Prix, all those guys at the bar are asking, 'What happened?'. They've all read in *The Times* or *Telegraph* what happened and who won, but they want to know all the funny stories, you see, and so that's what I write about. I think that the reader would like to be with me at the races, but he can't do that. And he would really like to be the next one down the bar listening to all the funny stories, but he can't do that. So I write it for him.

"The magazine's the next best thing to being there, or at The Barley Mow, and he can read it in New Zealand or Japan or wherever, all the funny, interesting and amusing things. I mean the whole fucking world sees the race on TV, which has tended to almost dilute the necessity for being there.

"Getting back to Denny and his gearbox. I never have been and never will be technically minded. And I've always thought that the majority of readers are like me, so why bore them? Why should I endeavour to describe a gearbox in the magazine? And if I tried there would probably be some words left over!

"At the first motoring paper I ever worked for the editor there said the credo of his publication was to entertain first and inform second. It's been mine ever since. If I don't get amused at a story, I won't write it down, or if there's something in the story that doesn't interest me, I won't put it in the magazine.

"People are interested in people. But it's getting harder to find the characters in Formula 1, the whole atmosphere has changed. Now, we almost never have dinner with drivers. We don't know any of them that well. They're busy with their sponsors. The night before the race they have got to be in bed, and the night after the race they're in their Lears going back. Now, I really enjoy going to the races, just for the company and the chat of the journalists."

DENIS JENKINSON

"There are all sorts of ridiculous things going on, all around you all the time, and you have to keep an eye on the silly people."

When you study photographs taken at the Grand Prix races of over 40 years ago, back when the World Championship series began, you can often find a small, bearded, bespectacled man hovering in the background. Then, as now, he can be seen observing the proceedings with keen interest, peering intently at the engines, kneeling down to look at the finer points of the chassis, watching the faces of the drivers and team personnel, and occasionally scribbling in a notebook.

This is Denis Jenkinson, the famed 'DSJ' of *Motor Sport*, whose venerable spectre still haunts the pit lanes of the world. His keen gaze undimmed by the passage of time, he continues to watch the machinations of the Formula 1 circus with a twinkle in his eye, taking everything in, usually with a grain of salt, and reporting back to his multitude of readers, for whom the Grand Prix gospel according to DSJ is all that counts.

Besides entertaining generations of fans, his musings in *Motor Sport* ('The magazine that gave its name to the sport') have helped inspire others to take up his profession (including this writer) and he remains a mentor to several contemporary journalists. But 'Jenks', as he is known to his host of friends, has his detractors. Those same outspoken opinions that endear him to a legion of enthusiasts cause some people to call him an antiquated curmudgeon. Besides some who accuse him of harping on about the glories of yesteryear, others take issue with his penchant for dividing the whole world into just two categories of people: racers and non-racers, and having little room in his universe for the latter.

However, no-one can deny that Jenks is a pure racer – in thought ("I'm racing 365 days a year in my mind"), word (in conversation he seems *always* on opposite lock, gesticulating frequently, laughing all the while) and deed (he still competes in vintage motorcycle events) – and he's been that way for about seven decades.

(Jenks does not consider a tape recorder to be a necessary tool of the journalistic trade and suggested I would learn more from him if I took notes during our interview. My notes were strewn with indecipherable squiggles, occasioned by outbursts of the Jenkinsonian wit and desperate attempts to keep pace with his rapid-fire delivery of profundities, but this is approximately what I learned.)

He was born about 20 years after this century began, in South London, into a not particularly affluent family. With only a bicycle as a means of conveyance he had trouble getting out to see the world, and sometimes felt imprisoned in his neighbourhood.

In 1931, Mr and Mrs Jenkinson took their boy, all dressed up in a new suit, to see a flower show at Crystal Palace. Little Denis (today, he still calls himself "about half actual size") quickly became bored with the tubrous begonias and welcomed the distraction of the sound of engines in the distance. He went around a corner and discovered motorcycle speedway racing, the spectacle of which left him breathless, and his new suit covered in cinder dust. Back at the flower show the sight of their boy in a sooty suit caused a parental "rumpus", but Jenks was already too far gone to be reclaimed. He was smitten by motorsport.

There followed a visit to the Brighton Speed Trials with his brother, more excursions to Crystal Palace to watch bikes and cars, and so on. A previous fascination with airplanes waned – they were too far away and inaccessible way up there in the sky – and from then on he concentrated all his boyhood energies and fantasies on motorsport.

At school he studied the writers and philosophers and decided that life was there to be grasped, or better still, ridden through at high speed. At race circuits he noted the techniques of the better drivers, saw their vigorous cornering manoeuvres and noticed that the door is only open once. You have to seize passing opportunities quickly, or be consigned to the role of a backmarker. At another Crystal Palace race Jenks suddenly decided he was on the wrong side of the fence and resolved to do something about it at the first opportunity.

He probably read more racing magazines than school books, and in one issue of *Motor Sport* he noticed an advertisement from a racing driver wanting a helper to work, unpaid, on his car. Jenks responded to the advert, was given the job, and went with the driver to Brooklands. That was about 50 years ago, and he's never paid to get into a race since.

Jenks now found himself inside racing circles, but there remained the task of earning a living. Coming from a Victorian family, he was expected to "get a respectable job" and, since he was always drawing things (mainly racing cars), he thought about working in commercial art. He scrapped this idea after meeting some pretentious "arty" people and decided to concentrate on another field with racing possibilities: engineering. In the early war years he studied that subject in college, then worked as an aeronautical engineer for the RAF, doing everything he could to help win the war so racing could begin again.

In his spare time he did technical drawings of racing cars and submitted them to magazines, and when he was asked to give a lecture at school he chose Grand Prix Racing. Jenks "went on and on" (about his subject) "they couldn't shut me up!", holding his audience enthralled for two days and was given a book as a prize: *Motor Racing With Mercedes Benz*, by George Monkhouse. (Later, DSJ wrote his own books, among them the classic *The Racing Driver*, which was 'Dedicated to The Driver over the Limit, may this book help him to recover'.)

By now Jenks had decided that the real heroes in motorsport were the road racers, not the speedway or oval track men, and he set about sampling the thrills of the open road himself. After the war he began racing motorcycles for a living, and in 1948 he went to meetings on the road circuits in Europe, because they paid starting money. In fact, he could get £30 for starting two events on a weekend in Belgium, while people in postwar England were earning as little as £5 a week. Another attraction for Jenks was that he could get to see the car races on Sunday, because his motorcyle races were held on Saturday as preliminary events.

Shortly after these European jaunts began, he met William Boddy, founder and editor of *Motor Sport*, who invited him to send contributions from abroad. In 1953 Bill Boddy asked him to cover all the Formula 1 races for *Motor Sport* ("since you're over there anyway," says Jenks) and the DSJ legend was underway. But his first missives were signed 'Carrozzino' – Italian for the man in the sidecar, and, indeed, that's where the author often found himself.

Writing about racing was a thoroughly exciting business but, for Jenks, the only way to really get the adrenalin flowing is to race. So he continued to do that, first as a solo rider, then achieving considerable success in motorcycle sidecar competition, wherein he was "the movable ballast" in what is surely one of the most dangerous types of motorsport.

And when he became a journalist covering four-wheeled events, Jenks found an outlet for his competitive urges at the wheel of his Porsche 956C in hillclimbs and as a navigator in the notorious Mille Miglia, where for three years running he rode as passenger to Stirling Moss, most famously in 1955, in a Mercedes-Benz sports car. With Jenks reading out instructions concerning oncoming hazards (which he had inscribed on a scroll and unravelled like a roll of toilet paper), the daring duo won the event at an average speed of almost 98mph. Jenks was quite pleased, indeed honoured, to place his life in the hands of the great Moss, and he describes that 10-hour trip of flat-out motoring over 1,000 miles of public roads between Brescia, Rome and back to Brescia as one of the greatest days in his life.

Jenks has been intimately acquainted with many top racing drivers over the years, but he tends to concentrate on the "real racers". Only a handful qualify for his shortlist of men he has most admired in each era he has witnessed: Alberto Ascari, Stirling Moss, Jimmy Clark, Gilles Villeneuve and Ayrton Senna.

And in Jenks' book, anybody who doesn't *race* all the time receives a black mark. In response to Alain Prost's decisions not to compete in heavy rain, DSJ likes to quote Mike Hailwood: "The throttle works both ways" and Gilles Villeneuve: "There's always some speed you can do, no matter what the conditions."

But Jenks disapproves of faithfully reporting a driver's every utterance. He doesn't interview people. He talks to them, but doesn't report what they say. "And if a name doesn't appear in my report it means he did nothing in the race. Period."

He also avoids the post-race press conference, considering it to be an abomination imported from America ("the American Disease"). He says they're always boring: "A lot of claptrap. The bloke who won only did what everybody else was supposed to do. Nobody else did anything. Period."

Though he remains fascinated by the current Formula 1 circus, in Jenks' opinion earlier times were in many ways the good old days. For instance, the mechanics: "Nowadays they get on planes wearing business suits and carrying briefcases. You never see a mechanic with a toolbox any more, and a mechanic without a toolbox is like a woman without a handbag." Nor does he approve of all the public relations shenanigans that go on. When Colin Chapman brought the first sponsors to Formula 1 in 1967 they brought their bad habits with them. Jenks says "Bravo" to Bernie Ecclestone's recent banishment of some PR people from the pressrooms. Also, at the circuits, the most welcome sound to the Jenkinson ears is the shriek of racing engines, firstly, because he loves the sound, secondly, because they drown out the strident voices of those bickering personalities who cause the internal combustions rampant in the sport these days.

Furthermore, says Jenks, the current trend to feature drivers as personalities is rubbish because most of the time it involves creating something from nothing. The average modern driver, who must keep his nose to the racing grindstone from an early age, has no time to learn about life so that he tends to be something less than a brilliant intellect.

According to Jenks, part of the problem lies with today's journalists, not enough of whom have any racing experience, and most of whom don't really know what they're talking about. "Eighty per cent of them are not really interested in racing, they're just sent to the races by their papers to get the news." DSJ is not a 'news' man, and is not interested in the minutae of current events, nor in the puffery of press releases. "Never take anything at face value," he says. "You've got to analyse and interpret."

DSJ says he is a reporter, talking in print to people who aren't able to attend the races. And to do that you don't hang around the pressrooms, which are too far away from the action. At Monza, where new, sanitized press and pit facilities have been built, he thinks he might just buy a ticket and go and sit in the stands among the *tifosi*. And at Silverstone: "I hop on my bike and go out to a corner to see what's happening. You either see it all, or you know it all. I prefer to see it all!"

And over a Grand Prix weekend, "if you keep your eyes and ears open, you get plenty of material. Then, if you put down 10 per cent of that, you've done a good job. You have to try to cut out all the waffle and piffle, all the superlatives, and be brief and to the point – rather like designing a racing car". As an engineer, Jenks was taught to think logically, and he likes to think his thought processes work along the lines of those of Colin Chapman. The Lotus founder was always pleased when he designed a part that could do five jobs, instead of one. The right word works in the same way, and if you string a few of them together to form an entertaining piece of prose that contains an element of humour – all the better.

In one of his 'Letters From Europe' in *Motor Sport*, DSJ once wrote that he never looked in the mirrors of his Jaguar while travelling down an autobahn at 150mph because, in his view, anyone trying to pass him could look after themselves. And on slower roads there were only ever three reasons for using the mirror in his Porsche: to watch for the police, to see if the engine was on fire, or to look at a pretty girl after he had passed her.

But times have changed, in everyday motoring and especially in Formula 1 circles, and now Denis Jenkinson believes you have to be more observant than ever because: "There are all sorts of ridiculous things going on, all around you all the time, and you have to keep an eye on the silly people."

MIKE DOODSON

"I've always had the feeling that if you offered James Hunt a World Championship point for running over his granny, he would get in his car and do it without hesitation."

A prominent figure in the pressroom, and always one of the last to leave, Mike Doodson, a former chartered accountant, is one of the busiest freelance journalists. Besides being Grand Prix editor for *Autocar & Motor*, he writes for magazines in half a dozen different countries. Perhaps his industry owes something to his previous profession and a concern for avoiding red ink. But Doodson's bottom line is that he is an enthusiast.

Over the years Mike Doodson has supplemented his income by making a specialty of ghosting magazine columns for several drivers, putting himself in their shoes, so to speak, and interpreting (sometimes inventing) their thoughts for public consumption.

In what follows, the tables have been turned on the ghostwriter, though absolutely no literary licence was necessary since 'Dood', like many of his peers, is a very articulate and entertaining spokesman.

"I regard myself as a fan who's lucky enough to be paid to do what he does. My mother always used to tell her friends that Mike was somebody who did his hobby, not just on weekends, but all through the week as well. She might have added that he's failed at pretty well everything else.

"For instance, while pursuing legal studies at Cambridge I spent far too much time with my friends in the university's automobile club and left after a year. Let's just say the impetus for the departure didn't come from my side. But my father was very determined that I should have a sensible profession of some kind, so I became a chartered accountant.

"I claim to have been 24 years old for 18 years. It was an age when you could have every justification for being irresponsible, and I was irresponsible for a very long time. I never had any money and didn't care about it. All I cared about was going to the next race. Though my wife Sally says I'm still exactly the same, I think I may have matured a little bit. I may have progressed to about 30.

"At first, I was determined to be a racing driver. I bought a very well used Mallock U2 Clubmans car and spent a lot of money, far more than I had, on rebuilding it. One afternoon I took it to Aintree to try it out. I wound that little car up to what I thought was the maximum possible revs and went into one of the corners, leaving the braking point to what I thought was the last conceivable moment. At that same moment I was overtaken by the entire Chevron works team: a sports car driven by Derek Bennett, the founder of Chevron, a Formula 2 car driven by Peter Gethin, and a Formula 3 car driven by Tim Schenken.

"And they all went past me as if I was stopped. They pulled in front of me, braked about 50 metres in front of me, and flew around the corner in perfect formation. And there I was on the limit. That was the moment I knew I wasn't going to make it as a racing driver. So, how does the saying go? "Those who can, do. Those who can't, write about it."

"I've always read everything I could lay my hands on about motor racing. I had two journalistic heroes: Henry Manney in *Road & Track* and Denis Jenkinson in *Motor Sport*. Manney had a very colourful and entertaining style, and he wrote about other things, including a visit to the nudist colony on the Ile du Lavant. Jenks inspired me because he was travelling around, doing something any enthusiast would give his eye teeth to do. At the beginning of the season he was on the ferry at Dover, sitting there in his Porsche . . . in a Porsche! . . . with a bag full of traveller's cheques, setting off on a great adventure. And Jenks transmitted his enthusiasm for what he was doing through his writing.

"What those journalists did struck me as being far more interesting than going into an office every day. So, after about two years of post-qualification practice in accounting, I took up a full-time job as a motor racing journalist with *Motoring News* in 1969. I started covering club racing, and the first day I went into the office they presented me with this object which filled me with dread. It was a typewriter. And I taught myself to type on two fingers – which is what I still do.

"I got no lessons in Formula 1. I just got flung in at the deep end. The first Formula 1 race I covered was the 1970 Belgian Grand Prix. Pedro Rodriguez won in a BRM in what was the fastest ever race. But all that just washed over me. I flew back to

London from Spa right after the race and ended up sitting in my flat that night realizing that I'd just seen a great motor race and knowing absolutely nothing about how to communicate it to my readers – in 3,000 words, by my deadline, 8 o'clock the following morning. Well, I would not like to look back on that race report.

"Nowadays, the crucial point of the whole weekend for me is still the deadline. And I have quite a few deadlines. For journalists like myself, when the chequered flag comes out and everybody else's work is over, that's the moment our work starts. And for years I really deeply resented the interference of deadlines which prevented me from enjoying myself.

"Tracking down the cause of significant moments, like driver retirements, can be a problem these days because they all vanish so quickly. By the time you want to talk to them they're halfway to Monte Carlo in their private jets. Many times I've been sitting in the pressroom with perhaps the last five or six guys and it might be midnight. I look up and say: 'What the hell happened to Caffi?'. And we all scratch our heads, then somebody says: 'Well, it sounded as if he was having gearbox trouble.' So we all scribble down gearbox. And that's how history is made in Formula 1. I've got many books in my collection, written by fairweather authors who never go to the races, which contain the most crass errors, misinformation or outright inventions of facts that I might have made in some of my early race reports.

"There's a tendency for some journalists, particularly British ones, to hunt in packs, probably because they're all worried that the others might get something they don't have. Now someone like Jenks never did that. He did it all on his own, and I think his stuff was the better for it. Even now, although there's some people who hover around him, I still think he's a lone wolf.

"I don't mix with the other Brits because I think I can do better mixing with other nationalities and try to use an international approach in my reporting. That's useful because it means that my stories have instant markets in different countries. I speak fairly competent French and I also do a lot of reading in other languages. I would say that the good Italian journalists are among the best. The shining example is set for them by Pino Allievi, who is a terrific writer. I also personally enjoy reading Jabby Crombac, because he's a man who continues to be fascinated and enthusiastic about motor racing. There is no sense of lassitude about him, though he's been around for a very long time.

"Most British journalists are trained in the same school as me: *i.e.* none. And we're doing it because we like car racing. The Italians and the French are nearly all trained, professional journalists. Quite often the guy who's writing about motor racing for *L'Equipe* will be sent off to do swimming, athletics, hockey, or whatever. And I admire that.

"I still think I'm a very poor race reporter, because of the time constraints. All my work is done under intense pressure, which makes it very difficult to get the atmosphere of the race. I think you need a night's sleep after a race to be able to get the proper perspective, to be able to filter out the important things from the unimportant ones. Sometimes that sleep is hard to come by. After the 1986 British Grand Prix was delayed (by Jacques Laffite's accident), I remember leaving Brands at 4 o'clock in the morning, still with my *Autocar* report to write. For a moment, accounting began to look attractive again to me.

"I would quite willingly give up race reporting and concentrate on writing racing news and features. Sometimes, when I go into the pressroom after a race and know the work I have to do before midnight, my heart does collapse a little. And, since I got married, my enjoyment has changed. I used to enjoy packing up and closing the front door and heading off to a race. Now, the high point is packing my bag at the hotel and heading towards the airport and coming back home.

"But I've *never* been disappointed by what I found in motor racing. When I first started writing about it I promised myself that if at the start of a race I didn't get that thrill, that kick, that rush of adrenalin, I'd give it all up and go back to being an accountant.

"And after 20 years on the job I still don't feel I'm an expert in this business. Because I have not sat on the starting grid with 25 other cars around me and gone down into that first corner with those guys. Throughout the years I've tried to find out what it's like to drive a racing car. I am *full* of admiration for the drivers since I'm just standing there, not even risking my butt, and they're out there doing just that. I want to know what's going through their minds, so I try very hard to get as close to the drivers as I can, so I can get the words they use to describe the sensations.

This is one of the reasons I enjoy ghosting columns for them.

"The first one I did was Denny Hulme, then Emerson Fittipaldi, Alan Jones, James Hunt and Gerhard Berger. The one I did for the longest period of time was Nelson Piquet, and he was the easiest to do. I learned very early on that I didn't need to talk to him. He just told me to go ahead and write it. I tried to pick up his mood and talked to the people around him. Since he never reads anything in the motor racing press, I could have written 'Nelson Piquet is a homosexual child-molester who overtakes under the yellow flag at every opportunity' and he would still have been friendly. Well . . . maybe he wouldn't have liked the homosexual bit.

"Although none of them are intellectual giants, I'm consistently impressed with the articulateness of racing drivers. Sometimes it takes a special effort to get it out of them. James Hunt is full of wonderful comments, but you've got to pitch a question at him first. He doesn't know where to start. You also have to choose your moment, that's *very* important. I'm a hoverer. A lot of journalists just plunge straight in with their tape recorder, totally unaware of the fact that the driver may be in a rage for some reason. I try to make appointments with them in advance, and I think I get more depth out of them that way.

"I think most of them are extremely bright people. They have to be. It's not just the racing itself – which requires a lot of mental analysis and thinking on your feet – but the politics of getting a new drive, persuading the sponsors to pay you more money, dealing with journalists, and so on. Drivers have got a lot of things going on in their brains at the same time and they're always cross-referencing them. That impresses me.

"Most of them are quite reasonable people, but a ruthless touch is absolutely essential for success as a driver. It's a consistent feature among the best drivers, and I find it quite attractive. James Hunt, for instance, is a charming man – not just with women – and he can be very understanding. I've gotten to know him quite well, first as a driver, and now in the BBC broadcast booth where I keep a lap chart for him and Murray Walker. I've always had the feeling that if you offered James Hunt a World Championship point for running over his granny, he would get in his car and do it without hesitation. He would stop when he'd done it, and he would back up in the hope of getting another half-point.

"I have a feeling that the people who do well in motor racing – the mechanics, team managers, drivers, anyone at the cutting edge – tend to be exceptional people. It has to do with the gladiatorial element. What they're doing is a matter of life and death. If they screw up they can kill somebody. I remember when Elio de Angelis was killed in a Brabham it destroyed Gordon Murray for a long time. Elio was the first guy who'd been killed in one of his cars.

"I think probably somebody who came into Formula 1 from the outside would say that the drivers and many of the people here are not really human beings at all, because they just live in the milieu of motor racing. That's where I live, for better or for worse. My wife thinks it's for worse and criticizes me for it. She finds I can't switch off, and I think most of the blokes in our position are the same. We're just so interested in it we can't look away from it and see anything else. And, when you're a freelance journalist, you can't *afford* to look away from it because things happen so fast you've got to be there to keep track of what's going on."

JOE SAWARD

"If you are going to a party of extraordinary people all the time it is quite hard sometimes to make the adjustment to the real world."

The International Editor of *Autosport* once described a driver as tzigane (gypsy-like) and referred to certain of the Monza *tifosi* of the feminine gender as callipygous (beautifully bottomed). Besides a predilection for peppering his prose with such 'sawords', Joe Saward has another unique distinction among the journalists: he doesn't drive a car and has no desire to get a licence to do so.

Saward believes that may be an advantage because he doesn't think like a frustrated racing driver, hence the path to making better critical judgments is less encumbered. If his background contributes to any particular way of thinking, it may be that of a spy, since Saward's speciality while earning a degree in history from London University was the covert actions of the CIA in

South Vietnam in the '50s, particularly psychological warfare and black propaganda. Thus, Saward may be better equipped than most to infiltrate the shadowy world of intrigue that prevails in the darker corners of the pit lane and behind the smoked glass windows of the motorhomes in the paddock.

While still in school Saward discovered Formula 1 racing. "What first got me interested was in 1977, when I would turn on the BBC and there were these two crazy guys called Pironi and Patrese who kept crashing all the time, and I thought this was great. Then in 1978, at Monza, I watched the Ronnie Peterson accident and I suddenly thought, Jesus, this is serious! Before it was a game, and then suddenly there is a guy dead and I thought, why do they do it? And then I started buying the magazines, getting drawn into it, wanting to know the answer to the question, why do they do it? And that continued while I was at university, and I got to be the archetypal magazine reader."

By the time of his graduation Saward had his sights set on a career as a journalist for his favourite magazine, *Autosport*, but his scholastic achievement was no immediate passport to that already crowded vocation. But close scrutiny of *Autosport* revealed that no-one was reporting regularly on the European Formula 3 Championship, and Saward decided he would leap into that void. He sat in the grandstand at Silverstone for one event, submitted a report to the magazine, and was given the job "at an incredibly ridiculous figure that you couldn't live on".

The enterprising young man then went to *Motoring News* and told them, since *Autosport* now had a Formula 3 correspondent, *Motoring News* couldn't afford to be without one, and Saward was just the man to do it. That publication agreed, but his twin incomes still left him ill-equipped to finance a season in Europe, so Saward applied for, and was given, a university grant to cycle across America and write about it. That adventure had to wait, as Saward embarked for Europe with a borrowed camera and a tent in the summer of 1983 on an escapade that was "madness, complete madness!".

He mainly travelled by rail, then hitch-hiked to the circuits, and wrote his first magazine report "sitting in the middle of a station somewhere in Denmark at 4 o'clock in the morning. I just basically bummed all over Europe in '83 and again in '84, when I also covered the European Touring Car Championship. Didn't make any money at all. The bank managers were going bananas. They never knew where I was, and I never went to the same bank twice. By late summer I was completely bankrupt. I came home in a tyre truck at the end of the season. It was just ridiculous. I thought I was going to be arrested!"

Saward managed to escape the long arm of the law, and instead was given a temporary job in the production department at *Autosport* which staved off starvation until he was assigned to cover the British Touring Car Championship. His continuing excursions abroad to follow the European saloons were made much easier when Saward talked Tom Walkinshaw, leader of the Jaguar team, into giving him a seat on his private plane. In 1988, Saward finally went Grand Prix racing for *Autosport*, reporting on the qualifying sessions (and writing an occasional Globetrotter column), working with that magazine's Grand Prix Correspondent (and Fifth Columnist), Nigel Roebuck.

"All that secret service stuff is actually quite funny because, even with the nicest one in the world, when you are dealing with team managers, they like to keep secrets. Because to have a secret is to be powerful, and they use all kinds of methods to keep their secrets. So, if you ask a question, you have to ask the right question. I'm talking about wording, because if you ask a question that is slightly loose, they will slip out of the trap. The phrasing of the question is super-important because if you don't ask the right question, you don't get the right answer.

"When you first start out, you don't even notice the games they play, but the more you play the game the more you notice. And to be honest, some of the Formula 1 team managers are quite good about black propaganda. You get told a lot of things, and some of them are not true, and you have to work out what is true and what is not. And if you believed everything that you were told by the PR men, you would write absolute rubbish!

"So you have your own spies and you build up networks within the teams. And it is like, in a way, being a sort of mini-spymaster. Because I have got people in all the teams, whose names are never mentioned, who slip me bits of information. People love to spill the beans. They like telling secrets and all I do is, I just sort of massage the secrets out of them."

Besides his intelligence gathering, Saward loves language and words, and he enjoys communicating to an audience that is clearly defined in his mind. "I am writing, first of all, for the guy who I used to be, so that he knows what has happened and how exciting it is to be there. You have to tell them what it is like to be in Rio de Janiero because otherwise it can be anywhere, a report is a report is a report. What you have to do is feed the market, and the market is dreamers."

Joe Saward is still trying to find answers to the original question that attracted him to the sport. "I'm sure that the thrill and the competition are factors. But I think it is deeper than that, psychologically speaking. I think that the drivers all feel the need to prove something, whatever that might be. Why are Grand Prix drivers, generally speaking, womanizers? Because they are trying to prove something to somebody. Maybe themselves, maybe the world, I don't know. But they are all different, so you can get the motivation of one and you think you have got it sorted out, and then you see another one and you think, no, that doesn't work.

"The sport attracts unusual people. Most of them, obviously the drivers, but also the engineers, the journalists, all of them have taken massive risks to get where they are. That is something that only a limited number of people will do. Most people say, 'I will settle for a nice, comfortable life. I'll earn my £70,000, have a car, a house, a dog, a wife', not necessarily in that order, but they have security. But people who come and do this generally have no security, because it is a rotten kind of life if you want to have any sort of normal, stable existence. So they all are a bit nutty in their own way. It does attract a weird kind of person. They're a bit like the retired spies I've met: they have unusual minds, they think laterally, they think sideways, they have fun, they live for the moment, and it is a different kind of attitude to life.

"This is an interesting, fascinating world, that is why I'm here. Every little kid wants to join the circus, that is what I did. It is just a sort of grown-up kid's dream. And it affects your life. Sometimes, when I would go to a party in London, I would hate myself for writing everybody off as being boring. But at that party you might meet one extraordinary person, and if you are going to a party of extraordinary people all the time it is quite hard sometimes to make the adjustment to the real world."

JOHNNY RIVES

"I remember when I was a boy racing my bicycle around the house in Toulon. I was the driver behind the steering wheel."

For most Grand Prix journalists, covering motor racing is a way of life. For Johnny Rives, it gave purpose to his life during a time of deep despair. Rives, Grand Prix Correspondent for the French daily sports newspaper *L'Equipe*, is a *pur sang* (pure blood) enthusiast, whose love for the sport is nothing less than a deeply felt passion. His love affair began many years ago, when he was a boy in Toulon and a certain racing driver captured his imagination.

Little Jean Rives was called Jeannot by his friends, but his mother preferred Johnny, after Johnny Weismuller, the American actor who played Tarzan in the movies. Films were a familiar part of the Rives household, since Johnny's uncle, who lived with the family, owned a cinema. More importantly for Johnny, he was a rally driver.

"When I was not at school I was in the garage with him, polishing his Simca Sport. It was in '51, '52. I was 14, 15. And he told me about his rallies, and all the stories you can say to a young boy for his imagination. My uncle was 45 or 50 at this time, but very enthusiastic. For me, he was my best friend. He was like a poet. And from talking to him I had the idea to go to a race not far from Toulon. There I fell in love with motors completely because of the sports cars, the Jaguars and Porsches. For me it was a revelation. My life was there.

"And after that I read the books of Paul Frère (the Belgian racing driver/journalist). And the driver I loved at the time was Jean Behra, of France. He was driving for Gordini, and for us he was a great hero. And quickly, I wanted to become Jean Behra. But how to become Jean Behra? There was no money at home, no money at all. So I thought of the books of Paul Frère. That was the way to go. I will become a journalist, and after that I will find a car and get behind the wheel. Like Frère. Then like Behra.

"And I saw my first Grand Prix in '56 in Monte Carlo. I remember well the first lap where I was with a friend at Tabac corner. There was a mixup at Ste Devote between Musso, Fangio and some others. We did not know that, but at the end of the first lap Musso in the Ferrari was leading by 100 metres. Then came Behra. He accelerated to the Bureau de Tabac where I was standing. And when I saw him: no it's impossible he can turn, take the corner, because it's too fast. And he was very quiet sitting in his car. He turned the corner magnificently. Sideways. Yes. Yes. Brilliant! I fell in love again!

"I was 19 at this time, and I started three or four months later to write in a small newspaper in Toulon, though I was still in school. Then I went to the army. I spent two and a half years in Algeria, where there was a war at this time. I was in the infantry, a sous-lieutenant. I lost a lot friends . . . close to me. It was a very bad experience. And I was to come back from Algeria destroyed . . . really destroyed.

"I wrote to the chief editor of *L'Equipe* at this time and sent him my articles from the small Toulon newspaper. I knew nothing. He was very famous. But he wrote me. He said you know very well Formula 1 racing, it's just that you have to practice writing, then you have a big chance to become a journalist. So I sent him, I would say, 10 letters during this two and a half years, and he always answered me. And at the end of my military service I asked him if there was a chance to find a job with him in Paris. I had never been to Paris.

"That was 1960. I was 22. I telephoned to him and he told me to come to Monte Carlo for the Grand Prix and we would talk together. There, he asked me to make his lap chart for the race. And it was . . . it was a terrible souvenir. Because, I remember, I made the lap chart easily, but I could not find an interest in the race. I was still in Algeria . . . with my bad memories.

"I could not find an interest in motor racing. It was so far from the awful world I knew in the war. I could not find myself.

So, I thought, I lost my interest for everything. It was very hard. But I went to Paris to *L'Equipe*. They took me and I started to work, but it was not pleasant for me. It was very difficult for me for three years. I was alone.

"One day the editor introduced me to an old motorbike racer who was very famous in France. And he was with two young racers. They were Jean-Pierre Beltoise and Jean-Paul Behra, the son of Jean Behra! They wanted to meet me and they took me with them. They were a group of friends for me. I went to their races and we talked about motor racing, and everything. So I began to live again. That was at the end of '63. My life started again.

"Maybe motor racing is like a drug for me. It's very difficult to imagine that I could stop watching motor racing. The only thing for me is the cars on the track. I like to see the drivers driving. Only that. I hate the paddock. Too many people are involved in motor racing only because of money. Too many. Too many, 99 per cent. I don't like them. I don't like sponsors. I don't like the other journalists, too many journalists who do not love motor racing. They are here just because it's a big prestige. In French they are *poseurs*. I don't like them. I like to be in a quiet corner, with a good friend, a journalist or photographer who knows motor racing. And we love to speak, about a driver, about his car, about his tyres, about what can happen tomorrow if it rains . . .

"The best part of the weekend for me, after the race, is 9 o'clock on Sunday night. My work is finished! I'm happy that my article is in Paris. Maybe it's bad, but it is in Paris at least. Then I am ready to talk about racing again. You know, sons of some of my friends became journalists, perhaps because of my influence. I talked about my life with their fathers and they were inspired. I am very proud of that.

"I remember when I was a boy racing my bicycle around the house in Toulon. I was the driver behind the steering wheel. I was going very fast. I was driving a Gordini, a blue one. It was 1952. It was just after I had seen Behra in the *actualité*, the news, at the cinema. He was driving a Gordini, a blue one, when he won in Reims. It was a non-championship race, so he was not driving a Maserati. But everybody was there. The Ferrari team, Maserati team, all the British teams. Behra won and I remember the *actualité*, the movies . . . It was a black-and-white film, but I knew the Gordini was blue. The man who was at the camera was in front of a field of wheat. The Gordini was behind the wheat. And Behra was in it. And I was with him."

JEAN-LOUIS MONCET

"Each day, the tension becomes higher and higher and higher.
Suddenly it is all finished. Then I must wait for the next race."

A good friend of Johnny Rives is Jean-Louis Moncet, Sports Editor of France's *L'Auto Journal* and a race commentator on the TF 1 television channel. Moncet is also a close friend and confidant of Alain Prost, with whom he co-authored *Life In The Fast Lane*, Prost's autobiography. The seeds for Moncet's own life at speed were sewn shortly after he learned to walk.

"It was quite easy, you know. My father was born in Le Mans, so I remember, maybe at three years old, my family talking about sports cars. My father was a pilot in the French Air Force. My eldest brother is a captain of a jumbo in Air France, my first brother-in-law is a fighter pilot in a Mirage, another is a technical director in Air France. And in the Moncet family everybody talks about airplanes and cars. That's all.

"My family moved to Morocco for a while, and in 1956 came back to France, to Nice. I saw my first Grand Prix at Monaco in 1961. My study was literature, and when I was a student I worked on a newspaper and I decided to become a journalist. Then I did my school of journalism, and for me, journalism must also have travel. I wanted to discover the war zone. Except in sports, there was no travel, and for my career I chose automobile sports. I made the acquaintance of Jabby Crombac and, in July 1971, he said to me he needed an assistant at his magazine *Sport Auto*, so I did that. I grew up in *Sport Auto*, in Formula 3, then in Formula 2. I followed Lafitte, Jabouille, Arnoux, Prost. I began to do some commentaries on television for Tele Monte Carlo, and because of my friends, the drivers, it was possible to follow the Grands Prix.

"So I am here. And like my friend Johnny Rives I am completely an enthusiast. Completely. Not specifically the technical things about the race, but the men, the drivers. More than the technique, you know, it's something beautiful about them. The drivers are fantastic guys and they all have very different character. I had good friends, like Tambay and Villeneuve. He was Canadian, yes, but like family, you know. When we lost Gilles in Belgium, back in 1982, it was very bad for us. For Prost, for

Arnoux, we all paid the price. But our enthusiasm came back. Our pleasure. For the French, there is always someone. Prost, of course, and now Alesi.

"It is during the pressure of the Grand Prix that you can discover the character of the people here. All the mechanics, OK, they are very good, at a very difficult job. The drivers, we can see how they work. The team managers, some are not very competent, I think. The man I like very much is Ron Dennis. I prefer him because I think his first characteristic is he likes the race. He thinks for the race, he learns for the race, he works for the race. Not specifically for McLaren, but for Le Grand Prix. He is a racer.

"Some of the journalists also are not very competent. I am sorry about that. Johnny is very good. Allievi is very good. And some others. But many don't know about the race, about the drivers, about the technique. About Grand Prix generally. And only a few PR people are good. Like Agnes Carlier of Philip Morris Marlboro. When you know all the drivers it is quite easy to talk to them. But for television sometimes you need the PR people to arrange things, and only a few of them can do this.

"The best time for me, but the most difficult also, is the live Grand Prix on television. You have to go fast with no mistakes, with great enthusiasm. Because all the action is just at the moment. That's fantastic. It is after the Grand Prix, after the stories, that is the worst time. Because, on the weekend, during the practice and each day, the tension becomes higher and higher and higher. Suddenly it is all finished. Then I must wait for the next race."

JABBY CROMBAC

"One of the attractions of this sport is to meet the sort of people we do. Whether they are mechanics, or engineers, or team managers, or the drivers, they are all adventurers."

Given his incessant perambulations up and down the pit lane, Gerard 'Jabby' Crombac personifies a favourite saying in Formula 1 circles: to stand still is to go backwards. Crombac's forward progress has seen him chalk up more Grands Prix than anyone else, (400 of them as of the 1990 Monaco event). The pipe-smoking Parisian journalist has been observing the World Championship series since it was formally organized in 1950.

"One of the attractions of this sport is to meet the sort of people we do. Whether they are mechanics, or engineers, or team managers, or the drivers, they are all adventurers. They are prepared to make sacrifices in their life to have an exciting life. Sacrifice, for the drivers, is taking risks. For the others, it's working the way they do, with all the travelling. They haven't got a family life. That's why we see such a turnover in people, because many of them can only take this life for so long. Still, a few here have done their stint. Bob Dance at Lotus and Alan Challis at Williams have stayed on over the years. Apart from that, they are all fairly new people . . . at least to me.

"I've kept my enthusiasm because it's never the same here. You see, I'm especially interested in the technical side of it, and the evolution is absolutely flabbergasting! So there's always something new, something interesting to look at and write about. The most exciting Grand Prix for me is one in which there are new cars. I am in a *dream* for the whole weekend.

"I'm still here because I still enjoy it. And I was lucky to start my own magazine, *Sport Auto*, and make a success of it. So, you know, this is the one thing I have built in my life, and though I've sold it, and I am semi-retired, I kept Formula 1. It's my life."

Crombac was first introduced to the racing life when he was seven years old and his father, who had a chain of department stores in Paris, took the family on a picnic to a motorsport event. That was just before the outbreak of World War Two, and Crombac was also a spectator at the first postwar race in Paris, in September 1945. That winter he came down with a severe case of 'flu and was bedridden for some time. He asked his father to buy him some magazines, and Crombac senior presented him with stacks of *Motor Sport* and *Motor*, from which Jabby learned all about racing. From them he also learned English, and became something of an automotive anglophiliac.

A stint as a race mechanic trainee with the driver Raymond Sommer in 1949 soon lost its attraction when Crombac discovered it was not going to lead him "straight into the cockpit of a Grand

Prix car". He went to work for his father, ostensibly to learn about the department store business, but in Jabby's mind only to earn enough money to buy a racing car. Meanwhile, he fed his hunger for racing by becoming the Continental Correspondent for *Autosport*. In it he also read about the expoits of Colin Chapman, who was carving a swathe through English club racing in his self-built Lotus Mark VI. Crombac and a friend went halves and bought the car from Chapman and raced the first Lotus to be sold abroad.

Crombac became Chapman's 'man in France' and was such a pronounced Lotus afficionado (his late basset hound responded to the name of Lotus) that Denis Jenkinson once joked that one of his eyes was green, the other yellow, then the colours of the team. (DSJ has been writing longer than Crombac, but has not attended as many Grands Prix.) Jabby named his son Colin James, after Chapman and Jimmy Clark, who shared a flat with Crombac in Paris in the latter part of his career. When Crombac bought his second car from Chapman, in 1955, he came to the factory to assemble it. "Colin said the mechanics will help you, and this tall bloke with a moustache worked with me. His name was Graham Hill."

In 1962 Crombac and an ex-racing driver friend who owned a bar in Paris founded the magazine *Sport Auto*, but from the beginning Crombac seldom wrote about the drivers in the sport he loves. "Because I've been a driver myself, and a bad one. So in my mind there are two kinds of drivers. There are my gods, and they deserve a bit better writer than me, and the others. I don't care about them too much, because I have been a bad driver myself, and I think, of course, they are 200 times better than I ever was, but they are still not the top. And I am very elitist.

"Obviously, Jimmy Clark was one of the tops on my list. Before that, when I was at Reims in 1949 and someone introduced me to Tazio Nuvolari, my hands were shaking. Of course, I was a young enthusiast. But to me, he was the epitome of all that I had read about. Like Jimmy, I was very close with Mike Hawthorn, too, and whenever he came to Paris we would get together. We were both vintage car enthusiasts, so that linked us together. I don't think I could have the kind of conversation with a driver today the way I could with Mike Hawthorn, discussing the merits of the prewar Alfa Romeo with the swing-axle in the rear, and so forth.

"I was closer to the drivers when we were the same age. But nowadays we have a different era, a change in the driver's mentality. The drivers are not motor racing fans, they are sportsmen who are trying to make a career, and big money, and succeed, and be on television, and so forth. And that is something which I don't appreciate so much.

"I think you have to be realistic, of course. I do remember the days when there were no sponsors at all, but I also do remember that at this period, the drivers would change their clothes in the front of the truck, and this is where the debriefing would take place, too. And if you wanted a drink or a sandwich, you had to go and queue at the nearby restaurant. So, let's face it, the sponsors have brought us a very, very comfortable life. And financially speaking, you have a lot more butter upon your bread than you did in the early days."

Crombac helps earn his daily crust by contributing to the FISA news bulletins that are issued in the pressrooms several times throughout a race weekend. This is the reason for his stalking up and down the pit lane incessantly. "There are things the teams won't tell you. If you see they are doing something odd, then you can ask a question and get an answer. But if you don't prompt the question, I mean, prime them, you'll get: 'Oh, fine today, no problem'. They don't like any problem to appear in the *FISA News*. So you have to be on the lookout all the time. That's why I go up and down all the time. I never stop more than two minutes."

GIORGIO PIOLA

"In Formula 1 there are no normal people. Even the journalists, they are all crazy, or anyway sometimes not very well in their head!"

The sound of a telephone ringing in the pressroom might actually be Giorgio Piola, an Italian journalist whose melodic mimicry of the device has caused more than one of his colleagues to try to answer a non-existent call. Piola's other unique talent, the ability to draw the finer technical points of Formula 1 chassis in great detail, is the envy of even some of the designers themselves. His fascination with the technical aspects of the sport at one time posed something of a dilemma for the handsome native of Genoa.

"When I was younger I used to say I was more excited to see a new Formula 1 car than to make love with a girl I had already done it with. This is a joke! But I'm very excited when I see something new in design, to be able to be the first one who does the drawing and to be able to show it to the people."

Piola's engineering studies at university were interrupted by an accident suffered in his other main interest, show jumping. Injuries sustained in a bad fall left him unable to read for some time, but he could still draw racing cars, which he and his three brothers had always done. As to who was the best artist was in some dispute, and Giorgio bet his older brother that he could get one of his drawings published first. The two sent some of their work to a newspaper and Giorgio won, his reward taking the form of a free trip to the 1969 Monaco Grand Prix as an artist for the paper. Thus Piola's career was launched, much to the chagrin of his father, a lawyer for the Pope, who thought his son should continue university and become an engineer.

"But this Formula 1, especially then, was a wonderful world, it was more like a movie. So I was living like in a dream, and I lost completely my university, because I could have gone on. But I have to tell you that I prefer it like this because I could never be an engineer in racing, knowing that if I make a mistake the driver can be killed. I could not take the responsibility. While if I do a drawing for a newspaper, of course I try to do my work in the best way that I can, but nothing bad happens if I make a mistake.

"And, being an Italian, I like a lot the quality of my life. I could not work in a factory eight hours a day. I prefer to work, if I have to, all the night long on my drawing table, and then if outside is sunny, I take my boat out to sea. I live on the harbour near Genoa with the sea on two sides of my house. I also ride my two horses every morning, and I still do jumping competitions. I prefer to work like a freelance, even if the future is never sure, but I never think about the future.

"In Formula 1, I am most interested in the technical side. I find that here, even on the human side, I have more relationship with the engineers. I talk more about life, about feelings, with the engineers, not with the drivers. Because the drivers sometimes seem to be living in a sort of dream, or being like young boys, with not very big souls.

"I think in a good, and in a bad way, we can say that in Formula 1 there are no normal people. Even the journalists, they are all crazy, or anyway sometimes not very well in their head! There must be something wrong in their mind, because you can do a lot of other jobs easier. But probably we like the pressure.

"There is a lot of competition. Especially in Italy. We have at least 12 daily newspapers. For example, *La Gazzetta dello Sport*, which I work for, every Grand Prix has two whole pages. It's a lot. And people say that in Italy you have to talk every day about Ferrari. It's very difficult sometimes. The people consider Italian journalists the more pushy. But you have to understand we have to do what we have to do, because we are in such a big competition. But I am not writing in the scandalistic way, and I prefer to lose a news story than to write something that in the end is rubbish.

"In Italy you need to write a completely different story from what you need to write in France and what you need to write in England. For example, in France they are more nationalistic. They even talk about the slowest French driver as if he could be World Champion. Even a driver that never qualifies in the points. And if you read an article in a French magazine, you believe this must be God. This must be the best Formula 1 driver.

"The English press are a lot more quiet than the French and the Italian. For example, some of them are always trusting the press releases. They never try to go beyond the press release. In Italy you can't do that. There is such a big competition that you must have something more than the other journalists, and the English don't understand this. When they see a quote, they write it and they stop.

"The public relations people are useful for people who don't speak other languages. I don't like to be considered arrogant, but for the inside people like myself, Jeff Hutchinson, Nigel Roebuck, Pino Allievi, and a few others, for us they are nearly useless. OK, when you have too much to do, then you ask Eric Silbermann about Honda, and that is very useful. But the press releases they give out in the pressroom, I never read them. It is more important to be able to talk with Nigel Mansell by yourself. Not in the middle of other people. For the same reason I don't like too much the press conference. Because the driver always makes stupid answers, just to get it over with, and you don't have the real answer.

"I like to consider that I try to give to the readers the truth, the pure truth. I consider that a journalist for a daily newspaper – not for a weekly or monthly magazine – has to be like a photographer of what has happened. He is a reporter, writing a very short introduction, and then it is the driver who has to talk so you can understand if this driver is nice, if he's mean, if he's a son of a bitch, or whatever he is.

"I'm doing this job now for over 20 years, and sometimes I don't have as much enthusiasm as before, because it's completely changed. I know it's the first feeling that I'm becoming old, but I remember when it was a wonderful world, like a family. There were no motorhomes, no helicopters, and Ken Tyrrell was eating sandwiches. And Ken Tyrrell is the person who has changed less than everybody else. I remember that Colin Chapman was a wonderful man to talk with. And there is no more Enzo Ferrari. And Ferrari is a big loss. To go into a press conference at Ferrari, for me, the interest is 20 per cent of what it was before. Before, even writing sometimes against Ferrari was a pleasure. Because you knew that you were making fed up the Old Man. Now you are only making fed up the Fiat people!

"But one thing I like a lot in this work, especially in my technical side, is that I'm a little bit like 007, James Bond. There is always a fight between myself and the engineer. The engineer doesn't want to show me anything and, of course, I have to try my best. But there are some rules. I will never steal a drawing. I will never listen to a conversation hiding behind the door. But very often I come to the race track at 7 o'clock in the morning, before all the mechanics, and sometimes I find out a very important scoop on the technical side. Fortunately, it's changed now, but in Italy they used to say I was a spy from Honda, and in England they thought I was a spy from Ferrari!"

PINO ALLIEVI

"The drivers often say that we ask stupid questions, but I often think that I am wasting my life asking some stupid drivers normal questions to which they don't want to reply."

Pino Allievi was born on the shores of Lake Como, in the Italian lake district, not far from where the illustrious authors Pliny The Elder and his nephew Pliny The Younger had homes nearly 2,000 years ago. In university, Allievi studied sociology, but he was, and still is, very interested in literary criticism and Italian literature. His own writing, about Formula 1 racing in *La Gazzetta dello Sport* (where he has been since 1968), is of the highest standard, and he is one of the most highly respected racing journalists working in any language.

It was only a coincidence that his father was the administrative director for Enzo Ferrari (for three years beginning in 1937), but the connection helped Allievi gain Ferrari's confidence, providing him with a fund of exclusive material with which to entertain the multitude of Prancing Horse fans in Italy. It was also the best possible training for Allievi to develop his skills as a chronicler of the human side of the sport, which is now his speciality.

"I was very close to Ferrari, he was very nice with me because of my father. Of course, it was very difficult to know his secrets. He was a very complicated man. Not an easy man. He had a very complicated head on his shoulders and very sophisticated kind of talk. Ferrari had a big, big, big sense of humour, of course, and it was funny to be with him. Today, in Formula 1 there is nobody with his culture. Nobody at all. Because Ferrari had total culture, from literature to history. He was a very sophisticated man. He didn't make so many studies, but he was reading books and newspapers, magazines, till 5 o'clock in the morning, sleeping only a few hours. So he was informed on everything. And today there is nobody like him.

"But you have some very kind, very clever people here, like for example Frank Williams. Even Ron Dennis, I think. I have a lot of respect for Ron Dennis, because today he has no more the arrogance that he had in the beginning, and I continue to ask myself why he wants to show the people only the worst face that he has and not the best one. Because during the time span of 10 years I have discovered that Ron Dennis is a very nice person if you talk with him. Another very clever man is Gerard Larrousse, for example, and Giancarlo Minardi.

"I enjoy to talk with clever people, like Senna. Definitely, a very, very clever guy, very complicated, but very clever. He has qualities that are difficult to find in other drivers. Prost is also very clever but he always suspects people. I want to include Gerhard Berger because he is one of the few drivers with a sense of humour. And that's very important. He has a sense of the limit of the job that he is doing. Like Niki Lauda, who was my close friend. Among the drivers, I also remember with a lot of affection Mario Andretti. Because, in my opinion, he had the best compromise between a man, first of all, and a driver.

"Generally, the people in Formula 1 are normal and average. But plenty of them think they belong to a special kind of people. There are a lot who want to be in the jetset. You see a lot of people who want to show themselves, for the prestige, to have a satisfied ego. There are plenty that have a lot of complexes. I see that in the journalists, the constructors, the drivers, plenty of people who have chosen their career because Formula 1 goes on the front page of the newspapers. If Formula 1 was on page 16 they wouldn't have chosen this career. Maybe they would have gone to be an actor, to work in the theatre, in Hollywood, and so on. So, it's necessary to watch this kind of world with an ironic point of view . . . otherwise you get crazy!

"I think that the average person in Formula 1 has a big head. A very, very big head. I think you see that when they are interviewed by television. They look around and they see how many people are watching them, and they think to give special secrets like they are a researcher on cancer. They forget they only do a sport, with all the limits of a sport.

"I think that the human quality of the engineers in Formula 1 is the best. Maybe because they did university, they did studies, they know something outside Formula 1. I only see 30 per cent of the drivers that are with their feet on the ground. All the others are, I don't want to say stupid, but like children. I often write that and I have a lot of enemies because of it.

"But I want to be very realistic. I think that it's very easy to think that you can educate the people through the press. Maybe you can't, but you can describe the true side of the sport. So I try to describe the truth. But I have a lot of secrets, shocking things, I will never write because I have respect for the consequences this could have on certain people. Still, I write about the drivers with their positive points and their negative points. And you get many people who don't want you to destroy their heroes. And that's very delicate. And then, I don't think that the people reading sports have a sense of humour. They don't want to have compromises, they don't want you to make jokes about their idols. That's a problem.

"Because we must do a very special job with a lot of people around, it's very difficult to work in this crowded atmosphere along the pit lane, to have contact with the people that you want to talk to. You have five minutes of two people talking, and that's a big shame. And so, when I walk around, first, I ask myself what am I doing here? That's a demonstration that I may be in the wrong job, because sometimes I am disgusted. The drivers often say that we ask stupid questions, but I often think that I am wasting my life asking some stupid drivers normal questions to which they don't want to reply. It's very depressing to make some interviews with some people. But in Formula 1 you have sometimes to make interviews with them, and that is very boring and depressing.

"I don't accept the way to make an interview is only by making jokes with the people that you interview. If you see some of the press speaking to Mansell, for example, they try to show him how nice they are, how clever they are and so they make jokes. It could be that they admire too much the driver, and if the driver feels that you admire him too much, he puts himself in the position of a star, not of a man. But if you talk on an equal level to him, everything changes. So it must be clear that we need a mutual respect. He is not the star and you are not the stupid journalist in a hurry to lick his feet.

"I think that the Italian press is the more international press, because we write about everybody. For us, Ligier gets the same space as Minardi. Of course Ferrari gets the biggest space, but even in other countries Ferrari is important because they are the only team doing all the World Championships since 1950. The French people have a complex because they don't have a competitive team. They don't want to write that, but they have this kind of complex.

"The British are very nationalistic and most of them are writing about very light things, stupid things, except for four or five journalists. These people are very definitely on the top and, personally, I think Nigel Roebuck is one of the best informed in the history of Formula 1. But there is a big gap between them and all the others. The most stupid things that I ever read are in the British press. Some of the daily press of Great Britain is terrible, it is disgusting, it is the worst in the world!

"The American press is very practical. They don't know anything about Formula 1, but when they write, they write serious things. Then you have the South American press, that is the press of the drivers, not of Formula 1 racing. But I think that the average of the Brazilian and Argentinian press is very, very good. Because I am lucky enough to read in Spanish and Portuguese, and so I read a lot what the other people write, I can tell you that 90 per cent of the time I read serious things there. Then you have the Italian press that you can divide into two sections: the sports newspapers that are very well informed – there is a big competition that makes the level go up year by year – and then you have the daily information press. The average is not bad, but you find a lot of writing only about the worst things of Formula 1, and it is very easy to find the negative things here."

FRANCO LINI

"Formula 1 in the last 10 years has become like the Harlem Globetrotters in basketball: a big circus."

The dapper figure of Franco Lini, always nattily attired in a jacket with a scarf or a tie at his neck, has been a fixture along the pit lanes of Grand Prix racing for over four decades. Given that as a boy he lived in Mantua, home of the great Tazio Nuvolari, Lini thinks it was inevitable that he would somehow become involved in the sport of his hero. "You have to keep in mind that in that age, when boys were seven or eight years old, motor racing was something absolutely special, like the space adventures of today. It was not a normal thing, you know. So you have just a god. In Nuvolari sometimes we saw a big man, with a cigarette. He was a big man to a small boy, but in fact Nuvolari was a small man."

The Lini family moved to Milano, where their home was destroyed and all their possessions lost during the war. The hostilities also interrupted Franco's university studies, and the machine tool factory where he had planned to work in sales was also levelled by bombs. So he turned to sports journalism, specializing in motor racing. He covered his first Grand Prix at San Remo in 1949.

In emulation of his hero, Nuvolari, Lini also raced motorcycles, a pursuit that ended in disaster in a mountain enduro race in 1950. "I broke three vertebrae, four ribs, I was totally broke! In fact, the doctor, when he saw me, he believed I was to die before the next morning and the next morning, when he saw me alive, he believed I was to be paralysed all my life. I am very lucky."

His own life as racer now over, Lini concentrated on writing about those who still did it. He covered all types of racing and by the early '60s he was a regular touring member of the fledgling Grand Prix circus, one of the first journalists to travel to every race. When he arrived at Watkins Glen, for the 1962 US Grand Prix, the parochial Americans misunderstood his name and believed he was Irish. "They thought I was Frank O'Lini!"

There was no mistaking his nationality a few years later, for Lini was then the manager of the consumate Italian Grand Prix team. "One day Ferrari called me and, brutally, just like that, he said: 'How much you earn a year? Listen, I believe you are the most knowing of Grand Prix, you know everything and everybody. I will give you the same money plus 50 per cent and you become the team manager of Ferrari.' 'Are you crazy?', I said to him. 'No, come on, you are joking.' 'No, I am serious', he said. 'No, I am not the man for that.' We fought for two days, but finally, at the end of 1966, I became the team manager for Ferrari for two years. I think he was satisfied, especially my rebuilding the image of the team, because the image of Ferrari was deteriorating before."

Over the years Franco Lini has seen the image of Formula 1 change dramatically, and in his view it has deteriorated. When the cars are actually racing, few journalists are more keen. When the engines are switched off, Lini is less enthusiastic. "Exciting, yes. Amusing, maybe not. Because to me, and it is not an old man talking, I believe it is a sport man talking now, to me the world of motorsport is going the wrong way, but especially the Formula 1. First of all the Formula 1 takes over all the other racing activity, which is not normal, is not good for other racing. Second, the Formula 1 in the last 10 years has become like the Harlem Globetrotters in basketball: a big circus.

"Yes, a big circus, but no more a sport. Advertising people have money, and they bring in money here. They bring also a very special type of people who are not interested in motorsport, an ethical sport, or in the technical side. They are just interested in smelling dollars. That is the big problem. I don't like it at all. I don't like the exaggerating. You are exaggerating for advertising in many ways, which is sad. They destroyed the tradition. For an example, in America, Watkins Glen was a very popular Grand Prix for many, many years. Over 200,000 people came there because it was a tradition. They cancelled Watkins Glen only for the money. They don't pay enough money so they go to Las Vegas, Dallas, Phoenix – no tradition, no people. That is happening also in Europe. In Spain, nobody is around, no fans, but they go there because they have money. This I don't agree with because of the destroyed tradition.

"People don't come to a Grand Prix to see Marlboro. They come to see a fight in the race. I say, when in heaven you will call back a memory, it will be of something exciting in a race, something good, not a sponsor's name. Remember '79, the famous last lap of the French Grand Prix, the fight of Villeneuve and Arnoux? It was fabulous! Two men fighting. This is not only me talking. I believe deeply everybody wants that. So I don't agree with the way they go, first of all money, first of all business. And when Bernie Ecclestone says to me, well I have to pay my bills, I say you have to pay your bills, yes, but you want to buy a jet or a helicopter!"

Sometimes Franco Lini would rather go fishing or golfing, "when some stupid things happen in Formula 1", but he vows to stay around as long as there is enough actual racing for him to express his views in the newspaper *Il Giorno* in Italy and several publications in other countries. "Being a journalist would be a fantastic job if you didn't have all the writing! When I am writing I try to give some message, always. I have never been a chronicler. I try to be keen and attentive and look for small details. I watch everything and write, just interpreting sights, interpreting situations.

"It is a tradition that the best writing is in England and Italy. England, in a way, better than Italy. The English, in style, are more deep, and quieter. In Italy you have some very good writing, but the majority has too much emotion. Up and down, up and down, you know: Ferrari is coming back – Ferrari is shit. We know only the up and the down. We don't know any middle."

GEORGE GOAD

"Every man has a secret belief that he is the world's greatest lover, the world's greatest chili cook and the world's greatest driver."

"A lot of these guys may have flat-spotted their brains." George Goad wonders if some of the Grand Prix people have been on the job too long. George himself has been a Formula 1 camp follower for about 10 years, though "I haven't the foggiest idea why I'm here. I'm not a car guy at all".

George is a laid-back Californian whose flowing blond locks are reminiscent of someone who might have driven one of the Little Deuce Coupes immortalized by the Beach Boys. But he didn't. He was an art major in college when his car-crazy room-mates dragged him off to Riverside to see some races. "I didn't know anything about it, but I loved it. Sound of the engines, and all that sort of thing."

When the Grand Prix circus first arrived at Long Beach in 1976 George was there and "got hooked", then found little in America to feed his habit. "Long Beach was usually at the beginning of the year, first or second race of the season, and we would get all excited and see everything and then the cars went away and Formula 1 would drop off the face of planet."

Even the *Los Angeles Times* ignored the sport, and George, with his girlfriend Pam Lauesen, a photographer, decided to do something about it. They formed the Formula One Spectators Association (FOSA). "I wanted it to be a kind of a spectators' union, and the attempt at first was to try and influence media because, if the damn fundamentalists could do it on TV with religion, we figured we would give it a shot. But the attitude in US network television was monolithic: forget it, there is no audience out there, we are not interested, thank you very much. So, faced with that, the job fell to us and the only medium we could afford was the telephone. So we started our hot-line service, and then we followed it up with the race reports and photos in a bulletin."

George finds the Grand Prix world "has very little to do with reality. A parallel might be old Hollywood back when a few people had charge of the studios, and invented the glamour, and had the money, and that was what was happening. And it is basically the same thing here. You have the moguls here in what is probably the last refuge of the robber barons.

"I very much admire the skill of the drivers. Every man has a secret belief that he is the world's greatest lover, the world's greatest chili cook and the world's greatest driver, but as you go through life you are quickly disabused of many of those notions. Watching this from a driver's point of view, threading their way through traffic, you finally have to admit, I can't do that.

"But I certainly admire those who do. Because they do what they do they deserve all the money they get – maybe they don't get enough – and the superstardom. You get a cult of personality over actors and rock musicians, and they are not putting their arse on the line.

"And the technology is fascinating – yet more money . . . all the millions that are pumped into this sport, which is accomplishing nothing. Everybody says that it advances the technology of the motor car, which it does, but that is like a spin-off. It's basically sport and entertainment.

"When Tom Wolfe was writing about the astronauts in *The Right Stuff* he came up with a beautiful scenario of the single warrior combatants. Like when the medieval knights would ride out to do battle in place of armies, huge armies. He said that the astronauts had become this, the same sort of image and I immediately thought that this is Formula 1. Because anybody that drives a Ferrari is carrying the entire colours of Italy, and so on. Nobody is fighting the American battle now. We are the Switzerland of Formula 1."

REBECCA BRYAN

"For anyone covering Formula 1, it is a bit difficult when you're first starting because it is a very tight-knit community."

"Oh, I always thought you were somebody's girlfriend." That was a typical response when people learned that Rebecca Bryan was actually covering Formula 1 racing for United Press International. A native of Little Rock, Arkansas, Bryan is a full-time UPI sports reporter, based in London.

"I cover most of the European races and organize all our Formula 1 coverage, all over the world. I've been doing this since 1986, but I also cover tennis, golf, swimming, track and field, and so on. When I first attended a Grand Prix, as a fan, I didn't think it was any greater spectacle than a track meet. But from inside, given all the hospitality and the way the teams one-up each other, you can't beat it as a journalist in that regard. With the motorhomes and all that sort of thing, every year it seems you've got to have something different, something a little bit better. They were doing lunch, so we're going to specialize in breakfast, and that sort of thing.

"For anyone covering Formula 1, it is a bit difficult when you're first starting because it is a very tight-knit community. Even now, because I don't cover all the races in person, there are gaps to be filled. If you miss a couple of races there are sure to be changes, new people around, people switching teams, and so on. So I have to spend a little time playing catch-up, and people don't automatically recognize you. But if I need a quote from a driver or team manager, and can manage to grab them, they're quite happy to talk to me.

"One thing that's quite interesting for me is that even though there aren't very many women journalists covering Formula 1, there are a few women involved in the photography and PR side of it. That makes it easier. At an international soccer match, you might be the only woman there, period. Which is a very odd feeling. No matter what anybody's attitude towards you is, it just feels odd. Here, at least, I'm not alone."

DAN KNUTSON

"It's a lot more work than I imagined. I thought you'd sit around and watch a race and then afterwards sip a beer and maybe whip out a report."

Dan Knutson was born in South Africa, to American parents, and lived there for 15 years. As a youth he cycled to the nearby Kyalami circuit and decided he would somehow become involved in the racing world. He began by racing a Formula Vee on his return to the States. "But I wasn't really very good and I realized no-one was going to pay me to do it. I grew up reading Denis Jenkinson's stuff in *Motor Sport* and thought, 'That's what I want to do. I want to drive a Jaguar around Europe, going to all the Grands Prix.' And here I am, minus the Jaguar. I found out it wasn't quite as romantic as that.

"It's a lot more work than I imagined. I thought you'd sit around and watch a race and then afterwards sip a beer and maybe whip out a report. I didn't expect to be sitting in the pressroom until 1 o'clock Monday morning. And some of the magazines pay poorly, but there are a lot of guys out there that'll work for free, just for a pass. So it is a struggle financially sometimes.

"When I got my BA in journalism, from the University of Minnesota, they taught us a lot of ethics, like never accepting free lunches. That might work if you're on the staff of *Newsweek* or *The New York Times*, where everything is paid for. But it's not like that out in the real world. It doesn't mean we're bought by the Formula 1 sponsors, but I will eat lunch at a motorhome, and if they give me a free shirt, I might wear it, maybe not at the race track, but elsewhere. At the race track I don't want to favour one sponsor or the other.

"Another thing I found, at first, is that Formula 1 is really a closed shop. There's definitely a lot of snobbery here. I covered some American racing and was used to the very free and open drivers with the media. Here, it was harder for me as an American, as an outsider, because I didn't grow up with these people, through Formula Ford, Formula 3 and Formula 2. I just came in and sort of jumped in at the deep end, while these guys have known each other since the '60s. And I'm also rather a shy guy, too, so it took me a while to get in with them.

"Once you get to know people, it's better. One of my favourite times at a Formula 1 weekend is late in the evening. Because that's when all the hubbub is finished and there's just the people, and then I can sit around and talk to my friends and visit. There are really a lot of nice people, and this is my family away from home.

"The travel sounds glamorous, but it's not. You hang around airports, spend something like a day and a half on an airplane. That's one other advantage the Europeans have over us, they only have a one or two-hour flight. We have a one or two-day flight to get here. It's tiring and it's boring and it's miserable, and you're sitting back there with the crying babies and people kicking your seat and everything.

"But once you get here it's good. I sometimes think if I won the lottery, I'd still do the same thing. And I could fly business class instead of coach, and I could rent Mercedes instead of taking trains. But I'd still do this."

PIERRE LECOURS

"Formula 1 itself is another world. And some people in it believe they are the end of the world!"

In countries where Formula 1 racing is not traditionally a high profile sport, a native son as a driver can suddenly make it newsworthy. Such was the case in Canada when Gilles Villeneuve's exploits made headlines which, in his home province of Quebec, were very often written by Pierre Lecours. Previously, Lecours had covered Villeneuve's high-speed adventures in snowmobiles, then followed him through his Formula Atlantic years, and the two Quebecoise became close friends. Now, Pierre Lecours (who, though he is not slight in stature, translates his name into English as 'Peter the Short') is Mr Grand Prix Racing in French Canada, writing for *Le Journal de Montreal* and contributing reports to a network of radio stations.

Lecours has also covered other types of motorsport, but finds that his Grand Prix involvement commands more respect among his peers on the home front. "It has been very good for my career professionally. I have more consideration now, compared to when I was doing stock cars, drag racing and rallying. The professional journalists, like the hockey guys, or the baseball guys, don't think much of those other kinds of racing. But now Formula 1 is a big thing, and they see how big Le Grand Prix du Canada is, all the travel around the world, and so on. Formula 1 itself is another world. And some people in it believe they are the end of the world!

"Coming from North America, what I don't like is the attitude of some people in Formula 1. Sometimes it's very bad and sometimes it's very funny. It's so pleasant to work with the Indycar people, because they are very available, they are friendly with everybody. They know they are there to give a show. Formula 1 is a really big show. It's a circus. But when the people, like the drivers, think they are more important than the show, it's bad to work here. And there are so many political affairs and so much money involved, that sometimes you have to just step back and try to analyze everything.

"The other day I saw a French newsman wait four hours and a half to have a two-minute interview with Alain Prost. That was really stupid. OK, they have meetings, debriefings, and stuff like that, but it only takes a second to say to you, 'Wait until I do these things, and then I will do the press things'. That's the stuff that I don't like very much about Formula 1.

"But I love the sport, this job is good, the money is good, and I am happy to be here. Sometimes, because we don't have a Canadian driver now, it's less interesting and has less motivation for me. It's much better when you can work with a driver from your country. People back home want to know what's going on with him, and you always have good stories. That's what I miss the most right now, a Canadian in Formula 1."

HEINZ PRULLER

"I love this sport, yes. The racing drivers, yes. But I think there are so many people around who are really unnecessary in the business."

Heinz Pruller is Austria's pipeline into Formula 1, covering the sport in print and on radio and television. Austrian interest began after Pruller's good friend Jochen Rindt became a winner. Prior to that, the situation was a bit different, as Pruller recalls. "I told the Chief Editor I was going to the Grands Prix with Jochen. He said you only call us if your friend is winning, or if somebody is killed. So a normal report was impossible then.

"I also do football, boxing, ski racing, whatever. I love this sport, yes. The racing drivers, yes. But I think there are so many people around who are really unnecessary in the business. We could do without the half of them. Jackie Stewart, 20 years ago, had very good words for them. He said they're professional spectators. And it's these spectators with the special passes who behave like being important and being noticed and pretending to work. But they don't work. I say they're wankers!

"The real work is Sunday nights, when you have to write the long reports when you're tired. That's a tough job. Look at the spectators after a Grand Prix: when they go home they are dull and they are tired, and they're completely blind and deaf. But you have to sit down and write and try to make it good. The other problem is the total chaos the first hour after the race. Like when you have to cross the Monza tunnel, to get to the drivers. They do television from the other side, so you have to go through the pits. It's 200,000 screaming people at Monza.

"And of course, the worst thing is if an accident happens, and it's even worse when it's concerning a friend of yours. Like Berger at Imola in 1989, or Niki Lauda at the Nurburgring in '76. But mostly, like Rindt at Monza in '70. And it was strange, the moment Rindt had the accident. I didn't hear it, I didn't know it, but I felt it. I was . . . shivering, all cold. And that was about two minutes before the loudspeaker said anything. But I felt something terrible had happened. And then he died. And the same thing I felt with Villeneuve at Zolder. I swore to myself, the night of the Nurburgring, if Niki's going to die, I stop this. And it was about the same for me with Berger. Because then it's difficult to defend this sport. A footballer can break his leg. But a racing driver can get killed.

"On the other hand, you can have dinner with a Grand Prix driver the night before a Grand Prix. I had this hundreds of times. It's very difficult to have dinner with a famous football player before a match. Because they have to be together, in a separate room, because they are a team. The skiing people are easier, because everything is about 10 years younger, the mechanics, the journalists, the racers. There's not so much money involved, or so much danger.

"But the easy days are over in Formula 1. Not so much with the drivers themselves. It's more or less the things surrounding them that are a problem, the people who sometimes feel they have to protect the drivers, against the journalists. As far as interviewing is concerned, I hate the press conferences, and all this kind of stuff. I remember when you could talk with the driver for hours and hours. Now it's become much more complicated for the driver, with all the technical briefing and debriefing. And sometimes, some drivers tend to become slightly arrogant. But this might be because of the big publicity that we give them, when everything that comes out of their mouth is a big headline."

ACHIM SCHLANG

"All the people here have to be different from normal because, not to blame the normal people, but if you are normal you probably can't stand it."

Achim Schlang, a journalist for the German magazine *Rallye Racing*, was just three years old when his father took him to the Nurburgring to see a race in 1949.

"I still remember parts of that event which means that I was very, very impressed. I was a fan from this day on. The noise, the atmosphere, the cars. After the first two or three cars crossed the finish line at the end of the race my father said, 'OK, let's go'. And I remember I held his hand as he walked away, and I said, 'Wait, wait, there is still someone coming'. And we waited until the last one came by. It was a yellow Gordini."

There were many more family excursions to the Nurburgring and other circuits around Europe, and the younger Schlang began to follow Grand Prix events in newspapers and magazines. In the German language press he found the coverage to be "a disaster. Very badly done. After you have seen the race in the grandstand as an interested spectator, you knew more about that race than you could read in the newspaper. One day I decided to try to do it better myself, and so it started."

After a term in the army, Schlang studied geography and eastern and asiatic languages, working as a freelance racing correspondent whenever he could. He wrote social-political and military articles for other magazines for a while, then joined *Rallye Racing* in 1984 as a permanent staff member, because "my heart is really in motor racing.

"My main interest is in the men and the sport, and after that the technical part, which also is very interesting. But nowadays you have to be really an expert. It is really necessary to study engineering or something to understand correctly what is going on, especially because the technical directors don't tell a lot about what is going on.

"Along the pit lane you need always to have your eyes open to see the things which are not normal. There is so much going on. Among the journalists there is collaboration and also competition.

And the collaboration works on an international basis. It is more easy to ask an Italian for a quote from Ferrari than getting it from German colleagues. We also help each other, but everybody keeps back the really special things.

"I think all the people here have to be different from normal because, not to blame the normal people, but if you are normal you probably can't stand it, or could only stand it for one year or two years, and then you would stop it. It starts with the travelling around, staying away from home, and spending an average of 120–130 nights in hotel rooms, and things like that. And to stand that is not normal. Probably in England people would say it is not necessary to be crazy to do this job. But it helps!"

MIKAEL SCHMIDT

"Sometimes I don't like that some Formula 1 people are not aware that the press is still very important for them."

Mikael Schmidt, who writes for the German magazine *Sport Auto*, became fascinated with Formula 1 as a 10-year-old, watching the Grands Prix on television. His prime interest was in the technology and, though he studied computer sciences at school, his desire to get closer to racing machinery prompted him to choose Formula 1 journalism as a career.

"For me, the technology is the peak of the sport. I admire the engineers, how they deal with downforce, with the horsepower from the engines. I would say that the contribution of the engineer is as big as the contribution of the driver. I'm a little bit disappointed at some people in the business who say it's just the driver who is the most important man in the team.

"The engineers are fascinating. I think that some of them didn't even study engineering. They came as a mechanic or as a technician into Formula 1, but then they got so much experience about setting up racing cars that they are probably better than people who studied it. And I think they also like the competition. I think there is no engineer in this business who doesn't like motor racing, who is just here because he is pleased to design a car or engine.

"The competition exits also among the journalists. I can just say what's going on in Germany, or in German-speaking Switzerland, and Austria as well, and there is a big competition among journalists as far as it concerns getting information. And if you have good information you never will give it to the others, although you are privately good friends. But I think this business is in every part – whether it's engineers, journalists, or drivers – is to be the best, to be in the top. For us, it's a very expensive job for your employer, because he has to pay all the travel expenses. And in the end, if he sees in the competition paper that they have more information, he will ask you what is going on. So you have to try to be on the top.

"Sometimes I don't like that some Formula 1 people are not aware that the press is still very important for them, and it's very difficult sometimes to get information. And I think that the CART series for Indycars in America is much more professional towards the press. I know it quite well because I am going four or five times to America a year. But some people in Formula 1, I think they feel that they are something better, that it is not necessary to give information to the press. This, I think, is not a very good attitude because, all the sponsors, they expect to be in the press, whether it's in photos, text, or TV.

"For us Germans, we have to be interested in everybody when we have no German drivers here. So we have to deal with the French, with the English, with the Italians. And I think that the press is different in each country. Italians, of course, they focus on Ferrari, and maybe they are sometimes exaggerating in their information. I think that the British press is different. I know a lot of their guys (one of the British press, Mike Doodson, is working with our paper), and I think they are quite open to everybody here."

DERICK ALLSOP

"Nice guys don't necessarily finish last. But, at this level, they tend to struggle."

Derick Allsop might have been a business lawyer, which he studied for, or a football player, which he would have preferred. When an injury ended his athletic ambitions he decided to do the next best thing and write about sports. Since 1980 he has been covering one of the most curious of all sporting endeavours and he is fascinated by its players. Besides working for several British newspapers, he has written three books (two with Nigel Mansell) about Formula 1 drivers.

"I think, certainly at the top and part way down, Formula 1 attracts some of the most strong-willed and self-centred people I've ever come across in sport. And particularly at the top end, the front-runners. It doesn't surprise there's always conflict, always acrimony. Because these guys, to have reached this far, have got to be extraordinarily self-centred people.

"And I cover a lot of sports, mainly football, but also athletics, golf, tennis, cricket, almost anything up to, or down to should I say, highland games and clay pigeon shooting. I've done everything in my journalistic career, though I'm doing more and more motor racing. I'm working now principally with *Mail on Sunday* and *Today*.

"Football is still very much in my blood, having always been a football lover from childhood, and always played football. I never really wanted to be a racing driver. But what I have done is appreciate more and more the pull of speed. The allure of racing. I can understand that. And when you mix with these guys you can understand a bit more of really what makes them tick, what does turn them on. Though I tend to prefer football as a sport, I find this travelling circus more fascinating. I mean, this beats *Dallas* and *Dynasty*. Knocks spots off those things. This is extraordinary!

"First and foremost it's a village. And in any village, any community, you're going to get a mixture of relationships. You're going to get very good relationships, very genuine relationships. You're also going to get an awful lot of animosity, and you get rows and fights. It's inevitable. Because we're in this enclosed community. Once you're in the paddock, here we are in this little village again. The in-fighting here is probably worse than in a village. That's probably down to money as much as anything. We're talking money and pride. Those are very strong forces.

"It's more noticeable here because they're all brought together all the time. Imagine, for instance, in football that you had, every other weekend, the top 26 players. Just doesn't happen. Even in the World Cup they're scattered around among the various teams. But this is a head-to-head situation. And in reality we're not talking 26, we're talking perhaps six or eight. And at the very top we're talking three or four. So when you're focussed like this it's not surprising you're going to get confrontations between Prost and Senna, between Mansell and Piquet.

"People ask me who do I like, who don't I like, of those guys. I actually like and admire them all. Because I see their strong points and I see their weaknesses, of course, and I wouldn't necessarily want to go on holiday with all of them, but I do find them all very, very fascinating. You do not get to that sort of peak in any sphere of life, certainly not in this game, unless you've got something fairly special about you. And I can sit for hours and listen to those guys. Alright, at the end of it you may say a lot of it is garbage, but I do find them genuinely interesting, and I do listen to them, all the time, because I'm all the time trying to find out just what makes them tick. What are their interests. You try to delve deeper and deeper and deeper. You may never get to the end of it. But, I've spent more and more time with Senna in the last couple of seasons, because A, I think he's being more accommodating, but B, I think as he's grown older he's also grown more interesting.

"People say to me he's difficult. Well, for a start, you choose your moments to talk with people. For instance, at tests, that's always a good time to deal with people. They've got more time, they're not under such great pressure. There are days when they actually welcome someone to talk to. Rather than mechanics, or the rest of it. So it's a change. I find that if you pick the moment, as with anybody, if you're courteous and reasonable, people do tend to respond.

"I don't think Senna's an angel. I think he's a very shrewd cookie, as well. But then, they all are. So is Prost. Prost has this lovely image, in general terms. But he's a very, very cunning man.

Very, very cunning. He assesses everything. He's got the whole situation assessed. He's got this great art of appearing totally calm, totally pleasant, but at the same time he's not survived all this long and got three World Championships and all those wins by being just a nice guy. Nice guys don't necessarily finish last. But, at this level, they tend to struggle."

MARK FOGARTY

"The track element of it I find extremely boring, but what's interesting is the politics and the intrigue behind the scenes."

In 1987, a refreshing new character appeared in the pressroom in the form of a tall, irreverent Australian who previously specialized in tennis and golf. Mark Fogarty brings Formula 1 news to Americans via the newspaper *USA Today*, as well as disseminating radio reports on international networks, and his byline appears in various magazines. This is what he thinks about the Grand Prix circus and its performers.

"I don't like the racing. I think the racing is boring as shit, as they say in Britain. Because you hardly ever see any real racing. So the track element of it I find extremely boring, but what's interesting is the politics and the intrigue behind the scenes. Unlike tennis, or even golf, you can dig out new stories all the time. It's very turbulent here.

"In 1989, for instance, you had stultifyingly boring racing, nothing but McLarens over and over again. But you had this tremendous story of confrontation between the warring team-mates Senna and Prost. To a journalist that is just a gift. I was trained as a news journalist originally, and in tennis and golf there's very little opportunity to exercise your nose for news. So I think to me the races are just an excuse to come and hound all these people and try and get them to tell you something that they quite patently don't want to tell you.

"Also I quite like the camaraderie of the Formula 1 press corps. It's a very difficult clique to break into, but once you do it's quite good. It's like all cliques, really, they're bitchy and everyone's talking about him, and him, and him, and gossip, gossip, gossip. Of course, you've also got your national bent here. The Brits are always going on about the British drivers: Mansell, Mansell, Mansell. And the Italians are Ferrari, Ferrari, Ferrari. The French on Prost. And I suppose I would glorify an Australian.

"I think the drivers are, to some degree, full of their own self-importance. I don't think it's entirely their fault. I think all the hangers-on promote that feeling, and in some ways it's getting harder and harder to get to talk to these drivers, yet in some ways it's easier. After having done about three year's worth of this stuff, I was able to talk to Mansell or Prost, or if I really had to, Senna. I don't like his attitude, I don't like the disdain he shows people. Apparently he can be a very warm and caring person, if he deigns to want to know you. He's hated by a lot of people and to some extent he's brought it on himself. If he would just spend a little more time and not be so snotty about things, he'd get an even break. But the way he behaves he's just tailormade to be a villain.

"I may not like people, but I try not to show it in my work. You just call things as you see them, workwise. You don't have to be in love with someone in this business. In fact, I think it's quite an asset not to get too close to the participants. If you just have an up-front working relationship they seem to sort out who is professional and who isn't, and so they'll give you the time, even if they don't particularly like you. The classic case for me was Alan Jones. I used to know him quite well from some of the Grand Prix races I'd do occasionally in the past, and also from back in Australia when he raced. And we hated each other's guts, which is pretty funny, considering I was at one time ghosting a column for him. But professionally, I've always found AJ really good to work with, and I wrote a lot of stories about him. But taking the great Australian gauge of how well you like someone, he's certainly not my guy to go down to the pub and have a drink with.

"I suppose it's inevitable that I compare the drivers to the players in tennis and golf. In tennis it's an advantage not to be a deep thinker and most of them aren't. They don't spend a lot of time analyzing, and if they do they're in trouble. They get so wound up in it all that they can't see the wood for the trees. They spend too much time thinking about it rather than just doing it. A lot of tennis is just some knowledge, but then it's instinct.

"Whereas in Formula 1, it seems to me, among the very, very top drivers, the common denominator is acute intelligence, and they think very deeply about things. And I think it's because it's not enough to have the instinctive skill to be a racing driver, the sheer reflexes. Because it's such a technical sport you have to know so much about the mechanics of the car, how to set things up, and so on. It's not just reacting to a shot, like in tennis (although you can be reacting to conditions on the circuit), but basically you're thinking a corner ahead, even further. You've got to project ahead all the time.

"Formula 1 drivers, to me, are more like golfers. Golfers have to be extremely intelligent. And if you listen to any golfer talk, they're very articulate and thoughtful people. And with golf, as I know just from learning the game, you have to think about what you're doing. It's not a reflex thing, unless you're extremely gifted. I don't think in golf you can just go out and swing and hit the ball. You have to think about it all the time. Interestingly enough, a lot of the top Formula 1 drivers are very keen golf fans, Mansell and Prost being the obvious ones.

"So there are some very bright drivers here. Prost, The Professor, is a notable example, and Senna spends a lot of time thinking. I think Berger's keenly intelligent. I don't think Mansell is unintelligent. I'm certainly convinced he's no Rhodes scholar. I just think he is probably the bravest man on four wheels, or any wheels, in the world. I think Mansell probably makes up for it in just sheer balls, as they say in Britain."

BYRON YOUNG

"There's a very personal element to what a journalist writes. I have to be honest and say it is sometimes coloured by the people that they know."

Freelance journalist Byron Young used to be a newsman working for an agency, covering "court cases, murders, fires. I think it was fairly useful training for having a sceptical mind and preparing for Formula 1. I always thought in my teens I would plot my life and it would go in a certain direction. But it never has done. The two things I said I'd never do would be work in PR and work in London. I ended up doing both of them at the same time."

That began in 1987 when Jardine Public Relations offered Young a job handling the Camel account with Team Lotus in Formula 1. Though he found working with Ayrton Senna and Nelson Piquet "fascinating", Young preferred straight journalism and returned to that profession in 1990.

"When I was in public relations I sometimes wondered why the hell I was doing it. Being a trained journalist of several years' standing, I was disappointed to be in a situation where I was running around doing photocopying for people. I felt that I had more qualifications and I could be using my talents in a better way. On the other side of it, I think I was very lucky actually working with Camel, and I'm not just saying this in a PR sense any more. They're nice people and they have a positive attitude. When push comes to shove, they make a decision. And I actually got to work with some very good people. The down side of it I think is the kind of secondary servility PR requires, which is not in my nature.

"There's a very personal element to what a journalist writes. I have to be honest and say it is sometimes coloured by the people that they know. Some journalists are biased that way, and if they don't like drivers or team managers, what they write can be coloured by that. So I think getting on with people is part of it. What I'm trying to get away from is doing everything with a vested interest. I'm trying to be able to write as an independent journalist. I'm trying to write the truth, which in Formula 1 is quite a hard thing to do. Because you're inevitably upsetting somebody along the way.

207

"The thing I discovered about PR, that I'd never realized while I was in it, is that it's a very necessary thing. Formula 1 is such a complex business now that you need to have information supplied to you and you need it fast. The media is very hungry for news and information. And you need to have a good PR agency to do that, and that requires a good personal touch.

"In PR I found it very difficult to walk from A to B to get something done without somebody wanting something else. I'm not talking scrounging, or anything like that. But to get a job done is very difficult. You found yourself talking to people every five yards, which is all part of the job, but it's difficult when you have a specific aim. I had some quite difficult times at Lotus because, as a PR person, you have to look on the sunny side. And I think for a lot of that time there wasn't a sunny side to look on. There were people trying at Lotus, just as hard as McLaren were working, but they weren't getting the results. And that was often the hardest thing.

"As for the cars, I don't care how many sprockets it's got and how many gizmos it's got. What interests me is people reacting, personalities. It's what makes it tick. The psychology of Formula 1. Not A and B finished first and second.

"At the end of the day, what happens on the track is the tip of the iceberg. Although 26 cars start a Grand Prix, I think the drivers of 20 of them know they have very little chance of winning. And they know that before they come here. But it's a development process happening on so many different levels. There's Ayrton Senna and the team racing for today. There's the test team working for the next event. There's management working for this year, and there's the marketing people working for two, three years ahead. And that's what I find interesting, all the different ways it all interacts."

STUART SYKES

"I think there is a large proportion of these people who are in fact quite blinkered and see only this world and don't know about what goes on in the outside world and don't particularly care."

Though Stuart Sykes was born near the home of golf, St Andrews, in Scotland, his boyhood interest soon strayed from the greens to racing circuits as he followed the exploits of his countryman Jimmy Clark. When his study of modern languages in university brought him to Le Mans to teach English at a French school he was distracted by the annual 24-hour race, where he eagerly acted as an interpreter for the accreditation officers. While his academic career flourished he continued to peruse the racing journals.

For his PhD in French, Sykes wrote a thesis, then a book, in French, on the 1985 Nobel prize-winner for literature, Claude Simone, though he was equally well versed on the lives of numerous Grand Prix drivers. Finally, after teaching French at Liverpool University for nine years and being promoted to Senior Lecturer, he gave it all up to devote himself to the subject he was most interested in.

Taking a large drop in salary, Sykes went to the BBC where he worked in the Ceefax teletex service, covering all sports, but majoring in Grand Prix racing. In 1986 he graduated to the inside of the sport, signing on with CSS Promotions, who had a public relations contract with the Tyrrell team. The French division of Tyrrell's sponsor, Data General, required a French speaker and Sykes was their man. He also did public relations work with Williams, wrote two BBC Grand Prix books, and in 1989 became editor of *Prix Editions International*, a glossy magazine devoted to Formula 1. Sykes is now Managing Editor of that publication, where his linguistic bent is still a major concern.

"I have great respect and reverence for our language, which is one of the few things that sets us apart from the common herd and from animals in general. And I think there is no reason, simply because you have to meet a deadline, to ignore the niceties of writing, from punctuation through to just looking for a different adjective now and again. I hope that what I write reflects a concern for language, and the shape of a piece. I think a lot of journalists do try to do that, but a lot of them don't have the time or the inclination. But just because you are reflecting high-speed events on the track doesn't mean to say that your writing needs to be quick, hasty and slapdash.

"I think there are a few people writing, Maurice Hamilton is one who springs instantly to mind, Nigel Roebuck is another, whose concern for language and ability to express themselves with humour and with elegance reflects well on the sport. And there are people like John Blunsden, for instance, who has been gracing the pages of our newspapers for many years. But I have the unfortunate feeling that perhaps they are in something of a minority, and there isn't yet a well-defined tradition of motor racing writing.

"Perhaps the effort to capture the drama of the sport has taken precedence over the desire to penetrate beneath the surface of the people that are involved in it. But I see more of that these days, and for me that is the fascination of all sport, and this one in particular: what lies beneath the surface of the people that actually operate in this peculiar little milieu.

"I think the psychology of motor racing is very interesting because at one and the same time it is a big, glamorous global industry, but it is also a tiny family which goes around the world together, 16 times a year. I think there is a large proportion of these people who are in fact quite blinkered and see only this world and don't know about what goes on in the outside world and don't particularly care. There is a certain degree of insularity, not to say xenophobia in some cases. But I think the unifying factor here is the ability to bring a sense of humour to bear on events that can sometimes be very sad and chastening. Most of the time it can be extremely exasperating, but a lot of the time it can generate a lot of fun. And there is a cross-section of very interesting, and sometimes quite fascinating, people that work in this game.

"The majority of really top sportsmen are enjoyable people, and I respect the pleasure they give to the ordinary mortal. I mean, Nigel Mansell is not going to come and watch me bashing a typewriter, but I would sure as hell go and watch him racing. The fact that these people not only have to master themselves, but also master a machine which could very well master them so easily, the quantum leap that an ordinary mortal has to make between driving down the fast lane of the motorway and what these people actually do on the tracks – that, and the reasons why they do it, fascinates me.

"I think that a lot of people tend to look down their noses because, let's say, your average Formula 1 driver is not capable of shaping profundities about what it is he does, and the meaning of life in general. But I think that is an unfair view, because we who are supposed to be wordsmiths are incapable of expressing ourselves as eloquently in our profession as they do in theirs.

"What I am trying to do with the magazine I edit is reflect all facets of what is a very colourful, technical but, surprisingly enough, a very humane sport. So I want to reflect what drivers are like out of a cockpit as well as in it. I want to reflect the high tech aspects of it. I want particularly to reflect the internationalism of Formula 1, which is why I am opening up the pages to writers whose native language is not necessarily English. I want to widen the scope of the magazine to take in this whole microcosm that Formula 1 is."

FREDRIK AF PETERSENS

"The big difference is the amount of money in this sport. It is putting more pressure on the drivers, the engineers and the designers."

"It is a kindergarten for grown-ups. I don't know how many hundred people are involved in this game, but a lot of them see it as if the world is made for them, and not the other way around. They are taking themselves too seriously."

'Freddy' Petersens does not take himself too seriously, noting that he is a "technical idiot" when it comes to the intricacies of Formula 1 machinery. Besides, he enjoys playing in the kindergarten and sending reports of the antics of its inmates back to his native Sweden on radio and in print, though he does not write for any of the 'comics' as he calls the specialist motor racing magazines.

Petersens terms himself "a failed racing driver", and maintains it was a lack of bravery that made him take up the pen and not the sword for a career. "I drove a couple of races back home in Sweden, and Denmark, and I found out that I really enjoyed it. First it was a Mini-Cooper and then I had a go at Formula Vee, all those open wheels and that sort of thing. No, thank you very much, that was too dangerous. And I even wanted to sign up for the United Nations Peace Corps, at that time for Cyprus, but it never happened. Because I saw very quickly I wasn't brave enough. Before I did anything silly, I stopped."

But he still wanted to be involved in racing, and he met Gunnar Nilsson, the Swedish Grand Prix driver who died of cancer in 1978, and became very good friends with him. Swedish interest in Nilsson and Ronnie Peterson, who was killed in 1978, helped Petersens begin his journalistic career in Formula 1, a task for which he feels he was not particularly well prepared.

"I am still surprised that they published my first story. I still have it at home and it is so bad it is a nightmare when you read it. So I learned on the job. And I started to read the comics, *Autosport* and *Motoring News*, and all that sort of thing, and I saw how they wrote their stories. Then I read the daily papers to learn to write a short story for the dailies. I was intrigued by the personalities in the sport, and the travelling as well.

"The travelling still appeals to me, and most of the people here, I enjoy their company. Wherever we go there are always the oddballs among them. You go out and have dinner and have a few drinks and a few laughs, and with some of them you talk about other things than motor racing. There are a few people who have other interests. But after about 20 years in the sport I'm . . . I don't know if disillusioned is the right word, but I think it might be . . . about all the money here now, and the politics. I also cover World Cup skiing and the golf tours, and the atmosphere is completely different there.

"The big difference is the amount of money in this sport. It is putting more pressure on the drivers, the engineers and the designers, though they must love it because there is no end to some budgets, and they can go experimenting with their little toys. And the human touch is gone as well, because everyone from the driver down to the greenest mechanic has to produce results. Walk down the pit lane and look at the mechanics. There are very, very few smiles among the mechanics, usually everybody has a totally blank face. And you used to walk into the garage and the tea kettle was whistling in the corner, at least in the British teams.

"After so many years in the sport I've found the English – since there are no Swedes now – the best to work with. It might be that they have a mentality that is closer to my own as a Scandinavian, than the southern, Latin temperament. This is no criticism, or anything like that, they just appeal to my way of thinking. They're the easiest ones to work with and talk to, and they've got a sense of humour, which we could use a lot more of here.

"Lately it seems that Nigel Mansell is the one who is cracking a joke or two, and seems really to be at ease with himself and life. He's taking himself less seriously, and I think that is why Nigel, in a way, is a better driver now. He has got his family, he has got his golf and he has got his business interests, and all that sort of thing. And so has Derek Warwick, who is a very good chap to talk to as well. They have so many interests outside of Formula 1 that their brain has to work, they have to think, they have to make decisions.

"But a lot of the other guys just live for motor racing, and that is it. They haven't got a clue about the outside world. This actually happened to me a few years ago: I asked a driver what he thought about Jimmy Carter, the American President at the time. This guy asked me what team is he driving for!"

JEFF HUTCHINSON

"Sometimes I am amazed at some of the things I see written by other journalists."

Jeff Hutchinson, who has been to every Grand Prix since 1973, covers the sport from every conceivable angle. Besides his contribution to the FISA news bulletins that are issued throughout each race weekend, the Hutchinson byline appears in an impressive number of publications around the world. He also does television and radio work, and his International Press Agency (with Jad Sherif) covers the sport photographically. An avid aviator, he flies his Twin Commanche to all the races in Europe, and for events further afield he is often in the cockpit alongside Nelson Piquet (one of several drivers Hutchinson has taught to fly) in the Brazilian's Lear Jet.

In charge of his own destiny in the air, Hutchinson is able to avoid all the delays commercial flying entails and theoretically he should be able to spend more time in the pastoral setting where he resides. He owns a house in a small farming village on the Swiss-French border, not far from Geneva.

"For me, going home after a Grand Prix is almost like going on holiday. Unfortunately, I am so little at home . . . that is probably the biggest change I have noticed in Grand Prix racing over the years. It is no longer a long weekend every two weeks. It really is a full-time job. After a Grand Prix you may be home a day, then you're off to another country testing. All the winter now is testing. There may be a week or two here and there but the rest of the time it is just non-stop."

At one stage Hutchinson had visions of a career change to full-time flying when he turned 40, but that milestone has come and gone. "And I keep saying to myself, well I'm doing as much flying as I would anywhere else. I enjoy going motor racing, though at 4 o'clock in the morning in the pressroom on the Monday after a Grand Prix, when you haven't slept for 18 hours, you sometimes wonder. But all my friends are here, and for me the pleasure of going motor racing is to enjoy going out and eating and talking and sharing their lives, and them sharing my life.

"The sport is certainly much better organized now than it was in past years, and your own ideas of what you like and what you don't like change as you get older. One gets to dislike the attitude of some of the drivers who are paid a great deal of money and then find it too much trouble to spend time talking to the press, as opposed to American racing drivers, who are brought up knowing what PR is all about.

"But the majority of drivers are usually very approachable and very friendly, obviously depending on how you treat them and how you are with them. They usually have short patience for somebody who either doesn't know the subject or doesn't treat them fairly. On the other side of that, the thing I like most about it,

I think, is getting to know the majority of the drivers very well, both on a personal basis and a professional basis. I've gotten to know many of them through our shared interest in aviation and when we go out to dinner they love to talk about something else besides motor racing.

"I have never been in awe of racing drivers. Racing drivers are just everyday people, and I treat them basically as a person before I think of them as a racing driver. So I can like the guy who is on the back of the grid just as much as the guy who is on the front of the grid. I treat them all with the same respect and I try to give them all a very fair crack of the whip. I don't care how good the racing driver is, if I find him dislikable as a person, it still won't affect what I write about his racing, but it will affect whether or not we have a friendly personal relationship.

"I enjoy all the aspects of what makes them tick, what makes anybody tick within the sport. And I think that's the key to understanding what goes on here. It is actually quite amazing, to my mind, how few people understand the sport that they may have been covering for 10 or 15 years. Obviously you can never know the inner workings of each team, because they are very secretive about things that are going on, but people who should know a lot better seem to miss the point about what is really going on, and why drivers are doing what they are doing. Sometimes I am amazed at some of the things I see written by other journalists.

"I think the problem is that a lot of the journalists tend to rely on press releases – like the type that I put out in the FISA bulletins! – and don't really go and talk to the people on a personal basis, especially concerning comments about drivers. I think that a lot of drivers are misunderstood simply because journalists don't take the time to get to know them and to understand them. And even though maybe sometimes you get a few rebuffs, at the end of the day a driver will respect a journalist far more if he keeps coming along and asking intelligent questions, and he will realize that he is talking to an intelligent journalist and then give him the information he wants."

PATRICK STEPHENSON

"You're always being subjected to the test of time. Every human being has a weak side to them somewhere, and it's often revealed by this severe testing process."

Patrick Stephenson has carved a niche for himself that neatly combines his three main interests: travel, publishing and racing. He is involved with a publishing company which produces and distributes the *World Travel Guide*, a mammoth publication for the travel industry, and on Grand Prix weekends he works for the UK newspaper *The Daily Mirror* and ABC, the Australian radio network.

Stephenson's racing travels began when he was a teenager and met some competitors who prepared their cars in his uncle's garage in Oxfordshire. For a while he assisted the racing commentator Peter Scott Russell with lap charts and timing at club events. His first trips to Formula 1 races were aboard a light aircraft piloted by Pete Lyons, then *Autosport*'s Grand Prix Correspondent. Lyons was learning to fly, and his back seat passenger was quite willing to endure a season of white-knuckle adventures because of the powerful attraction of the destinations for which they were bound: the Grand Prix circuits of the world. Though Stephenson now entrusts his journeys to British Airways, his enthusiasm remains undiminished.

"It is the passion of motor sport! This is the pinnacle of the sport and brings the most out of not only the drivers, but the designers and all the other people behind the scenes, who do not always get a lot of credit for their efforts. They are all working flat-out to just get that extra notch of performance, even the journalists.

"I think there is always a terrific competition to get that story that scoops everybody else. But also there is a lot of very good co-operation because, as the sport has got more and more complicated, people have realized that you cannot be everywhere at once. So they frequently compare notes and swap quotes and collaborate with each other, so that everybody can get the whole story – on time for their deadlines.

"Time is of the essence in this business, and I suppose that is the biggest pressure you have to contend with. You're always being subjected to the test of time. Every human being has a weak side to them somewhere, and it's often revealed by this severe testing process. I must admit that I sometimes find myself in rather a dither, particularly when taping something for radio purposes.

"On radio, nothing beats the recorded voice of a sports personality. But you can't really doctor up the garbled speech of a driver the way you can in print. And again, there's the time factor, and I must confess I had lots of trouble with Alan Jones from Australia. Alan was the sort of character that, if he'd blown it, or if the car had blown up, he was sick of the whole thing and raring to get as far from the scene as he could. And not too happy to talk about it, either. What he did have to say might often need to be censored!"

BOB CONSTANDUROS

"There is glamour in Formula 1 – for the people who want to bask in it – along the pit lane, in the paddock, posing around the motorhomes . . . they are welcome to it. Just as long as they don't get in my way!"

Bob Constanduros speaks to everyone at each Formula 1 race. His is the voice heard over the public address system, imparting the latest information to Grand Prix people and spectators alike. Constanduros also writes for several international publications and edits the FISA annual of the sport. Writing, racing and race commentating are traditions in his family. His grandmother Mabel was a playwright, and her nephew Dennis wrote a number of books. Bob's father and uncle were keen racers in the UK, then, after the war, uncle James Tilling was the track announcer at Goodwood, where the senior Constanduros helped him with lap charts and spotting duties. It was in their company that Bob saw his first race.

"I think it was about 1956 at Goodwood. I can remember taking a picture of Innes Ireland and Mike Hawthorn together, my two heroes. And it's funny that these days I'm a colleague of Innes.

After university I worked as a journalist in trade papers for a while, principally for the hotel and catering trade, then I worked for *Autosport* covering club racing at weekends. Next, I bought a Volkswagen Camper, and I installed my girlfriend in my flat while I just went off around Europe, eight-week trips at a time, from race, to race, to race, to race. Formula 2, Grand Prix racing, sports cars, touring cars, the lot.

"My first commentaries were in the middle of the night at Le Mans. Uncle James was commentating at Le Mans, as he always had for 25 years, and I started off helping him, doing the night stuff when he'd knocked off to bed and everyone was too drunk to care what was being said anyway! And then he decided that he really didn't want to carry on, so I took it over, lock, stock and barrel. After Anthony Marsh left Formula 1 I took over from him.

"Over the years I've known motor racing in its various amateur forms, but I must admit I prefer it in its more professional form, modern Formula 1. There are people who dislike what Ecclestone has done to motor racing. I think they've got their heads in the sand. I'm very much a progressive person. I don't want to live in the past. There are lots of people who harp on about Monza, and the atmosphere of Monza, and what a marvellous place it is, and it's not like one of these modern concrete edifices. Well, I've got to work there, and I prefer the concrete edifice because it's more efficient.

"I think there is glamour in Formula 1 – for the people who want to bask in it – along the pit lane, in the paddock, posing around the motorhomes. The people who do that think there is glamour there, and I sort of agree with them, and they are welcome to it. Just as long as they don't get in my way!

"The regulars here are very, very competitive people, and you will never find their level of determination outside. Not just the drivers. I think it carries over into the engineers, team managers, mechanics, even to the journalists to a certain extent. Their collective determination is amazing. This is such an amazing business because it's constantly changing. If you get out of it for five minutes, you're left behind. You're gone. You're history. People forget you. It's an incredible business, and you've got to be in there, beavering away all the time.

"Some people think everybody's only in it for the money. But when it goes wrong, you only have to see those people's faces to realize that they aren't in there for the money. They are in it because they want to win. They don't go out of their way to be unpleasant, but I think you have got to have a sharp edge in this environment. They say nice guys finish last. Well, my mother talks about it another way: about somebody who was a nice guy – but that's all he was!"

DAVID TREMAYNE

"You've got to keep on, and keep on, and the pressure is there and if you relax that pressure then you start going backwards."

Few journalists feel more deeply about the sport than David Tremayne, Executive Editor of *Motoring News* and a regular contributor to other publications. To satisfy the requirements of his readers he must pour forth a torrent of words about Grand Prix racing, but it was a photograph that originally captured his imagination.

"I know exactly what first interested me in Formula 1. It was a picture of Jackie Stewart in the H16 BRM that appeared in *Autocar*, I think it was the 5th of May, 1967. It was a real head-on shot that they used to be able to get while the cars were sliding around. It was a worm's-eye view and it just looked so big and impressive. The caption said: 'Jackie Stewart's fierce looking BRM, blah, blah, blah'. It was a very dramatic picture.

"From then on I just sort of followed everything and collected all the magazines. I discovered *Autosport* and *Motoring News* in '68. Up till then it had been *Autocar* and *Motor*, so I got a lot more detail from then on, and just kept reading, reading, reading, everything I could. I did economics in college. The only way I could remember my economics was if you went down the price curve you could get into a Philips' drift, and then you'd hit some barrier. A means to an end. Then I worked in publishing at a place called Marshall Cavendish, and heard that there was an opportunity at *Motoring News*, which I went along for, and joined them in December '80.

"In many ways I think you make your own lot in life, but I certainly was lucky in that I was around at the right time. As soon as the *Motoring News* thing started, that was it. It's a hell of a life. It's a hell of a busy life, and you don't get a lot of time for your private life and your family, but it's the kind of thing where it's something different literally every day.

"Now we get a lot of people writing to us at *Motoring News* saying, 'It must be terribly hard, but how do I get in?'. In actual fact, it's a lot easier to get in than I ever thought it was. There's an opportunity for young guys. We always say if people are really enthusiastic when they come for an interview, that's the biggest single key. You can always tell when people have got that burning enthusiasm. There aren't that many of them where nothing else matters but doing that job, never mind the conditions or the pay. I took a financial sacrifice to go to *Motoring News* which has since corrected itself. One has to eat.

"I think, after a bit, it's inevitable that you sort of lose that first naive passion. I am very cynical about motorsport in general because of the way the people in it are. That doesn't take away your initial enthusiasm. Nothing takes that away. I think, in a way, when you get closer to the people you've been interested in reading about, the reality is often very different. It's inevitable, people aren't quite what you expect them to be. I think that's something you have to come to terms with.

"I can see why people think it's glamorous here. I personally don't think it is, because a lot of the time the people at the root of it are often not just economical with the truth, but they're downright parsimonious. There is nothing glamorous about that. I mean, it's a game isn't it, between the press and the rest. You find out as much as you can, you establish relationships that are as good and as strong as you can in the hope that the lies will be diminished. All I'm interested in is writing what I perceive as the truth. You try and be as accurate as you can. I find it frustrating that people are out there who don't want you to be able to do your job as well as you can. So that's why I don't find it too glamorous.

"If their car breaks for any reason, or the wheels fall off, or whatever, they're not about to tell you why. I can understand that. That's when it becomes a game. But there are those who will deliberately mislead you just because they think it's amusing to see you get it wrong in print. I don't know quite why they draw any satisfaction from that, but some of them do.

"There are some people here who never cease to amaze me with their ability to fool themselves. The sort of peripheral people who like to present the benign view of everything, and they're the ones who may be economical with the truth at times. I find there are some you can relate to who know exactly how to do their job, but they're few and far between. The peripherals are the kind of people who are only in it because the sponsor has a passing interest in racing. I think the journalists and obviously a lot of the team guys, they would be here come what may. If there was no money they'd still be here. Because they believe in the sport, the sport is the thing to them. Whereas the peripheral people, they like the posing and the glamour and all that kind of shit.

"The guys that are very central, I think, are incredible. We think we work quite hard as journalists, but Christ, we're not living and breathing it every single minute of the day. Think of the personnel of the teams, where once the season starts there's no running away and having a week off here or there, if you feel you're overworked. That's what I admire about them. You've got to keep on, and keep on, and the pressure is there, and if you relax that pressure then you start going backwards.

"I like the sense of a deadline, because I'm basically lazy. If I didn't have to work hard I wouldn't. If someone says do it in three weeks, inevitably you leave it until the last day. One of the things that I think is a shame with the kind of writing we have to do for *Motoring News* is, it's what you might call a shopping list sort of report, where you've got to sit back and just make sure you get everyone in there. You've got to write it very fast on a Sunday night, and I do write very quickly, so that's not a problem. On a Grand Prix weekend I don't try and write a literary masterpiece. If I write something for *Motor Sport*, or a freelance thing where you're doing a story report rather than a pure blow-by-blow report, you've got more time to be clever and to try and put some kind of craft into it.

221

"In Formula 3 I used to be very much a lone wolf, and I'd go my own way and do my own thing. The journalists were friends, but you wouldn't ride around on each other's backs, and certainly you wouldn't swap information. Whereas here, it's kind of the way of the world. You keep some things to yourself and other things you don't. After a bit, everyone's so enthusiastic, you can't stop yourself telling stories that you've picked up. In that sense it took a bit of getting used to, because you tend to think, I've got to do it all myself, and what I get I've got to keep.

"Some people tell you journalists have tremendous influence. I think that's a load of bullshit. I think you are an opinion former to a certain extent. But if you write something they don't agree with, they won't necessarily take your view. They'll continue to hold their own view a lot of the time. So, I don't think it's a particularly earth shattering role we play."

ALAN HENRY

"I am amazed by the affluence. It is not a real world."

There have been suggestions that Alan Henry is actually several people, such is his prolific output. Formula 1 correspondent for *The Guardian* newspaper, Editor of the prestigious annual *Autocourse*, regular contributor to several magazines, author of over a dozen books about Formula 1, Henry is a veritable industry of Grand Prix words.

His first race-related writing took the form of a letter to the Editor of *Autosport* in 1968, wherein Henry suggested that the correspondent covering a certain club race was "an idiot". Henry had been there as a flag marshal and saw things quite differently. Some weeks later Henry's bluff was called and he was invited to set the record straight in *Autosport* by covering a meeting of the Romford Enthusiast's Car Club. The date is indelibly impressed in his mind: April 7, 1968, when Jim Clark was killed at Hockenheim.

Thus Henry's journalistic career was launched, fortunately enabling him to avoid being the solicitor his father had hoped he would be. Words about racing Henry understood, but "books on constitutional law and land law might as well have been printed in Cantonese. I grew up on a steady diet of Jenks in *Motor Sport*, and it intrigued me that people could actually make a living from being a racing journalist. Anyway, I would have made a bloody awful lawyer. The irony is there are so many lawyers now that I have done better financially being a motor racing journalist than I would have being a lawyer.

"So it's slightly hypocritical to have to say I don't like some of the qualities that the enormous infusions of money have brought into Formula 1. I sometimes walk down the pit road with a rather bewildered feeling, wondering how all this money is being channelled into what sometimes looks a rather specialized business. I am amazed by the affluence. It is not a real world.

"The journalists have benefited from the influx of money over the last 20 years, but my particular irritation concerns team owners and drivers who are super-critical of anything written which is vaguely critical about themselves. But, on the other hand, they won't give you the time of day to explain the situation. There is a big gulf of understanding between a lot of teams and drivers and the journalists.

"But I think it is important to remember that the pressure on them now on the Friday, Saturday and Sunday is so enormous. If you meet a guy that you perhaps think is a bit of a miserable sod over the weekend, and then you meet him on a Thursday, or perhaps at a test session, you are going to get a totally different impression of him.

"I think the drivers are superstars right enough, but I am not in awe of them. The last person I was in awe of, and still am, is Mario Andretti, who had more charisma in my opinion, more star quality, than anybody I have ever met – probably the sum total of the rest of the drivers I have ever met put together.

"I admire the mechanics and engineers and the design process, how they're all so committed and so thorough over such a long time. We have the winter off, they don't. But I don't think it is a problem for them, I think they thrive on it. Nobody comes into this sport unless they are totally obsessed with racing and in fact a lot of people work phenomenally long hours.

"There is a lot of competition among the journalists. Even your closest friends, you try to pull the wool over their eyes every once in a while. It sometimes gets a bit catty. We're all biased in our own ways, but I think the British press are more objective than the Italians and the French. The Germans are alright, but the Italians and the French, in my view, are so prejudiced towards French and Italian drivers that it is a joke.

"But all this is only a game, at the end of the day. I mean, our life isn't on the line. Everything is just a footnote to the race. As Jean Behra said: 'Life is racing, the rest is waiting.'"

JOHN BLUNSDEN

"The first thing a driver wants to do after a race, especially if things have not gone too well, is to get away from the circuit as quickly as he can. It's understandable, but it's also extremely frustrating for those of us for whom the hardest part of our work is just beginning."

The life of the man from *The Times* has always revolved around words and wheels. And earlier in his life John Blunsden often took a turn behind the wheel of racing cars, wringing out whatever performance they were capable of, then writing about it. He was one of the pioneers of motor racing track tests in the UK, and such was his prowess in the cockpit that sometimes he went faster than the regular racers.

"I was extremely fortunate. By about 1970 I suppose I had driven more than 100 different racing cars, from Formula 1 down to modified saloons, so this had given me quite a broad experience. I think I developed a bit of a reputation for being able to bring them back in one piece, so from time to time I would be invited to have a few laps in someone's car just to give them a second opinion, even though there was no question of writing about it.

"It could be fairly nerve-wracking at times because some of them weren't screwed together terribly well, but most of the cars of the really professional teams were a treat, they gave you every confidence. For example I particularly remember the tautness of one of Ken Tyrrell's Formula 2 Matras – it was actually Jacky Ickx's car – from the very first lap you just knew it wouldn't let you down."

Blunsden had been active in club rallying during the '50s, but his plans to switch to racing went terribly wrong. "A friend, Bill Lambert, and I went half-shares in a Jaguar C-Type, the idea being that he would just sprint it, because he was married, and I would race it. But shortly after my first race we discovered that Bill had terminal cancer and we had to sell the car. Then came the Suez Crisis, and I didn't get back on the track until I started to do the odd test for *Motoring News*.

Blunsden's entry into the world of speeding wheels began in an unlikely way with some advice given to him by a prospective employer. After he left school he was offered work as a junior clerk in a shipping company in London. "It was being run by a larger-than-life Canadian, and he told me I could have the job if I really wanted it. Then he said, 'But do yourself a favour – don't take it. Walk back through the outer office and look at the expressions on the faces of all the people working here. They're not living, they're just existing. They're old before their years, and if you come and join us you'll soon be the same. You know what I would do? I'd wander down to the London Docks, get myself a job on a boat and see the world'."

Instead, Blunsden wandered into the editorial offices of a motoring publication, introducing himself by presenting plans he had drawn for making scale models of cars. His skills at this hobby were impressive enough to gain him employment as an editorial assistant. After doing his National Service, in Egypt in the Royal Engineers ("that really accelerated the growing-up process!"), Blunsden returned to the world of wheels in 1950 as a salesman of secondhand cars, eventually establishing his own small dealership.

He also wrote a motoring column for his local newspaper, *The Croydon Advertiser*, and when the motor trade slumped badly during the Suez Crisis in 1956 Blunsden took up his pen in earnest, joining another motoring publication, *Commercial Vehicles*. Meanwhile, he had been active in motorsport and belonged to several motor clubs, so when a position as Associate

Editor of a new newspaper called *Motoring News* became available in 1957 he grasped it. Blunsden was Editor of that publication when he left it in 1961 to become a freelancer, which he has been ever since.

He joined forces with Alan Brinton to form Motor News and Features, a partnership which continues today, at first working out of offices at Brands Hatch, where they provided editorial services and produced several magazines for the circuit owners, as well as serving their other clients throughout the world. Then in 1968 Blunsden also became a book publisher when he acquired a majority shareholding in Motor Racing Publications. But he remained an active journalist, and in 1972 he was invited by *The Times* to become their Grand Prix Correspondent. He began with the Italian Grand Prix, chronicling the victory by Emerson Fittipaldi in his Lotus-Ford (which brought him his first World Championship) in the elegant prose that is his hallmark in that paper.

"I think it is important for any journalist to be aware of his or her audience, to understand their needs, and then to write accordingly," he says. "I was fortunate with *The Times* because I took the paper long before I wrote for it, so I suppose I was writing for myself, explaining the sort of things I would want to know if I had not been at the race. Accuracy and comprehensiveness, I think, are two of the keynotes for those of us who write for the 'serious' papers, whereas headline-making sensationalism is so often demanded of those who serve some of the more outrageous tabloids. I do not envy them their jobs, in fact I sympathise with them, because they are highly talented and professional journalists and they *know* that a lot of what they are forced to write is garbage. They also know that if they tone things down too much their copy will be doctored out of all recognition before it appears in print, and their byline will still be attached to it. That is something which I would never be prepared to tolerate.

"The impact of television has had a profound effect on many of us in the Formula 1 pressroom. Today you have to assume that a significant percentage of your readers will have been watching the box the previous afternoon or evening and will have been told by Murray and James the 'nuts and bolts' of what happened. So these people will not want to know 'What?' so much as 'Why?' when they pick up their papers. But others will not have watched television, so for them the 'What?' element is the more important. This is where we have to compromise within the limits of the space allocated to us, perhaps 600 words. It is important to recount the basic structure of the race, and of course give comprehensive results, but then I think it is necessary whenever possible to build in some driver and team quotes – the 'Why?' factor.

"For us the hour after the race is the most hectic part of the whole weekend, when tight deadlines mean you are sometimes forced to cut corners. The first thing a driver wants to do after a race, especially if things have not gone too well, is to get away from the circuit as quickly as he can. It's understandable, but it's also extremely frustrating for those of us for whom the hardest part of our work is just beginning.

"In times like this a certain amount of information is exchanged, it has to be because you can't be in 26 different places at once. So during the minutes after the chequered flag, while champagne is being sprayed from the victory podium, chaos reigns in the paddock as teams push hot cars, used tyres and all the paraphernalia of the pit garage towards their transporters, and pressmen, notebooks brandished, scurry from pit to pit, looking for drivers and wondering, if they're not there, whether they haven't returned yet, or whether they've already disappeared into their motorhomes (which is more often the case).

"This is when rivalries are temporarily forgotten. 'Have you seen Donnelly?' I might be asked. 'Yes,' I'll answer, 'gearbox,' without going into the detail I may have gleaned from Martin. And when I ask in reply, 'What about Piquet?', I'll be content to be told 'electrics', then decide whether or not I need to follow this up with someone on the team (much would depend on how significant a part he played in the race).

"At times, because of our tight deadlines, it must look as though we hunt in packs, and of course in a sense we do because we are usually after the same people at the same time. What I do find rather strange, though, is that after the facts have been ascertained, some journalists remain in a huddle, comparing notes, even while they are compiling their stories. I sense that there is an underlying sense of insecurity there, that they want to protect themselves from the wrath of their sports editors by agreeing not only the facts of

227

the story, but also which slant to adopt. For years, Alan Brinton and I have written for rival newspapers, but even though we are business partners, and have probably exchanged pieces of information after our separate fact-gathering efforts, we become competitors the moment our fingers touch the keyboard, and often the first we know of what each other has written is when we read the following day's papers.

"The press conferences are very much a mixed blessing. On the one hand you know that the first three in the race will all have something to say, but you also know that everyone will get the same quotes, and as often as not there will be more than a touch of PR in the remarks, which needs to be filtered out. Without doubt, the best material comes from a driver when you get him on his own, but these days those moments are rare indeed. At times we curse drivers for their elusiveness, but the plain fact is that their work timetables simply do not dovetail with the needs of the media.

"After every practice or qualifying session there is the dreaded debrief, which sometimes can go on for hours. Then there's the commercial pressures – the corporate handshakes, the 'meet our special guests' sessions in the Paddock Club, the contract negotiations (don't kid yourself this happens only once a year, some of them are at it all the time). Then there's the between-sessions massage and medical check-up – a sensible idea for a top driver in what has become such a highly physical activity (I almost said 'sport', but of course it ceased to be that a long time ago). I still remember with considerable affection the days when not only were the drivers very accessible, they were genuinely pleased to see you and talk at length about driving to you."

Would Blunsden like to be able to turn back the clock and climb aboard a Formula 1 car again? "Who wouldn't? But I'm under no illusions, it would probably give me a heart attack! I was very lucky. During the 1960s tyres were still relatively narrow, wings were only just coming in and ground effects weren't even thought about, so there was not a vast difference between the behaviour of a tightly suspended and powerful road car and that of a racing car. Now there can be no comparison, which is why I have the greatest respect for the skill and stamina of any driver who can just qualify one of today's Formula 1 cars, never mind score points with it.

"A long time ago I remember having a friendly altercation with John Surtees, the only man I've ever known with white hair who could really perform in a Formula 1 car. I had written to the effect that professional racing drivers should be prepared to drive in any conditions other than fog or flood and should adjust their speed accordingly. He was one of the bravest blokes around on two wheels or four, but for some reason he disagreed with what I was saying. 'You've never tested a Surtees, have you?', he said. 'No,' I replied. 'Right, we'll remedy that. The next time we're testing at Silverstone I'll give you a call, and if it's wet I'll let you have a few laps. I'll be interested to see what you make of Woodcote. Oh, and by the way, you'll be on slicks!' It was an offer I felt able to decline, but it made me realize that perhaps driving a typewriter had its compensations after all. At least if you get it all wrong you can go back to the beginning and start again!"

ALAN BRINTON

"There is a very strongly held opinion that in order to be a really fine racing driver you've got to be a bit of a bastard. I'm afraid this is so."

In a former life Alan Brinton was a parliamentary correspondent for a London newspaper for seven years, experience that serves him well in covering the high-speed politics of Formula 1. "It was in the days of Churchill, Macmillan, Bevin and Bevan, all the big guns. It was an exciting time. Some very dramatic things happen in Parliament and it really got the adrenalin going, particularly when you were near a deadline. Very often a big debate on a subject would end at 10 o'clock. One went straight onto the phone and dictated the front page lead from notes, because the deadline was a quarter past 10. You learn how to cut corners, go for the throat."

Brinton's background makes him unique in another respect: he is one of the few who was a professional journalist before coming into motorsport. He began by teaching himself touch typing and shorthand, and he served as an apprentice in a news agency, a general reporter, then a Night News Editor, prior to the sojourn in the Halls of Westminster. When his newspaper, *The News Chronicle*, folded in 1960, Brinton embarked on a freelance career in motoring, a subject he had previously been "shanghaied" into covering. At first he worked on general motoring topics of a non-sporting nature, then his career veered towards racing. He became Editor of the magazines *Motor Racing* and *Sports Car* and soon afterwards formed a partnership with John Blunsden to provide a variety of writing and editorial services. "We've had a jolly good time."

Possessed with a highly developed work ethic, Brinton became a prolific wordsmith on motorsport matters, capable of changing his style to match the tastes of his audience. Until recently he was indeed two people at Formula 1 events: Brian Allen of *The Daily Telegraph* and Alan Brinton of *The Sun*. Brinton also mastered the spoken word on radio, where his authoritative voice was heard far and wide. At one Belgian Grand Prix he reported for three radio networks, ABC in America, BBC in the UK, and CBC in Canada, hardly ever repeating himself.

Having travelled with the Grand Prix circus for over 30 years Brinton has a fund of anecdotes. While the spectacles he wears are not rose-tinted, the earlier times he recalls sound suspiciously like the good old days. "When I went to my first Belgian Grand Prix, at Spa in 1956, I was very much a Lone Ranger. Nobody knew me. I was talking to Stirling Moss beforehand and asked him the best way to get to Spa from Brussels. Moss said, 'Look, tell my secretary the time you plan to get there and I'll come and fetch you'. He was going to be in Switzerland. He set off early in the morning from Switzerland, bypassed Spa and went all the way up and met me at Brussels. It was quite a journey, and there were no motorways in those days. He took me back in his car to Spa, then he took me around the circuit as well. You remember those things.

"When Jack Brabham, driving for Cooper, won the 1960 Portuguese Grand Prix in Oporto, John Cooper said, 'Right, we're all going out to dinner'. And it lasted until 2 o'clock in the morning, a real old rave-up. When Brabham won the French

Grand Prix at Reims, they held the prizegiving in the Town Hall. There was a symphony orchestra and champagne flowing. And John Cooper insisted on conducting the orchestra.

"And I remember after Jim Clark had won the World Championship, I can't recall the year, but he won by whatever result it was at Monza. I was there with my wife and my two boys, and we were staying at the Hotel de Ville. We were sitting in the hotel and this quiet little man came up to us, the new World Champion, having escaped everybody else. He said, 'Would you mind . . . it would give me a lot of pleasure if I bought you all a drink'. So, the two boys had orange juices and we had something else. You don't get that nowadays.

"One time at Rouen, at the 1962 French Grand Prix, the motoring journalist Basil Cardew was with us on the opposite side of the fence from the start-finish area. Basil said to Jim Clark and Graham Hill, 'Now look, when the race is over we want to know what's happened. We are on the wrong side. You come over and tell us what happened.' Neither of them won, but Jim Clark came across – left his car – came across the barrier and he told us what had happened.

"The journalists tend to be a different sort now. Those who write for the enthusiast publications, in particular, these are the dedicated. These are the chaps who, from the age of seven, start reading *Motoring News* and they know it all off by heart. On some of the daily newspapers, and in radio as well, there are still a few people who were journalists first, and then they were recruited to cover motor racing.

"One of the reasons there are little cliques of journalists is that they tend to cover themselves. If one of the popular newspapers gets a scoop, the opposition demands it too. Back at the hotel they will get a phone call at 11 or 12 o'clock at night, saying, 'Why haven't you got this?'. So they all try to get the same quote from Mansell, the result of which is that there are exclusives to be had for the Lone Rangers.

"What has pleased me, now I'm being chauvinistic, is the interest the British newspapers have taken in motor racing which has built up in recent years, with Mansell coming to the fore. Quality papers like *The Times, The Guardian, The Independent, The Daily Telegraph*, they have a lot of space for Formula 1. A lot of this is due to television. People see the racing there and then they want more, particularly about the drivers.

"But the drivers are so distant now. There used to be prizegivings on the Sunday evening, and if you didn't go to the prizegiving you didn't get your cup, and you didn't get your money. Now it's into their choppers and off they go. I think it's sad when they become unco-operative. Because they owe their millions, really, to the things which we have done. They will say, of course, 'We've got where we have because we are good'. But we've packed their money bags for them and, generally speaking, I think we tend to build them up a bit too high. They are just too busy being involved in themselves and their money.

"There is a very strongly held opinion that in order to be a really fine racing driver you've got to be a bit of a bastard. I'm afraid this is so. But there have been some exceptions to that, and Clark was one. Jackie Stewart was both things. He was friendly, but he also applied himself to it. He very much realized the importance of the media. And Jack Brabham was a very decent man.

"In 1968, I was at Rouen for the French Grand Prix, and John Blunsden, who had just taken a call from England, came to my room early on the Saturday morning to tell me that my wife had been killed in a car accident. The next caller was Jack Brabham. He said, 'You'll want to get back, won't you? I'll fly you in my plane. Meet you at the airport in half an hour.' This was the last day of practice, remember, and Jack Brabham flew me back to Biggin Hill. He didn't even put in a flight plan, just bowled his way through everything. Then he flew back to France and got there in time for practice. Would anyone do that nowadays? You remember these things."

INNES IRELAND

"People talk about the glamour and the mystique of Formula 1 . . . But I've been around it, I suppose, so long that that has all worn off."

One of those drivers who provided lots of copy for Alan Brinton and his colleagues in times gone by was Innes Ireland. As a Grand Prix driver from 1959 to 1966 Ireland was noted as a colourful, free spirit who enjoyed himself in and out of the Lotus, Cooper and BRM cars he raced. Now, covering the sport as a journalist for *Road & Track* magazine (sharing the duties with Rob Walker), Ireland finds the current atmosphere quite different from his driving days, and the Grand Prix people rather a different breed.

"Today most of them are in it for the money they can get out of it, rather than for a pure love of seeing motor cars being raced around a circuit. Now there is so much money involved in motor racing, and there is an enormous number of people who see it as a very convenient and pleasant way to make a lot of money themselves. There is very, very little sport left, very little.

"And I see very little evidence of any camaraderie among the drivers. The drivers of my era, we all knew each other. We would laugh and joke about things and fool around, and have fun in an evening, and so forth. I don't see any of that. Nowadays, if his car breaks down before the end of the race, the driver is in his jet aeroplane or helicopter, or whatever it is, and he is gone.

"From the point of view of the financial aspect, I'd very much like to have been paid even fractions of what they get paid today. I say that very light-heartedly. But I'm glad I drove in the era I did. If one was given a decade, I would have liked to have driven from '50 to '60. I started in '59 and I saw all this sponsorship business coming in in '65–66. Knives flashing in the dark, and all that sort of thing. And I didn't like what I could see coming.

"Nowadays, I enjoy being able to write what I see and what I feel, but there is no point being negative. My own personal feelings, like the ones I've just outlined about lack of camaraderie, and so forth, I don't have to bring that out. It is not necessary for my story. So I confine myself to what I see on the track and what I see in the workshops, and the technical aspect of things.

233

"But I find it quite difficult talking to many people here. I always get the feeling that they know, or most of them know, that I'm a writer. Some of them know that I used to be a racing driver myself. But I always get the feeling that they would rather not talk to any journalists. They'd rather do their own thing and not talk to anybody, other than the chief engineer or the mechanics. So I never like to feel that I am intruding. I very often get that feeling, even talking to team managers.

"Obviously, there are times when I know to keep well away because they are in trouble with the car or whatever. And certainly during official practice times, and so forth, they don't really want to talk to you. In my day there were far fewer journalists around, so one wasn't being constantly harranged by people. But certainly, when people would come up, of course you'd talk to them, because they were often friends.

"We weren't under the same pressure. I never had any financial pressure on my shoulders – thinking I bloody well had to do so and so because of my sponsors – I didn't have any sponsors. So one wasn't under the same sort of pressure that the people are under today. That is obviously part of the reason that they are always too bloody busy to talk to you.

"So now, having lunch is a highlight of the weekend! But, really, the start of the race still has a tremendous impact. I can feel it inside – not in the same way as when I was actually taking a start myself – but I certainly feel very excited by it, and I think it is an incredible thing to watch and to listen to. It is far more impressive and meaningful if you are actually at the circuit. Television can never convey the feeling that one gets, if you are actually standing there watching it.

"But I don't like flying anymore. Flying is a pain in the arse, now. You have got miles to bloody well walk to get to the aeroplane. You have got all that hassle with X-raying your luggage and this, that and the other. I used to be able to turn up at London Airport a quarter of an hour before the plane was going to take off and I knew I'd get straight on. But now you have got to be there a minimum of an hour before, and preferably an hour and a half. So there is so much hanging about and waiting – then everything is late. And the service on aeroplanes is pathetic unless you are in first class. And even then, in the middle of the night, if you press the old button nothing happens.

"People talk about the glamour and the mystique of Formula 1. I know what they are talking about, and I know what they mean. But I've been around it, I suppose, so long that that has all worn off. I can see that people, having watched it on television and so forth, sense this mystique and the glamour of it, but from where I sit there is no glamour at all."

JAMES HUNT

"The only reason I ever walked up and down the pit road when I was a driver was to look at the crumpet."

To his role as colour commentator on the BBC Formula 1 telecasts James Hunt brings all the experience of 92 Grands Prix and the authority of a World Champion (1976). But Murray Walker's sidekick also brings his press-on-regardless style, which intimidated opponents, some of whom thought he was "barking mad", and which now takes the form of foot-to-the-floor and often caustic comments about what he sees on the TV monitors. And Hunt's pithy observations liven up even the dullest race.

Early in his career his penchant for crashing earned him the title of Hunt the Shunt. Later, in deference to his public school background, he was Master James and, during his tenure as a driver for Lord Alexander Hesketh, Hunt was the ringleader of a riotous Grand Prix team that seemed to consume as much champagne as petrol and where the nubile young ladies occasionally outnumbered the mechanics.

Hunt retired in 1979 "for reasons of self-preservation", and his formerly flamboyant lifestyle is now tempered somewhat by the responsiblities of fatherhood – he has two lively young sons – and having to tend a large flock of budgerigars, which he breeds in an aviary at his home in Wimbledon. But on race weekends Hunt turns his attention back to the Grand Prix circus.

"If I was driving now it wouldn't do for me to turn up, as I used to for a Grand Prix, unshaven and not particularly tidy in my civvie clothes. I was really only there to do my job in the cockpit and around the car, which of course one doesn't have to dress up for. Presentation is all-important now, because it's all so publicity-oriented, which is of course where all the money has come from, and it has to be respected. The teams are much more professional businesses. As a result, that's taken a little bit of the character out of it, because everything is so professional and organized.

"The only reason I ever walked up and down the pit road when I was a driver was to look at the crumpet, I used to be looking at the pretty girls. But with the modern pass system there aren't any in the pits now, so now you have to go outside. Pity, that. They've sort of managed to get that out of the pits now. There's so much professionalism.

"I was jolly happy with life in the '70s, really. We certainly had a lot of fun in those days. But I think my way of living when I was driving would be difficult today. I was entirely responsible about my driving, and never misbehaved there, but after that, when the job was done, I led a fairly laid-back lifestyle. I think modern sponsors in this day and age would find that a bit of a strain, and it would not be to my advantage in my career. People would hesitate before hiring me. And I would probably have to curb my behaviour, and certainly put on a different public face. I don't think that the way I lived then affected my driving, and I don't think it would if the whole thing was happening now. But you would just have to go a bit more under cover.

"Funnily enough, when I first retired and started commentating, I was very uncomfortable with Grands Prix. I think, having been a driver, two factors contributed to that. One was, I actually felt like a spare prick at a wedding! A lot of standing around with nothing to do. But what really compounded it, and made it particularly unpleasant, was that the general public was still treating me like a driver. And that was one of the reasons I retired. That was specifically one of the things I was trying to get away from. So there I was, walking back into the fire, having just got out of the frying pan.

"But people have very short memories, and by five years after I had retired I was able to walk quite happily and freely around the paddock without any aggravation. That's fine now, and I am very comfortable at Grands Prix, and I thoroughly enjoy my TV commentating. I enjoy the racing. It's a good way to watch the race because I'm actually involved with it, which is much more fun for me than just sitting and watching it, which probably wouldn't even hold my attention, most of them.

"On the weekend, basically I'm most interested in the final qualifying, and that's only an hour on Saturday. Then I've got a 24-hour wait until the race starts. There's actually nothing to do other than stand around and socialize and try not to start drinking too much out of boredom. But there's not a lot else to do!

"Even in my day, as a driver, one had to stay under cover, so you had your hibernation points. My hibernation point ever since I drove for McLaren has always been in the Marlboro hospitality unit in the paddock. They're particularly good friends of mine anyway. And the atmosphere in there is exactly the same as when I was driving, and I still stay under cover most of the time. I find it varies from race to race, but I like the paddock atmosphere at Jerez, for instance. It's got a nice wide open layout, and everybody always seems relaxed and in a good mood. And you can see people coming a long way off!

"But, basically, all the people here are mad passionate motor racing enthusiasts. Ninety-nine per cent of them are would-be racing drivers themselves, expressing their enthusiasm in other ways. They either haven't had the opportunity to become one, or they've tried, or they've just preferred in the end to express their love for it that way. Really, for everybody I know in the business, it is primarily an act of love. That's aside from the fact that nowadays it also happens to be a good job, with good working conditions and decent pay. But even if the conditions hadn't improved I'm sure the same people would be here."

MURRAY WALKER

"My heart is in the sport, I am passionately interested in it, I like the people and everything they do."

'Mr Grand Prix Racing' to millions of television viewers who follow his BBC commentary, Murray Walker was "born into it really. My father, Graham Walker, was racing motorcycles very successfully before I was born in 1923. He carried on until 1935, so I had several years when my life as a schoolboy was associated with a father who was a public figure who raced motorcycles. He was, in effect, World Champion in 1928, I say in effect because he won the European Championship, which was the only one at the time. He also won the TT on the Isle of Man and many other events. When he retired he became the motorcyle racing commentator for the BBC. I went everywhere with my parents to the races, and as far as I was concerned that was what little boys did. So it was literally in my blood when I was born, and it has stayed there ever since.

"I went to Sandhurst, the military training academy, and I came out as a Second Lieutenant thinking I was God's answer to soldiering. I joined the Royal Scots Greys, one of Britain's premier cavalry regiments, and went and did the invasion of Normandy. Then we fought our way up through France, Belgium and Holland into Germany. My regiment did the link-up with the Russians. I finished the war as a Captain and I came out in 1947.

"Previously, while waiting for training in tanks during the war, I got a business scholarship with Dunlop, the sort of thing where they put you through every department of the business – distribution, sales, accountancy, advertising, everything – for nine months. When I got out of the army I hadn't the faintest idea what I wanted to do, then I remembered Dunlop. And I decided I liked the sound of advertising. Probably because it seemed glamorous and I liked the people. I got a job in the Dunlop advertising department and I stayed there for eight years.

"Then I went to Aspro, an analgesic firm, and flogged Aspro all over India, Pakistan, Burma. Next I went to McCann Erikson to work on the Esso account, and I did that for two years before joining Masius Ferguson, a smaller advertising agency. I was there from 1959 to 1982, when I retired from advertising, and I helped build up the business from one office in London into 54 offices around the world. I was on the management committee and also a shareholder. Those were exciting times.

"My parents had given me my first motorcycle on my 14th birthday, and I started off doing one-day trials and six-day enduros. I won a gold medal in the 1949 six-day international trial, which was the high point of my achievement. But because of my parental background, I wanted to broadcast, I wanted to commentate.

"My chance came at a hillclimb in Worcestershire in 1949. My father was still doing the radio commentary for the BBC but, for a reason I can't recall, had to drop out. So they gave me the job and away I went, advertising from Monday to Friday and the broadcasting at weekends. At that time the BBC's cars motorsport commentator was Raymond Baxter, so I became number two to my father in motorcycle sports, and number two to Baxter in cars, doing Formula 3 and so on. I did radio until 1978, then the BBC started covering the whole Grand Prix season on television, and I've done that ever since. I cover all kinds of motorsport, from kart racing to truck racing, but of course Grand Prix racing is the most demanding.

"I appear in the pit lane in Spain, or wherever it is, on Thursday before the race, and I am continuing a never-ending dialogue. My job, as I see it, is to talk to anybody and everybody who has got anything to do with the sport – officials, organizers, sponsors, drivers, mechanics, team managers, team owners, suppliers – and become as knowledgable and authoritative about it as I can. Because at some point in the commentary there may be the need to draw on my knowledge, and if I haven't got the knowledge I can't draw on it. That, of course, is the obvious reason. The other reason is that I like doing it.

"Formula 1 is colourful, noisy, exciting and involves a great deal of travel and a great deal of money, and if that is the definition of glamour in motorsport, and it is not a bad definition, then I do see it as glamorous, and am delighted to be part of it. My heart is in the sport, I am passionately interested in it. I like the people and everything they do, and I want to be involved with it.

"I am involved with it by talking to people on television. I'm talking to a majority of people who know absolutely nothing about the technology, and it is my job to educate, instruct and entertain them. But I am also talking to a minority of people who are extremely demanding, the dyed-in-the-wool enthusiasts, who want me to tell them about valve overlap and camshaft construction and gear ratios. Somehow or other I have got to find, or try to find, the correct communication blend between talking about the cars, the drivers, the circuit and the politics.

"I am sad, I think that is probably the right word, about the deviousness of the politics, which we have seen all too much of in Formula 1 recently. In my opinion, Grand Prix racing is the ultimate distillation of life, because it is more competitive than anything I have ever seen. The rewards for success are higher than in any other walk of life I have been involved with. The penalties for failure are greater than in any other walk of life I have been involved in. And all of life, if you stop to think about it, is politics. Therefore, the politics in motor racing are going to be more intense. But that doesn't mean I like it. It is something I regret.

"In the telecast booth I stand up for the whole time. It's a psychological thing. I feel freer and able to express myself better if I can stand up and actually move about the box. I am not static, just standing like a graven image for the whole two hours. I am actually moving around and jumping up and down and pointing at the screen. I have a lot more power to my voice when I am commentating than I do in conversation, because I get excited.

"I was quite flattered when Clive James, who is a very big wheel in the British world of writing and entertainment, said that I always sound as if my trousers are on fire. I was impressed that he was even aware of my existence! But, no question about it, I do get excited, and I am usually jumping up and down and going berserk, while James is very laid-back.

"I am very lucky with James. I did the commentating on all the Grands Prix by myself for at least two years before the BBC told me there was going to be two commentators, and the other one would be James Hunt. And because I am a human being, my immediate reaction was one of great concern: They are trying to get rid of me, they are easing me out, what have I done wrong? What the hell does James Hunt know about commentating? – all these defensive reactions. But because I like to think first and act afterwards, I did nothing. I did not do a prima donna act and flounce off, and I very rapidly discovered that the producer had actually made an inspired move. Because if there are two commentators it means that the one who isn't talking has a chance to change gear mentally, observe what is going on, have a little think, before he comes back again.

"James was given the job because he knows the sport, has done it, has won 10 Grands Prix, umpteen pole positions, been World Champion, and James could add another dimension. I have never done it. I could tell them what was happening on the circuit, but I couldn't tell them what it was like from the driver's point of view. And it so happens that we genuinely get on very well together. He is very easy to work with. We try, and it is very difficult, not to hog the microphone, because the bloke that has not got it thinks he should have it. But we have learned to operate in a particular sphere. Thus, I do the commentating and James does the comment, and they are two very different things.

"I certainly can't comment with the authority that James can, and James is a particularly good bloke to do that job. Because unlike a lot of people who have been very good at the sport, he can talk about it. And I am not wishing to sound patronizing, but James is extremely well educated, he is extremely intelligent, he is eloquent and provocative and he can comment far better than I could, so that is a plus. And the other benefit is that because it would be difficult to find two people who, in terms of background, attitudes, beliefs and all the rest of it, are more different than James and I, because of that, the way we talk and the way we commentate is so different, there is no confusion in the viewers' mind about who is talking to them.

"On a Grand Prix weekend the thing escalates in intesity through practice and qualifying so that when the race actually starts you are running flat-out. And then you run flat-out for an hour and a half, two hours, or whatever it is. And when you put down the microphone, you're exhausted. But you realize you haven't finished because you have to get round to the teams to find out why so and so retired on lap 12. We do a BBC post-race show and I also need all the details for the book I write about the Grand Prix year.

"At home, sometimes my wife Elizabeth wonders why I'm reading magazine and newspaper reports on races I've just come back from. I tell her it's because I might have missed something and I like to see what other people saw. I must say that I certainly wouldn't have been able to do what I have done if I hadn't got a very tolerant and understanding wife. Elizabeth came everywhere with me for 12 years, and I think our record was 36 weekends in one year. One day she came to me and said she had had enough travelling. She said, 'I haven't got your enthusiasm and commitment and I want to go off and do other things'. And that is what she has done. But I am very lucky to have been able to preserve my marriage, and I think the women behind the men in racing deserve the recognition, and not very many of them get it.

"This is a hectic pace for a man not far removed from 70. I certainly don't do this for the money. I don't need it. But if I was divorced from motorsport it would leave an irreplaceable hole in my life. I would always be a fan. When my reflexes have gone, or I can't take the travelling, or whatever, I can see myself quite happily sitting in front of the box, and reading the papers and the magazines, like an ordinary enthusiast . . . like I used to be. Like I still am."

ROB WALKER

"I've lived in the circus really all my life and it is a way of life for me."

R.R.C. 'Rob' Walker is the resident aristocrat among the Grand Prix people, and he alone remains from the days of the gentlemen racers. He used his family money, from the Walker whisky business, for the sheer pleasure of being involved with motor cars in competition. A former driver himself, he then became a private entrant, fielding cars for others, notably Stirling Moss. Now over 70, and a journalist for *Road & Track* magazine (where he alternates with Innes Ireland), Rob is a wonderful raconteur of the many fascinating experiences he has had.

"I've lived in the circus really all my life, and it is a way of life for me. In the old days you'd leave Monaco and everybody would

242

shake hands and say, 'Goodbye', and a week later you'd all be shaking hands and saying, 'Hello' in Zandvooort, and so on. Everybody knew everybody, literally. It's much less so now, of course. Of the original people still here, I think you could count them on about four fingers. Among the journalists, for instance, there's Jenks, Alan Brinton, John Blunsden and Jabby Crombac.

"As one gets older I suppose one's enthusiasm for anything gets a little bit less, and the atmosphere here is absolutely no comparison to what it used to be. But of course, we've got all these sponsors in now. It rather spoils the close affinity among the people. I think there's much more jet-setty stuff – it's the place to be, and that sort of thing – than there was in the old days when the people were very special. But I still get very excited over the races, as long as Senna is driving. If Senna wasn't driving, I don't think I'd be so interested. Still, I love meeting everybody and knowing a lot of the people. And a lot of them know me. All that is very, very pleasant.

"I go back an awful long way, you know. My mother took me to a Grand Prix in 1924, the Bologne Grand Prix, as a child. I found it all absolutely fascinating. And I think that was the start of it all for me. We were taken by the taxi driver round the circuit. He was highly enthused by the whole thing, and my mother was terrified, while I was encouraging him as much as possible. And he was pointing out the places where people had been killed with great delight, the trees that they'd hit, and so on.

"Then my mother gave me a car when I was still quite young, and we had a long drive where I used to drive up and down, up and down. I used to time myself for the drive, and then I began to tune cars. My mother, seeing that I was very keen, gave me the second chauffeur to look after my car, to tune it up and that sort of thing.

"This was while I was under the age of being able to drive. I was on my own private property, so it didn't matter. And this sort of thing went on for a long while. Well, you can imagine how it grew, and the very first time I was able to have a car legally I put it in for a race. And then I got the Delahaye when I was up at Cambridge. I saw it in a shop window in Park Lane, in London, and I absolutely fell for it. And, although it was far more money than I had, I was introduced to hire purchase, and I bought the thing. Without telling my mother or anybody, I entered it for a race at Brooklands. That was in '38 and the next year I raced at Le Mans, the last one before the war.

"When I got married, one of the things my wife said to me was I must give up motor racing. She said, 'You can do speed trials or hillclimbs, but not circuit racing.' This was during the war, when I was a Fleet Air Arm pilot, and our losses were phenomenal. Out of our batch, where there were 260 people, 25 eventually came out alive. So I had no hesitation whatsoever in saying, 'Yes, I won't drive after the war,' because I didn't think I'd ever see another motor race, let alone drive in it.

"Well, when the war did finish and I was still alive, I still had the Delahaye, which was the fastest road-racing car in Great Britain, and I wasn't allowed to race it. So what to do but find somebody to drive it, and that's what started me as a race entrant. I got Tony Rolt, he really was a magnificent driver, who won Le Mans with the Jaguar team, and he drove single-seaters for me. We got a Delage, and then we worked up to Connaughts. After Tony Rolt retired I had Peter Collins, then Tony Brooks, and then I had Jack Brabham, who was the first one who drove a full year's Grands Prix for me. And then Stirling Moss came to me, and we had this wonderful relationship for five years.

"I was fairly well-known by this time. I'd been the first private entrant to win a Grand Prix, I was the first person to win a Grand Prix for Cooper and Coventry Climax, and I won the first four for Lotus. Actually I was the first chairman of FOCA, only because they were such a rabble! They had to have somebody, and I was called in for a short time until they organized themselves.

"Towards the end of the time when I had Siffert driving for me and we were doing very well, *Road & Track* sent a man over from America to interview me. And I must be honest, I'd never heard of *Road & Track*, but the chap interviewed me and the last thing he said to me was, 'If you weren't in Formula 1 with your team, what would you like to be?'. So I thought for a moment and I said, 'Oh, I think I'd like to be a journalist to keep my interest in motor racing'.

"By return post a letter came and said, 'If you meant what you said in the last paragraph, we'd like first refusal of your efforts'. And then they wrote a whole list of things for me to write on. Well, I tore the whole lot up and threw it in the wastepaper basket and never thought any more about it. Then they sent a letter and said Henry Manney, their Grand Prix man, had got tired of going around Europe and would I try doing Monza for them? So I said I would have a shot at it. I was still running the team, but I did it, and they were very pleased with it. When Henry Manney decided he was going to stay in America they asked me to go on doing it. And it was the first time I'd ever earned any money in motor racing!"

BETTY WALKER

"The whole sport seems to have become a social thing. I think there is quite a sort of cachet to it now."

After extracting her husband's promise not to race himself, Betty Walker was able to enjoy herself in the sport for which she still has great enthusiasm. She accompanies Rob to most of the Grands Prix because, "I love the race. I enjoy the whole weekend, really. The nicest time of all is when we take a motorhome to some of the races and we go along in the evening when the mechanics are working. That's really great fun, because we know lots of them. Many of them worked for Rob in the past, so we know masses of people here. At the closer Grands Prix I will take along about 100 to 200 brownies for the people we know. I work very hard making them. I wouldn't eat one for myself for anything on earth after the smell of them! But Rob and Mario Andretti used to joke about how they were a secret ingredient of Mario's success.

"In the race, one doesn't like the thought of the danger of accidents. And this is really why, when Rob and I got married, it was one of our stipulations that Rob would not race any more, because I couldn't have borne to be one of the wives watching their husbands race. Of course, to keep busy, I always used to work when we had our own team, and did lap charts and timing and so on.

"But everything is very different now. It was all frightfully cosy in those days because the drivers did not have motorhomes and aeroplanes and they all used to talk to everybody here. And there was much more rapport with the public. Now, they are rather sort of gilded heroes who are untouchables, but in those days they were very touchable.

"It was more fun then. Now it has become smart. For instance, at Monaco, it is some people's one aim in life to go to the Monaco Grand Prix. We did it 16 or more years on the trot. And, of course we won it three times, or whatever. Now, I wouldn't cross the road to do it any more. The whole sport seems to have become a social thing. I think there is quite a sort of cachet to it now.

"And some of the people here, I think they think they are a bit special. Of course, Formula 1 is rather the elite of racing, the top of the tree, as it were. And I think Formula 1 people think they really are rather the top of the tree. However, I don't think the journalists are like that because I think journalists work too hard at everything to be snobbish."

NIGEL ROEBUCK

"I've always felt in motor racing writing there's a comparative lack of humour. And I think a lot of what happens in motor racing is very funny."

During the Spanish Civil War one of Franco's generals, Emilio Mola, was leading four columns of troops against Madrid. In a radio broadcast Mola boasted that he had a 'fifth column' of sympathizers within Madrid who would support him in a rearguard action. Shortly after that a war correspondent named Ernest Hemingway wrote a play called The Fifth Column. Nowadays, in his Fifth Column in *Autosport*, Nigel Roebuck writes from behind the lines in Formula 1.

Like a war correspondent, Roebuck brings news of the in-fighting along the pit lane and the intrigue in the paddock. He is the fans' man on the spot, passionate about the sport, and sometimes amused, sometimes angered, by its players. In his introduction to a collection of his columns, published in a book, *Inside Formula 1*, Roebuck notes that he is fascinated by the pit lane 'scandal' and *'gossip.'* And this fifth columnist makes no bones about the perspective of his point of view: 'Unbiased journalism, if it exists at all, is doubtless terribly worthy. But it sends me to sleep.'

"At least I'm fairly nakedly biased. I don't think I'm devious about it. For instance I am a *blatant* Prost fan, just like I was a *blatant* Villeneuve fan – even more so with Gilles. In those days, in every pressroom I used to walk into a barrage of criticism about what I'd written. People like Doodson would be saying, 'Villeneuve is a rock ape'. And didn't I realize that? And, what's the matter with me?

"But I just always loved reading opinions. I get bored with facts. I *love* reading people's opinions of people. I love reading profiles, whether it's film stars, or politicians, or whatever, especially if it's written by someone who's prepared to say, 'Well, I didn't think he was very interesting', or, 'He can't laugh at himself'. So I always try to get it across that I'm not necessarily saying A's a better driver than B. What I'm saying is that I like A, and I don't like B, and this is why I like A."

Roebuck was just six years old when he discovered the first driver he liked. It was Jean Behra, who caught and passed Trintingant's Ferrari to win the 1954 Pau Grand Prix. Little Nigel saw it on BBC TV and was "absolutely spellbound". From the ages of 10 to 18 he attended private school, where his favourite subject was English, though he specialized in the extracurricular study of motor racing. As far as the boy Roebuck was concerned, those school years were merely a necessary interval to be endured until he joined his Formula 1 heroes.

"It never really dawned on me that I would be anything other than a racing driver. What else would I be? I hadn't quite worked out how this was going to happen, being a racing driver, but I did realize that you didn't leave school and a week later show up at Lotus and ask for a job. And I thought, 'Well, I'll have to do something *until* I'm a Grand Prix driver, so I'd like to be a journalist."

But, according to The Public School Appointments Board, Roebuck was ill-suited for the journalistic profession. He was interviewed by a career counsellor, who told him: "'Forget it, forget it. I don't think from talking to you that you are the sort of person who could go and speak to a grieving widow six hours after her husband's been killed and ask her how she feels. I just don't think that's you.' And I thought about that, I thought he's right actually, that isn't me at all."

Roebuck joined a management training scheme with Bowaters, the paper company, and worked there for five years. Meanwhile, he continued grooming himself for his first choice of a career by enrolling as a pupil at a driving school at Brands Hatch. There, he came to realize he might not have the right stuff to be a Jean Behra. "I had all the classic signs of a kid who'd quite like to be a racing driver, but isn't desperate enough. For instance, one of my grandmothers left me some money and I spent it on a Lotus Elan. I *didn't* spend it on anything to do with racing. So I think probably it had already sunk into my head by then, that either I didn't want it badly enough, or I wasn't good enough, or whatever."

So, if Roebuck was not to race himself, then he would write about those who did and, ignoring the advice of the career counsellor, he fired off letters to racing magazines offering his services as a journalist. Only *Autosport* replied, and he declined their suggestion of beginning as a cub reporter, covering club events. He wanted to start at the top, writing about Grand Prix racing, and he thought he saw an opportunity in *Car and Driver* magazine. He wrote a letter to the editorial offices, in New York, informing them that a particular Formula 1 story was terrible and that he, Nigel Roebuck, could do much better. The author of that letter is still amazed at his audacity.

"I mean, it's totally out of character. It's just not in my character at all to do something like that. But I said, 'You can't afford to be without me any longer'. *Car and Driver*, to my astonishment, wrote back and said, 'Alright, if you think you're so clever, go to Barcelona on Sunday week and write us a report of the race, and if we like it we'll use it'. It amazed me and, since this was about 10 days before the race, it frightened me stupid!"

From his school geography lessons Roebuck knew approximately where the Iberian peninsula sat on the map, but he had no idea of how to get to Montjuich Park in Barcelona, let alone how to report on the 1971 *Gran Premio d'Espana*. Nonetheless, with the weight of thousands of American readers resting on his shoulders, he set off, alone in his Elan, and drove non-stop "on pure adrenalin" from London to Barcelona. In the early morning hours he spotted a Ferrari transporter outside a cafe. Inside, he recognized the Ferrari mechanic Guido Borsari, and spoke to him. Borsari welcomed him warmly and gave him a Ferrari yearbook ("the kind Eoin Young now charges telephone numbers for!") and the would-be journalist was encouraged by this good omen.

At the circuit, Roebuck, the enthusiast, knew who everyone was. The problem was nobody knew him. "Very timidly, I set about introducing myself. And I remember the first two guys who were kind to me. One was Rob Walker, who at that time was associated with the Surtees team. He gave me a lot of advice. And the first of the drivers, whom I took to instantly because he was so immediately friendly and helpful, was Chris Amon. And you know, people, colleagues of mine now, still don't believe it, that the first race I ever covered was a Grand Prix. I can't really believe it myself sometimes."

The *Car and Driver* audience became believers. That first race report, chronicling Jackie Stewart's victory in his Tyrrell, was a success, and Roebuck's career was launched. He finished that season with *Car and Driver*, then moved to a new British magazine, *Competition Car*, where he eventually became Editor (and gave Maurice Hamilton his first break). When *Competition Car* folded in 1974, Roebuck spent the next year working with Quentin Spurring (who later became Editor of *Autosport*) doing public relations work for Embassy, the sponsors of Graham Hill's Formula 1 team. That ended tragically when Hill, Tony Brise and others were killed in a plane crash. In 1976, Roebuck went to *Autosport* as Sports Editor, a move that coincided with the departure of the Grand Prix Editor, the American Pete Lyons. Roebuck leapt into that breach and there he remains, a race reporter and intrepid Fifth Columnist. Though some of his youthful enthusiasm has worn off and his writing has a sharper edge, he tries to temper that with humour.

"I know I can be very sarcastic, and I suppose over the years I've certainly become more cynical. But in the right circumstances it amuses me a lot and I just hope it does other people. I always try to write the sort of piece that I would like to read. Just as simple as that. I mean, I've always felt in motor racing writing there's a comparative lack of humour. And I think a lot of what happens in motor racing is very funny, unconsciously. It's ripe for satire."

Though he is still entranced by the spectacle of racing cars at speed, Roebuck is not a 'nuts and bolts' man. He is fascinated by the personality traits of the characters in the sport, several of whom rub him the wrong way. "I mean, I don't like brash, arrogant people. I certainly would never want to become a friend of one. When you meet people, in any walk of life, you either find them *simpatico*, or you find they get your hackles rising. And drivers have done that to me for as long as I can remember. But I think the whole sport is infinitely more aggressive than it was. I think there's much more of a jungle feel about Formula 1 than there was 10 years ago."

Roebuck thinks commercialism is the villain here, and finds the heart of the jungle is in the paddock. "When I was a kid, when I was a fan, it gave me a huge thrill to buy a paddock pass. Half the thrill of being there was actually being able to see your heroes and get their autographs, and that sort of thing, which is terribly difficult now. In most cases, the only way you can get into the paddock is via the wretched Paddock Club syndrome. That's what I really resent. This is the sort of financial aspect of the sport that I absolutely detest – the 'corporate guest' syndrome.

"I mean, it's some guy who sold more typewriters in the southeast between May and November last year who gets rewarded with a day out at the British Grand Prix. I'm not saying he has no right to be there, he certainly does. But I am saying it sickens me that he has access to places, and perhaps to people, which the real fans, *real* fans, just don't have. I just find that very sad.

"Then there is the motorhome thing. For a driver, it's very tempting once you have a motorhome, when you're not actually driving the car, to stay in there, because it gets you away from all the hassle. But I *detest* them! There is nothing I hate more than knocking on a motorhome door, and the door is opened about 6 inches to see who it is. And when you sort of sidle in there it's like the classic western movie when a stranger comes into the saloon and all conversation stops.

"I think it's demeaning. You're made to feel like: 'What do you want? We can give you 15 seconds'. I don't think it's too strong to say that journalists are by and large treated with a fair amount of contempt by the people in racing. Not, funnily enough, by the drivers, anything like as much as by some of the team managers. I think some of the Formula 1 team managers are among the rudest people I have ever met in my life!

"I think there are a lot of people who have Formula 1 teams who genuinely love racing and just want to do this with their lives. But I also think there are a lot of people who regard it as just a means of making an extremely good living. And a lot of them make an extremely good living from doing it spectacularly badly!

"Some team owners I do like a lot. Ken Tyrrell is the classic case. The lovely thing about someone like Ken is that you can write something he *thoroughly* disagrees with, and he'll ring you up and complain about it and argue with you. But you know at the next race it will be completely forgotten and he'll come up to you and the first thing he'll say is, 'Have you heard the cricket scores?'

"I think team owners have a tendency to regard journalists as PR men for their team. And I've said this repeatedly to them, 'You *must* understand that I'm not here to write that everything in the garden's rosy if it isn't. I'm supposed to be here to write about this weekend, and all the teams this weekend, including *your* team, and if you screw something up in the last session, I'm not writing a press release for you. I'm here to write the story of what happened.'

"The PR people, I must confess, I look at a lot of them and I don't really know what they do. But there are others whom I recognize do a good job and do it well. I think, inevitably, there's a tendency among all journalists to think all PR people have a fairly easy way of life. I think we have difficulty sometimes with that, believing there is somebody at the races employed to do *nothing*. Taken there, and flown there and everything else, and it *appears* they do nothing beyond write a press release every day. I know there *is* more to it than that. I just know from the year I had doing it there's no way in the world that I'd do that now. Because so much of it is, I'm afraid, having to be friendly and polite and solicitous to people you probably can't stand!"

While Roebuck's strong opinions delight his readers, they sometimes leave those on the receiving end of his barbs less than amused, though he has never been involved in a physical altercation. The late Elio de Angelis once got into a shoving match with Denis Jenkinson over a DSJ item in *Motor Sport*. Another confrontation between an Italian journalist and Michele Alboreto left the driver with a fat lip. But Roebuck has only ever been subjected to verbal use, or in the case of Ayrton Senna, silence.

"That's not from choice, I hasten to say. It's a curious thing in fact. In '85 I actually got on with him remarkably well. And he had so much to say in those days, and he was very enthusiastic. There was something quite attractive about the way he was then, because he was the 'spoiler', he was shaking up the establishment. He obviously had this *blinding* talent, that was the main reason why they didn't like him. They didn't like his arrogance, either, which was there even then. And of course it was the end of that year that everybody wanted Warwick in the other Lotus, apart from Senna, who simply vetoed it.

"Now Derek is a friend of mine, but I also thought he was the logical choice for the drive. Yet I think Senna had valid reasons for not wanting him there. I mean, he was perfectly right about Lotus not having an ability to turn out two cars of equal standing. I just felt for a guy who'd been in Formula 1 two years, it was a bit high-handed. And that's what I wrote. Well, that was *it*. After that, I can remember going in the Lotus pit and Senna just looked right through me.

"But I can't really blame him. I mean, I think he puts people very much in two camps: you're for him or you're against him. And I'm afraid I'm guilty of that, too. This is a problem if you're a racing journalist. But people are only rude to me once. And I *never* forget it until they apologize. And if they apologize, then that's fine, and I'll shake hands with them and forget it. For instance, I get on fine now with Patrese, but I didn't speak to Patrese for years.

"I once asked him a question after a race. And he was in a bad mood, and I get very annoyed with people who are in a bad mood all day and give everybody the benefit of it. I think you should be capable of having an argument with somebody, and then be perfectly polite with the next person you meet. I think that's not unreasonable. You might not feel like having a long conversation, but you don't get in a bad temper talking to someone and then scream at the next person you see. I don't like that. So I don't know what put Patrese in this bad mood, but I asked him a question and he just turned around and said, 'Fuck off'.

"And in fact exactly the same thing happened with Piquet. It's happened with Piquet with quite a few people, Maurice Hamilton among them. And I just thought, 'Well, you know, I can probably scrape by without talking to you."

Riccardo Patrese and Nigel Roebuck have since shaken hands and Roebuck now finds him "a very pleasant man". And he has had close friendships with several drivers over the years, notably Gilles Villeneuve, for whom he became a confidante. It was in a Fifth Column, entitled 'Bad Blood At Maranello', that Roebuck revealed the depth of Villeneuve's despair and his feud with Pironi that set the stage for the final chapter of the Villeneuve tragedy at Zolder in 1982.

"It might sound ridiculous, that a magazine article could have a huge effect on Grand Prix drivers, but I think sometimes we do have perhaps more influence than we appreciate. And, you know, I think that ours is a reasonably honourable profession. But when Pete Lyons left *Autosport* he wrote a sort of valedictory piece, explaining why he was leaving. He thought he was changing, and he didn't like this and he didn't like that and so on. He said at one point, 'The big problem with being on the inside is that you can see the seams.'

"And that's absolutely right. It's an enormous disappointment. It was to me when I first got into this. You assume that anybody who's a Grand Prix driver has got to be incredibly interesting. And the realization that, in fact, they are just people, that some have a good sense of humour and some have none at all, some are barely capable of expressing themselves, and not simply because of maybe speaking a language which isn't their own. A surprisingly high percentage appear to have very little interest in the outside world at all, beyond the business. It's like show business people. It amazes me how unworldly a lot of them are. And I don't mean that in any sort of fashionable sense. Just how they have a relative unawareness of *life*."

Still, if a driver has anything of import to say, Roebuck has a knack of drawing it out and into his tape recorder. Unfortunately, he can't always put it all into print, something which bothers a man who confesses to having great difficulty keeping secrets.

"Not keeping a confidence, I don't think I've ever been guilty of betraying a confidence, but I'm hopeless at keeping secrets. And it can get absolutely maddening. I remember doing an interview with Mansell at the height of the Mansell/Piquet feud. And I mean some of the stuff that he came out with was absolute dynamite! I thought, Jeez, this is marvellous, unbelievable stuff. Then when I played the tape back to write the story, literally 70 per cent was prefaced by 'off the record'. And what I was left with was actually not a whole lot."

Nevertheless, his off-the-record information is invaluable for providing an overview of the sport and the insightfulness he is noted for. "I think the way you really get insight is by being around a long time, so people get to know you, and eventually confide in you. They'll realize they told you something sensitive and you didn't blow it, and therefore it's OK to confide in you again. That's where the real insight comes."

While Roebuck's self-censored material might never see the light of day in print, he takes great delight in replaying the taboo tapes for his own amusement. He finds himself particularly in need of comic relief during times of Grand Prix glut, a condition that reaches its peak shortly after mid-season.

"By then you've done Rio, which is a long way, and Mexico and Montreal, they're sort of longish flights. And you're well into this thing of a race every two weeks, sometimes consecutive weekends, and that sort of thing. You get to August and you've done nine, and there are still seven to go. Hockenheim is not terribly interesting, and overtaking is not easy in Budapest. It's the height of the holidays, so the airports are chaotic. The planes are late and you just think, Jesus, this is never ending! But then I always sort of pick up again, at Spa. Such a wonderful place. And Monza, I *love* Monza. I could very happily do without Spain and Portugal. And then you finish the year. Japan is alright because the track's so fantastic. And everybody loves Adelaide because it has this terrific atmosphere.

"I think, by and large, we are enthusiasts getting paid for doing what we love. Alright, we want to make a living out of it, and you can make quite a good living out of it. Sure there are easier ways of earning what we earn. But I think there has to be a love of what we do, or else we just would not put up with the travel and put up with occasionally being treated fairly contemptuously!"

Over the years Roebuck has built up a network of colleagues in the press with whom he shares information. This pooling of resources is international in scope and he regularly confers with people like Pino Allievi, Heinz Pruller and Jean Louis Moncet. Roebuck has great respect for them (and the feeling is mutual), though he thinks the various nationalities tend to have certain character traits.

"The French press is incredibly chauvinistic, I think. I find it quite endearing, I'm not offering it as a criticism. But they are also quicker to turn on their own than any other press. You find, for instance, that some of them are incredibly loyal to Prost, and I must say I'm as guilty of that as anybody. But then you get the other side, the other French, who built Prost up into a hero and now are busy writing that he's finished. I think they destroy their own heroes quicker than any other nation.

"The Italians are the most fun by a long way, because they just revel in this sort of machiavellian intrigue and they see meanings in everything, and everything is of great significance. Piccinini's wearing a red jacket today, which means bad news for Tambay, or whatever. And sometimes I just find myself laughing, but the Italian mentality is a law unto itself. They're also the most cynical of the lot, and what they're not is chauvinistic. They tend to be very straight with themselves about Italian drivers. If they think the guy's no good, they will say so. They tend to analyze their own drivers very deeply.

"I don't think the Brits are particularly chauvinistic, either. I think the daily paper journalists are . . . I was going to say they're guilty of having a Nigel Mansell complex, but you can't really blame them because, presumably, that's what their editors want. After every practice session there's the sight of eight or 10 British journalists standing there, obediently queueing up to speak to Nigel, all going to get exactly the same quote. So, it's for that same reason I never, ever ask questions at press conferences. Because I always think, why the hell do I want to ask a question and then share the answer with the world? If you've got a question, then ask it in private.

"The photographic equivalent of this is about 15 or 20 minutes before the start of a race, when it seems that 90 per cent of all the photographers set off for the first corner. And they stand there like that, jammed in together, and they're all going to take exactly the same picture. And I just think that seems so *incredibly* unimaginative. And that's why I so admire a bloke like Bernard Asset.

"A few years ago he took a picture in Rio which I thought was extraordinary. It must have taken him hours to get to where he got to. Walked halfway up a mountain. And instead of having the traditional first corner shot at Rio, he was miles away, but he had the start area and the first corner, and it was the most striking photograph. I thought, Christ, you know, here's a bloke *thinking* about what's going to look good. Asset uses his imagination and, in fact, I think of him as a genius."

BERNARD ASSET

"When I see a place where many photographers are, usually I don't go there, because I think all the magazines are going to get the same picture."

Bernard Asset's reputation for being an artist with a camera is hard earned, and he feels his art is the result of as much foot-slogging and patience as creative talent. He is an incessant prowler along the pit lane, through the paddock, and all around the circuit, keeping a discerning eye peeled for potential subject matter to commemorate, and constantly on the alert for exactly the right instant to snap his shutter.

When Bernard Asset walks down the pit lane he is looking for, "a nice portrait to shoot for, nice light coming in the box (pit), or maybe a nice girl, waiting near a car or near a driver. For any little details. So the only way to find this kind of opportunity to make a good photo is to go and come back, like this, all the time. It might be just a few seconds at the right moment. But you have to be present, many times. You can not go and have a seat, have a drink and wait."

Noted for portraying a unique perspective of Formula 1, Asset thinks that one of his advantages is that he was a photographer before he was an enthusiast. "That is why, maybe, I look at everything as a photographer, not as a fanatic. I don't like to do news photography. I don't care if something is happening at the other side of the track. I will not run to get it. I try to do nice photos first. When I see a place where many photographers are, usually I don't go there, because I think all the magazines are going to get the same picture. I like to work alone."

As a teenager in Paris, though he followed the exploits of local heroes like Jean-Pierre Beltoise on TV, Asset was more interested in other sports, admired those who photographed them, and decided to make that his career. While attending a photographic school he rode a motorbike, which inevitably took him to competition events. His camera was always with him, so Asset began photographing the two-wheeled action for his own amusement. He then branched out into rallying and regional car racing events in France, and began to see the photographic possibilities of motorized sport. He got a job processing film in the lab at the magazine *Auto Hebdo*, then emerged from the darkroom to cover Formula 3, Formula 2 and some sports car races. His first venture into Formula 1 was in 1979, with *Grand Prix International*, the glossy magazine noted for its striking photos, many of which were credited to Bernard Asset.

Now a freelancer for Agence Vandystadt, in Paris, Asset notes that the passage of time has not made his job any easier. "In the beginning I liked more to make portraits of the drivers, and I had a reputation to be a good ambience photographer. But now it's so difficult to be close to the drivers because they have so much pressure. Of course, it's always easier with the beginners because they need more publicity and they don't hide, and there are not so many journalists and photographers with them. We are so many who must work together that I like much more to go out on the track. There are three or four times as many photographers now, and the Japanese are coming. They are very good photographers.

"Also, the team people, the engineers and mechanics, are always careful. They suspect you. They think maybe you are working for another team. I mean . . . sometimes you come, you want to make a nice photo with an engine, but sometimes they make it so you cannot see any details. So in this way it is very difficult to work – more and more difficult."

Asset can see the beauty in Formula 1 hardware, but sometimes the impediments placed in his path make him long for more compliant subjects, like beautiful fashion models. "Sometimes I really don't like it, I want to stop. Sometimes it's a very bad weekend where everything is going wrong. Especially when you start on the Friday morning, and you get fired out from two or three boxes – pushed out by mechanics, because you are too close.

"But sometimes everything is going well, and you think you had the nice shot, so you feel happy. And if the race is interesting, you feel you have the good shot. Sometimes you have a chance to have the very nice light. Very often it's going bad during the weekend, but after, when I see the photos in Paris, I feel happy with them, I feel I want to go back."

PASCAL RONDEAU

"You have to understand drivers who are on a Grand Prix day very tense."

The competition factor, which permeates every nook and cranny of the Formula 1 circus, is particularly evident among the photographers. As it is with the drivers, an enthusiastic brigade of young lensmen keep the frontrunning veterans on their toes. One of the newcomers most keen to make his mark is Pascal Rondeau, an enterprising young man who was born within the boundaries of the Le Mans circuit in France.

Rondeau caught the racing "virus", as he calls it, at an early age, and his decision to become a racing photographer came when his father gave him his first camera. But putting his plan into effect would not be easy in his native land, so Rondeau decided to circumvent the system.

"In France it's difficult because people ask you to get experience. But you need to get the experience somewhere so it's like a circle. I couldn't get anywhere, I was wasting my time. So I decided to go to England and see what happened. I didn't study photography at all, I just went straight to London and found work with Allsport, the company I'm working for now, as a darkroom assistant. So I did that for a while and then followed photographers around and basically learned by practising."

After a year of Formula 3 in England, and a couple of excursions abroad for Formula 3000, Rondeau leapt into the Formula 1 fray where he quickly set about carving a niche for himself. He soon learned to temper his artistic ambitions with the need for practicality, though he relishes the opportunity to create a memorable photo. "The studio may want some standard shots, so basically you play safe and you bring back some boring pictures. But you try to take a gamble at every Grand Prix to get some very different pictures. And if you can make a good one that's going to be published, that is very good.

"They work by country, the photographers, and each photographer from England tries to get the best in the race if they can, because there are not a lot of magazines around, so you have to fight to get the best pictures, for sure. But this I love, and at the moment I am very happy and feel very good when I'm on the track."

Rondeau is less happy with certain obstacles in his path, such as areas of the circuit which are off-limits, and the over-zealous officials who guard them, though he has worked out a formula for dealing with camera-shy drivers. "You have to understand drivers who are on a Grand Prix day very tense. And so I think if you do what you can with them, they give you back the service. If you hassle them every time, you can't get anything from them. If you work cleverly with those guys, it's fine. They are very nice guys."

DOMINIQUE LEROY

"I prefer the men, not so much the machines. They have faces of great interest."

Dominique Leroy, reporter photographique of Nimes, France, has three Grand Prix heroes: Ronnie Peterson, Gilles Villeneuve and Jean Alesi. "For me, they are fantastique, because they are very, very spectacular. For me, this is the essential quality to photograph. I have many pictures just of Gilles, because he was so acrobatique.

"But I prefer the men, not so much the machines. They have faces of great interest. Prost and Senna, they reflect a lot in their faces, in their eyes. The eyes are very important for a picture. But it is very difficult to know the drivers here. I also do rallies and Le Mans, where it is easier to photograph the drivers.

"With the cars, some are very nice for colour, like Benetton and Ferrari, of course. I try to perfect a picture with the car in the landscape. To show the speed, the artistic speed, and the ambience of the circuit. I don't like some circuits. Silverstone is very flat. Hockenheim is flat and straight. I prefer Monaco, Montreal, Jerez.

"Sometimes I don't like the ambience with all the other photographers in Formula 1. The French photographers are sometimes very crazy. With other countries I have no problem. But the French mentality I don't like. It is hard to keep harmony. It is like a fight. They push from behind. Too much stupid competition. It is sometimes like a war!"

PETER NYGAARD

"Many people like to do motor racing photography and that's why there are so many 'semi-pros' around."

Denmark's only regular representative along the pit lane means that his country has one less lawyer, for that was to be Peter Nygaard's profession before he turned his legal mind to covering Grand Prix racing. In fact, he never practised law, for the day he got his degree in 1985 was the day he decided to become a full-time photojournalist.

Prior to that he had been earning a living of sorts by covering certain races that were within reach of his limited resources.

"I travelled only by train. I had a tent and I had only one camera, a Russian one. Very heavy, very old-fashioned. Actually my first race as a photographer was Belgium in '82, a tragic race, of course, when Villeneuve was killed.

"Taking pictures for the English magazines was the first solution because journalists in Denmark can see the race on TV, and make their reports from TV and from the press agencies, and so on. But they can't do the pictures. As I was the only one from Denmark going to the races some of our magazines asked me to do reports and small stories. And now I enjoy writing even more than photography."

Nygaard loves the atmosphere of the sport, especially the start, and enjoys the camaraderie that exits among the regulars. The problem is the powerful attractions of the Grand Prix inner circle bring an influx of interlopers who want to join in the fun, and "everybody is standing on top of each other. That's a problem. Many people like to do motor racing photography and that's why there are so many 'semi-pros' around. They get their passes by having a local newspapers write in for them".

As a one-man show for a country out of the mainstream of racing, Nygaard has none of the networking benefits and ready markets available to those of other nationalities, where the sport is more popular. He doesn't need a tent anymore, but he has to make all his own travel arrangements and find outlets for his work. The latter task would be made much easier if there were a Danish driver to photograph and write about. "When our Danish national team qualifies for the World Cup there is enormous interest in Denmark. Now the football team is not so good, so there is really room for a new superstar. If there was a Danish driver here I'm sure interest in Formula 1 would explode."

JAD SHERIF

"When you're in it the glamour obviously goes away. It's harder work than people expect."

Jad Sherif's international background is appropriate for his work as a photographer with the International Press Agency. Born in Lebanon, he lived in Cyprus, Switzerland, the USA and England. After attending boarding school in England and Switzerland he studied photography with a view to finding a job in motor racing. In 1980 he met Jeff Hutchinson, who gave him a job in his darkroom and the two formed IPA. Based at his home in Geneva, Sherif gradually took over the photographic side of the business, though he found the reality of Formula 1 somewhat different from what he imagined.

"When you're on the outside you think it's very, very glamorous, and fantastic, and when you're in it the glamour obviously goes away. It's harder work than people expect. The three days that we're at a Grand Prix are fairly tough, hard-working. But it's still fun. It takes time to actually get accepted within the circus. The ones in the limelight, like the drivers, have so many demands made on them. But when we have to work with them all the time, sometimes they kind of open up, after a photographic session or when we're out to dinner. But it takes time to get their confidence.

"There are sometimes hassles when we're trying to work. Mechanics will push you, they'll send you out of the garages, they'll be rude to you, even to some extent if they know you. And then, waiting for drivers is no fun. If you need to do a picture of them, you've got to wait a long time, wasting your time. I do motorbike racing as well, and I think bikes are probably what Formula 1 was 10 years ago, where you could build up a relationship with a rider much easier. They're more friendly and they're more down to earth, maybe because there's not as much money in it. That's part of the problem here.

"Take for example the VIP Club, where people pay a hell of a lot of money to probably just see one day of the three. And it's all just to be able to say when they go back home, 'I went to the Grand Prix'. I wonder how many of these people are really interested in motor racing? It's really just a big show.

"I'm still an enthusiast, but probably not as much as some people. I can't say I know the history of motor racing like a character like *Autosport*'s Jeff Bloxham. I think everybody sometimes has difficulty keeping their motivation up. And if you're not motivated enough your pictures suffer. Somebody like Nigel Snowdon, I don't know how he does it. He's been here so long. With all the travel it's hard on personal relationships. During the season we're probably at home two or three days a week.

It's hard on me and on my girlfriend. I think that's why we see a lot of divorces in Formula 1."

NIGEL SNOWDON & DIANA BURNETT

"We're all very competitive, though it's a very, very friendly competition, and we still all go out and eat together and drink together."

"When I started I used to occasionally have problems at circuits, where they used to make you stand further back than the men."

Nigel Snowdon and Diana Burnett have solved any problems of trying to preserve a marriage while one of them travels with the Grand Prix circus. They do it together. Snowdon, born in England and educated in East Africa, first started photographing Formula 1 in 1963. Formerly an aircraft engineer, his entry into the sport was accidental.

"It was at a touring car race in Australia, where that is the big passion. I brought along a camera, though I wasn't even a photographer, and a car crashed quite near where I was. A guy from a newspaper came running along and asked did anyone get a picture of it. Actually, I said, 'I think I have'. The next day it was on the front of the Sydney Morning Herald. And, I thought, My, this is marvellous, what an easy way to make money!

"I came over to England and took another job so that I could have more time off. I was actually a messenger, going around to advertising agencies, and things like that. And I had a friend who had a photographic business and taught me the basics of printing and developing. I used to run around everywhere with a camera and take lots of pictures and it built up from there. But I was only ever taking pictures of motor racing.

"Then I went back to Australia with all my pictures and Diana said, 'Why don't you do a book?'. So we did a book, but Australia in the 1960s was very Victorian in attitude. The book was called

The Ultimate Excitement, and we had it printed in Hong Kong. When the shipment came to Australia and Customs saw the title they seized the whole shipment. It's the only motor racing book that's ever been seized by customs as pornographic!"

The book was eventually released when it was found to be non-titillating, except to those with racing passions, and the Snowdons returned to England where they set up Snowdon & Associates, though Diana kept her maiden name. She had originally met her husband-to-be on a boat and, besides marriage, he talked her into becoming a Grand Prix photographer. "I started doing it in a small way, and worked in a photographic studio in London to learn the business side, so that I could learn how to run our own business eventually. Gradually I went to more and more races, and then we finally both did it full-time starting in 1978.

"At the races I've always been treated like an honourary man, as they sometimes say. When I started I used to occasionally have problems at circuits, where they used to make you stand further back than the men. In those days they used to let a lot of girls have passes, who were just walking around with photographers and not actually working. That's tightened up a lot since then, and everybody that does it now, one assumes, is fully professional, but they probably thought I was just wandering around, too."

Diana enjoys all the global wandering her job entails, since as a native Australian she's "a nomadic person at heart". And after nearly 30 years of photographing Grand Prix racing, Nigel Snowdon has seen many changes. "Apart from the cars, it's much more commercial now. You used to sell to magazines and books and make very little money, but now, with the big sponsors, people pay realistic rates. But the whole atmosphere has changed. In the old days you could sit and talk to Jim Clark and it's not terribly easy to sit and talk to Mr Senna here. But there are still lots of characters and the young guys coming up, like Alesi. And Nigel Mansell, if you talk to Nigel while playing golf he's a completely different person, a tremendous person. But at a circuit you're lucky if you say 'Hello' to him.

"But I still enjoy the racing, actually much more than practice, because I think we probably work harder in practice. You have a lot of things you've got to do, while in the race you go from A to B, you know what you're going to do . . . except when you've done two days with beautiful sunshine in practice and race day it's raining. Then you've got a slight problem because it wipes out all the previous shots.

"The worst part of the business is going home wondering whether you've got everything you should have, and whether other people were there to get anything you missed. We're all very competitive, though it's a very, very friendly competition, and we still all go out and eat together and drink together."

KEITH SUTTON

"There's a lot of us doing it. You look around and you think, How is everyone surviving in this world?"

"Girls!" That's Keith Sutton's answer to a question about his favourite photographic subject. Particularly the ones in Brazil because "they seem to wear less".

While the Grand Prix photographers all seem enthusiastic about capturing the actual racing for posterity, Sutton and some of his mates also have a keen eye for pulchritude. Though many of the old timers bemoan the lack of women in the modern version of the Formula 1 circus, Sutton and several other observant lensmen assembled enough photos of pretty ladies to publish a book called *The Glamorous World of Grand Prix Racing*.

The proprietor of Sutton Photographic started covering Formula 1 in 1986 after several years' apprenticeship in various lesser formulae in England and Europe. Nowadays his brothers Mark and Paul do that work for the family enterprise, while Keith concentrates on sports car and Grand Prix events. There he finds a great deal of competition and sometimes wonders how everybody makes a living.

"There's a lot of us doing it. You look around and you think, How is everyone surviving in this world? I'm doing fine, but they're probably looking at me and wondering how I'm getting on. I suppose there are more people here, at the pinnacle of motorsport, because there's a lot more to photograph. You're not just photographing the cars, and the drivers. There's a lot of personalities in Formula 1 and there's a lot more atmosphere for offbeat pictures.

"Besides the girls, and the crowd, there are the team managers, and the designers, and so on, and they're all personalities. People want pictures of them. Some of them are difficult to photograph. With some drivers you need patience. If you want to do a set-up shot, where they're looking directly into the camera, you have to stand back with a long lens and be patient."

One of those he must now be patient with is Ayrton Senna, whom Sutton befriended when the Brazilian first came to England to race and Sutton did all Senna's photos and public relations work.

"I found him great in those days, we got along fine. We haven't got a lot in common, these days. He's doing his thing and I'm still moving up in my career, moving up the ladder as he has done."

Still, Sutton frequently sees Senna through his lens finder as the proverbial pole sitter leads the pack away at the start. "The start of the race is still the big moment. Then you just hope that the cars stay together so you can get some nice group pictures of cars. You do the first 10 laps at the start area and then you begin wandering about. Unless it's a close race, and then you stick to your corner. You don't move too quickly if you've got lots of cars dicing together. You find out how the race develops and take it from there."

STEVEN TEE

"The bit that still is really the most impressive thing is the start. It still sends a tingle down your spine, every time."

Steven Tee may have Formula 1 photography in his genes, since his father Michael lugged cameras around the circuits for many years. Steven attended photographic college as a darkroom junior, then emerged into the light of day when he was 20, joining the senior Tee's LAT company. "I guess it's always been in the blood because I saw my father doing it when I was growing up, and it was always something I fancied doing myself. I enjoy photography, I love motor racing and I love travelling, so the three things tie in very well."

"I suppose sometimes it's difficult to get inspired every time when you do 16 races a year, and I've been doing it now for five or six years. But then again you can have a bad race and then the next race you go to can be fantastic. Maybe you've had a boring race, the weather's not too good, and the circuit is not particularly interesting for pictures. Then you go to Monaco, or Adelaide, or somewhere like that, and it sort of reaffirms the reason you're doing it. Racing cars always look better when the sun's shining on them, they seem to come alive then. So if you've got a sunny day, blue skies, and a good circuit, that's what it's all about.

"It's a sort of friendly rivalry among the photographers. It's not cut-throat, like the world of Fleet Street, or anything like that. But there is certainly a rivalry. People look at other people's pictures and sometimes they think, God!, that was good. How did he get that? Though everybody gets on quite well, everybody's always trying to get one over on everybody else, photographically. That's the name of the game.

"You're trying to get something that nobody else has got. There are standard shots that people do which everybody is going to get, and sometimes you can't afford not to be there. But you can still find new angles. It's just a matter of wandering around and thinking, Yeah, maybe that will work, maybe it won't. So, you've just got to look for new things all the time.

"The bit that still is really the most impressive thing is the start. It still sends a tingle down your spine, every time for me. Then sometimes you haven't got a clue what's going on in the race, you lose touch if you are wandering around from corner to corner. You don't detach yourself from it completely, but you certainly can't afford to really watch it. You try to know what's going on, but through the lens rather than as a spectator."

JEFF BLOXHAM

"You're always trying to be better than the man next to you."

As a teenager Jeff Bloxham often attended the races at the Crystal Palace circuit in London and decided to photograph what he saw. He bought himself a cheap camera, turned his parent's bathroom into a darkroom, taught himself how to process film, then discovered he could sell his work. He took a photographic course, spent a couple of years "self-unemployed," a couple more as a computer programmer, then turned his race photography hobby into a vocation by joining *Autosport* in 1977.

Bloxham quickly found that covering a Grand Prix event was hard work, lugging a heavy assortment of camera bodies and lenses around the length of a circuit over three busy days, seeking photographic opportunities all the while, but very often playing a waiting game. His race day usually begins with a hurry up and wait situation. "You have to get there say at 8 o'clock in the morning before the traffic. You have the warm up about 10 or 10:30, then you have something like a four-hour gap to the race. The start tower for photographers has a limited number of places so if you want that you have to be up there one, two, sometimes two and a half hours before the race, and you just sit there waiting. After the start you try and cover two or three different corners, then the podium, then you rush back to the car and drive like a lunatic to get the plane for Heathrow, drop the colour into the lab so that it will be delivered to the office at 9 o'clock in the morning. I then get home, if I am lucky, maybe 12 o'clock – 1 o'clock in the morning. Get myself sorted out, get to bed about 2 o'clock, get up at 5 o'clock to go back to work to get the black-and-white sorted out for the week's magazine."

As the magazine's staff photographer Bloxham operates outside the cut-and-thrust of the freelancers, where life can sometimes be a bit ruthless. "There is so much money involved that there is a certain amount of money-grubbing in the PR side of photography. If you see a chance you will go for it. Say you have a contract with someone like Canon Cameras and you are their photographer. Then I am sure over the winter period half a dozen guys will pitch for that contract, even if you have it on a three-year basis. People will undercut you or whatever."

When it comes to photographing drivers, all the lensmen are in it together, and Bloxham finds the new boys among the drivers much easier to handle through his lens. "You've just got to point a camera at them and they all stand at attention almost, smile at you, sort of zip up their jackets, get all the right sponsors' logos showing, very helpful. At the very top, Senna is always a hard guy to photograph. I don't think he likes doing it, but I suppose being at the top he should expect it. He will pose, under duress. Maybe it's the wrong time and he has got other things on his mind. Mansell always used to be a problem like that, but I have been told he became better once he became more relaxed. He had this thing about flash guns a couple of years ago where if you flashed at him, it sort of gave him a headache or something, so anyone with a flash gun got jumped on by two of his mechanics.

"In the race itself, nobody likes seeing a really nasty accident, but it's my job to shoot it. If anything happens my editor wants to know why I have not photographed it. If it is a bad race with no action, like one car every 10 seconds, you think, Why am I doing this? When you don't know until the finish line who is going to win, that's my idea of a good race. To photograph it you like to get somewhere where you can take a good exciting photograph ever if it's a simple car shot, sliding or maybe just grazing a curb, something that makes the photograph stand out from just an ordinary one.

"You're always trying to be better than the man next to you. But if I see some guy taking a better photograph, you know, I'm not above trying to copy him. There are a lot of good guys out there. The guys at Zooom Photographic, like John Dunbar, are very good, very professional. I think Steven Tee gets some very good photographs. And there's a German guy, Rainer Schlegelmilch, some of his work is stunning."

269

RAINER SCHLEGELMILCH

"In these faces I see a lot more expression than in normal people."

"When I had to do my examinations for photo school in Germany, a friend took me to my first race at the Nurburgring, in 1962 or '63. I only did portraits. And I was excited by the atmosphere, so next time I tried to get there by myself, and to get passes. I started to do good photography on motor racing. Not like a reporter, more from the art of photography, and this was the beginning. To get passes, I had to sell these pictures, to American and foreign magazines. And when you are in you can't get out. It's like a big family and when I think of not going to a race, like Monte Carlo, I would miss it a lot. You know, it became very normal. When you think to retire, you can't do it. It's impossible.

"I think the most dramatic is the start. And, yes sometimes, when it's a real fight in the race, that's something. But a photographer often doesn't get all the news information. He's going around and he's missing a lot of good things. That's a pity. So I try to do pictures that are interesting, not only a few days after the race, but for a long time. I like to draw with the camera, like an artist.

"I went to an art school for photography, and I still feel more as a photographer and second as a motor racing photographer. I do advertising and all this kind of thing in Germany, from Frankfurt. On weekends, when there is a Formula 1 race, it's my main business. But I do a lot between. A lot with cars, too, in advertising, but also I do still lifes, and I think in photography everything goes a little bit together. People, and advertising, and still lifes, computers, everything goes together for me. I do a lot of business reports. You train your eyes always, for everything.

"At the races I'm always looking for new places, for new ideas, for new possibilities. Because if you do always the same you get tired of it. Sometimes I like the beauty of a good machine. Some have beautiful ornaments, beautiful colours, shapes. It's a kind of technical art.

"To photograph the drivers is for me the most interesting. I like the impression, the concentration, the typical character of a driver. Some have eyes like piano players, like Caffi. For me, he looks like a Russian concert pianist . . . a player of Tchaikovsky, him in a black suit sitting at a piano. He's fantastic. Not because of his long hair. He has beautiful eyes. I see that just through my camera. It's fantastic to see the difference of the drivers. The most beautiful eyes had Niki Lauda, very sharp, very light blue. Piquet, he looks like a wolf sometimes. Very, very angry.

"You have all kind of characters in these racing drivers. Some are very gentle, very soft. Prost has a fantastic face. Like an actor. It's like a wooden face carved with a knife. Like Pinocchio, or in French, like Marcel Marceau, the pantomime artist. In these faces I see a lot more expression than in normal people. Because they know that they can live very short. It makes them very serious and they live very concentrated, I think. And this you see in the faces."

NIGEL ROEBUCK sometimes can't write all he hears, but he always writes what he thinks.

MIKE DOODSON abandoned accountancy for the racing life and has never looked back, while agency writer REBECCA BRYAN divides her time between Formula 1 and several other sports.

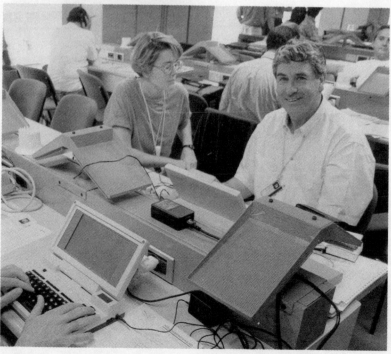

Honda's ERIC SILBERMANN seems to be convincing FREDDY PETERSENS, but finds a more sceptical response from JOE SAWARD, who studied pyschological warfare and black propaganda before he turned to journalism.

For JOHNNY RIVES motor racing is like a drug, but it helped him to shake off the horrors of war.

Designer GUSTAV BRUNNER finds that competition in Formula 1 begins with the scramble for the best seats at the airport, but he always has time to spare for technically minded journalists like JABBY CROMBAC.

JEAN-LOUIS MONCET, who combines magazine journalism with television reportage, thinks Formula 1 provides the ultimate test of performance and notes that sometimes it is lacking.

Technical artist GIORGIO PIOLA's talents include car design and telephone mimicry, but he has an aversion to press conferences.

Respected journalist PINO ALLIEVI says he sometimes asks himself why he is doing his job, but such doubts have never entered JEAN ALESI's mind.

FRANCO LINI, who once took a spell away from journalism to manage the Ferrari team, has seen many changes in Formula 1, not all of them for the better.

GEORGE GOAD, who founded the Formula One Spectators Association, thinks too much racing can flat-spot the brain.

DAN KNUTSON has found covering Formula 1 rather different from what he was taught in journalism school.

Canadian PIERRE LECOURS longs for another Gilles Villeneuve to write about.

ACHIM SCHLANG read German race reports and decided he could do better; now he thinks it helps to be crazy to do his job.

RAINER SCHLEGELMILCH thinks Nelson Piquet has eyes like a wolf, while MIKAEL SCHMIDT gathers much of his news in English then writes it in German.

Journalist and author DERICK ALLSOP's first love was football until Formula 1 put the boot in.

A Formula I family gathering. Journalists FREDDY PETERSENS, REBECCA BRYAN and MARK FOGARTY with Honda's ERIC SILBERMANN and an unseated ALAN HENRY take a break from the action.

BYRON YOUNG has returned to journalism after doing PR for FRANK DERNIE's Lotus team while DAVID TREMAYNE remains unmoved.

JEFF HUTCHINSON and DAVID TREMAYNE hear what life is like on the other side from former journalist IAN PHILLIPS.

Magazine editor STUART SYKES PhD thinks Formula I should inspire great literary efforts.

PATRICK STEPHENSON's journalistic profession neatly combines his love of travel and racing.

Track announcer BOB CONSTANDUROS collects the latest on Ferrari from STEVE NICHOLS before another session on the public address system.

Prolific wordsmith ALAN HENRY finds that some of his slower rivals suspect him of being several people.

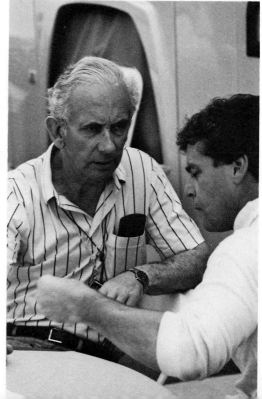

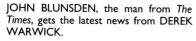

JOHN BLUNSDEN, the man from *The Times*, gets the latest news from DEREK WARWICK.

ALAN BRINTON used to mix with cabinet ministers before he and his pipe moved from Parliament into the paddock.

INNES IRELAND laments many of the changes since he was a Grand Prix driver but tries not to let this bias his writing.

JAMES HUNT, World Champion driver turned television commentator, admits his former lifestyle would be frowned upon now.

TV star MURRAY WALKER was not displeased to be described as speaking as if his trousers were on fire.

BETTY WALKER, whose 'brownies' have been used as secret weapons by drivers, extracted a 'no racing' promise before marrying husband Rob.

BERNARD ASSET, a photographic artist who is always seeking and finding new angles.

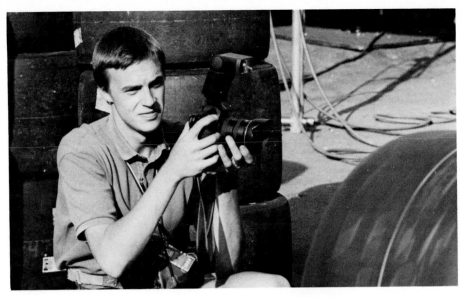

PASCAL RONDEAU was born in Le Mans so he just had to take his cameras motor racing.

PETER NYGAARD of Denmark may have an unused law degree but his cameras are well-worn.

DOMINIQUE LEROY, whose speciality is people rather than machinery, finds the photographic competition can be like a war.

Globetrotting photographer JAD SHERIF was born in Lebanon, educated in England and lives in Switzerland.

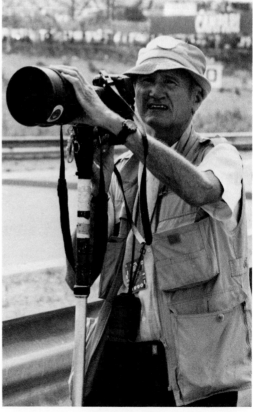

DIANA BURNETT gets down to work in the pit lane while husband NIGEL SNOWDON fires the long-range shots at the trackside.

KEITH SUTTON specializes in Grand Prix glamour, especially the girls.

STEVEN TEE continues the family tradition of motor racing photography.

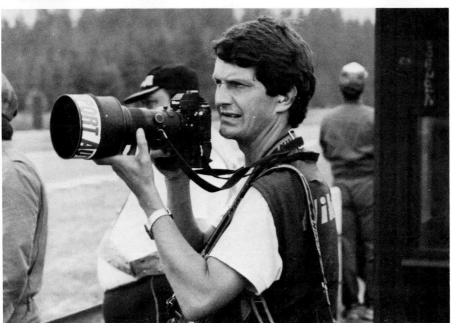

The newer drivers tend to stand to attention when they see JEFF BLOXHAM's camera.

JACKIE STEWART: an eloquent spokesman for the sport of which he was three times the World Champion.

FRANCOIS GUITER hates noise, though he has endured it since 1967 when he brought ELF into Formula 1.

LEE GAUG was a fighter pilot in Korea, but now he fights for Goodyear in the Formula 1 tyre war.

Goodyear's BARRY GRIFFIN explains all about tyre choices, but prefers running shoes for his own laps of the circuit.

MICHAEL KRANEFUSS, head of Ford's Special Vehicle Operations, has travelled the long journey from a dry cleaning business to Detroit.

SIMON ARKLESS, the Champion spark plug man on the firing line, says it would be better if the stars socialized more.

PAUL TREUTHARDT, "the correspondent who covered wars and motor racing", has moved into advanced technology as a Courtaulds spokesman.

R J Reynolds' DUNCAN LEE is always prepared to listen, but more often than not he has to say "No".

Marlboro's AGNES CARLIER always dresses in red and white and invariably wears a serene smile.

Ligier's DANY HINDENOCH wonders how some people in the paddock manage to get their passes.

3

OBSERVATIONS
IN THE PADDOCK

ORTWIN PODLECH's business is managing racing drivers; his office is on Ibiza and in his briefcase.

NORAH TYRRELL always supported her husband's racing habit because she has one of her own.

PAM WILKIE and her husband DAVE have been running hospitality units for Grand Prix people for 15 years.

STUART and DIANA SPIRES have no children, but they are "Dad and Mum" to a host of people at the Benetton motorhome.

When the circus leaves town people like DAVE MORGAN do the driving.

FISA's technical man CHARLIE WHITING sometimes wishes people would just shut up and go away.

FISA press officer FRANCESCO LONGANESI CATTANI, formerly ADC to Prince Rainier, thinks it's a bit of a laugh having photographer JOHN DUNBAR sign for his pass.

ROLAND BRUYNSERAEDE "can only pray" after he has pressed the green light button to start the race, but Professor SID WATKINS, the Grand Prix people's "family doctor", will be on hand if the worst happens.

JACKIE STEWART

*"I don't care how many times you've been to a Grand Prix,
you still feel the calm before the storm at the start, and that's
very special . . . There's nothing like it to get the adrenalin
pumping. I certainly still feel it."*

He is probably the most recognizable racing driver in the world,
though it was back in 1973 that the ubiquitous 'Wee Scot' saw his
last chequered flag. In all, he competed in 99 Grands Prix,
finishing up on the top step of the victory podium in 27 of them,
and Jackie Stewart still has about him the aura of a winner. During
his career a briefcase was as much a part of his equipment as his
famous helmet with the Stewart hunting tartan on it. In his
retirement he has parlayed his business expertise into a wide range
of successful enterprises.

He lives a jetset lifestyle (complete with his own jet), operating
business offices in London, Geneva and New York and
hobnobbing with the wealthy and the well-known in many fields
of activity. His home is near Geneva, he has a place in the sun in
Hawaii, "several other temporary places around the world", and he
lives in the Grosvenor House when in London, where he also
keeps a chauffeur on permanent standby. He performs consulting
and public relations duties for Ford, is on the board of directors of
Moet and Chandon, works with the Rolex watch company, runs a
chain of clay pigeon shooting schools (he was a champion in this
sport in his youth), has contracts with several TV networks as a
race commentator, operates a group of racing teams with his son
Paul, and keeps a breathless schedule of public appearances that
has him in seemingly perpetual motion.

But he never strays far from the pit lanes and paddocks of the
Formula 1 world, where journalists watch keenly for opportunities
to pounce on him with their tape recorders. For Stewart is an
eloquent spokesman for the sport and eagerly probes its nooks and
crannies with his quicksilver mind.

"I think Formula 1 is an exceptional situation and an exceptional
environment for exceptional people. But I do believe the people
are exceptional because the sport itself is so rare. People flock to it
because of the glamour, the colour, the excitement. For sponsors

the demographics are very positive. The lifestyles of the rich and famous, if you like, particularly at a place like Monaco. And the affluence that surrounds it is far in excess of anything that occurs in any sport, even Royal Ascot or the Kentucky Derby. Even the richest events don't have the kind of style or opulence and class that you get in Grand Prix racing.

"Formula 1 drivers are a rare breed. When I watch Ayrton Senna getting on pole I see a man at the outer limits of his ability. And when you see that, you think how that man is living a normal life outside of the racing car that's totally contradictory. He's got a jet, he earns $10 or $12 million a year, he's got all the toys that he ever wants in life. He doesn't have to do it. But he chooses to do it. That's an enormously interesting human factor. And I don't blame people for wanting to know what makes a man like that tick.

"You have to have a pretty hard streak in you to win in this business consistently. You've got to be fairly ruthless. You've got to be hard-nosed. That doesn't mean to say that you should not have some sympathy in you, that you can't be a nice person. It doesn't mean you've got to be aggressive all the time. But you've got to be able to focus your attention when the moment is right, selfishly, in the bullseye of your interest. And everything else must sit second. Whether it's your family, whether it's your loved ones, whether it's other business, whether it's other people, whether it's fans, whether it's sponsors, whether it's mechanics, or team owners.

"The driver is behind the wheel. And he's the only man responsible. To be like that, you've got to be a self-centred, selfish man, in many respects. You're paid to do a job. And you've got to do it better than anybody else. And in order to do that, sometimes there are sacrifices that have to be made. People say that's hard-nosed, and it's unsympathetic and they're not nice guys. In comparison to some fuddy-duddy, who's a wimp, maybe so. But in real life terms, they're real men.

"There are no other sports today with the following this has, a live audience as well as an enormous television audience, where life and death situations still exist, so clearly and obviously. And for the drivers to live that style of life in a society that's today so over-protected and wrapped in cotton wool is in itself a human interest factor which, for me, transcends all the other sports.

"Formula 1 attracts what I call professional spectators, some who have been in it as long as I have. And they're very professional. They know how to get the right credentials. They know how to get the best tables in the restaurants where the Grand Prix insiders go. They know everybody who's important. They survive because they're not a threat to anyone. They're just nice people. And they're completely engrossed and in love with the sport. With Formula 1. Not with any other part of motorsport. It's almost beneath them to go to a lesser event. They might be tempted to go to Indianapolis. Once. But they'll follow the Grand Prix tour for years.

"They love going to the pits, and maybe walking round part of the track, seeing and being seen. And looking comfortable, not obtrusive, and not being a bother to anybody. If they're a bother to somebody, then the sport spits them out. They're usually very well off, although there are some people who have managed to achieve it through friendships with other people in the sport, who have ensured their continuing presence.

"They love the excitement. I don't care how many times you've been to a Grand Prix, you still feel the calm before the storm at the start, and that's very special. Everybody feels it – the drivers, their wives, the team managers. Everybody wants to look cool, calm and collected and they're not, they're scared, and they're highly strung and there's a tension in the air, which is electric. There's nothing like it to get the adrenalin pumping. I certainly still feel it."

FRANCOIS GUITER

"Formula 1 has made big changes. It was friendly, and now it is not . . . It's only because we have been so successful."

Francois Guiter hates noise. He prefers the silent world beneath the sea where he has prowled around as a diver since he was 14 years old. A kindred spirit and compatriot of Jacques Cousteau, Guiter was a professional diver, a frogman in the French navy, and an underwater film maker. Now over 60, Guiter still dives for pleasure, though "my two ears are dead from diving, and from motor racing".

He was for many years also the marketing manager for ELF France and, while he is now retired from that position, he remains as a consultant to the company which he first brought into Formula 1 racing. Under Guiter's guidance ELF sponsorship helped restore French representation (drivers, technicians, engines, chassis) to the forefront of the sport which was originally given the name of Grand Prix by the French, at Le Mans in 1906. Over the years Guiter was also instrumental in such developments as getting the sport on television and beginning the distribution of press release information to journalists. But when he first surfaced in this noisy world of racing Guiter was like a fish out of water and had little knowledge of it.

"It was a marketing project. We had to launch the new trademark, ELF, in '67. We are an oil company, very big in drilling and refining and we are a very, very technical company. The company is directed by engineers and they asked me to concentrate on promoting ELF products. We made a big inquiry to see what for the general public was a synonym of good oil and fuels. And we found racing. We had never seen a race in our whole life.

"Now I have seen many hundreds of race weekends and I still enjoy it. For me, the best time is when the race is finished and we have won it! (In 1990 ELF sponsored Williams, Ligier and Arrows and provided fuel and lubricants to Brabham, Onyx and AGS.) One of the things I prefer is the last qualifying on Saturday because, for professionals, it is quite interesting to see how people act. For the race, maybe you can see it better on TV, if the broadcast is good.

"The worst part of the weekend is when somebody is hurt, but racing is a lot less dangerous than it was. When I started in racing in '67, there were two or three drivers killed each year. And in fact we lost our own. We lost Francois Cevert, we lost Patrick Depailler, we lost Didier Pironi after that in boat racing. We were very close friends. Now, I think the car, which is a lot faster, is a lot, lot safer, too.

"Still there is risk. I was a professional diver. I lost my brother in diving, and I still dive, and my three kids dive. So, when you

296

like something, you have to accept that there is a certain risk, you cannot hide from that. You have simply to try to restrict the dangers so the sport is at the best. Maybe it will be soon a little too much again, and we will have to limit the racing of the cars once more. To protect the drivers, and to protect the environment.

"Since I began, Formula 1 has made big changes. It was friendly, and now it is not. I used to stay after each race and all the big drivers, and all the team managers had dinner together. And the driver who won was making a speech. And that time is lost. Now, the technical exercise is at its best, but the friendship is not the same. I think that's sad, but it's a general trend of life. If you go to a Formula 3000 race or a Formula 3 race out in the country somewhere, it's still the same. You can find it. But it's something lost somewhere in Formula 1. It's only because we have been so successful.

"I remember when Jackie Stewart was having lunch, sitting on a tyre and eating a sandwich. The drivers today are hiding in the motorhomes. They want to protect themselves. Because you have something like over 1,000 journalists. If the people don't protect themselves, they could not have five minutes for themselves, to think about what is the main purpose of what they do. That is winning a race.

"But when you know them, they are very good people. Including the drivers who are supposed to be very difficult. Like Senna. Myself, I like very much Senna. He is a very nice man. Outside the race, he is charming. Inside the race he does not want to be bothered, and I think that is normal for him. He's dedicated to his job.

"I will give you a small example of Senna. Several years ago, when he was racing for Lotus-Renault, he won at Jerez in Spain. He won by centimetres from Mansell. Just a nose. He was so exhausted we had to take him out of the car and put him on the rostrum. That night we came back to the circuit at 9 o'clock. And there we saw a small rental car on the track. It was Senna, still with his overalls on. All the drivers should have been in Switzerland, or in their bed. Senna won the race, he was exhausted, and six hours later he was with a little car, cruising around trying to see where he made mistakes."

LEE GAUG

"It's big business. *It's big time* showbusiness . . . Hell no! It's
the most expensive travelling* circus *you've ever seen."*

Though very few of them have actually engaged in military
combat, Grand Prix people are fond of saying that going racing is
like going to war. Well, Lee Gaug has been to war, as a fighter
pilot for the United States Marine Corps in the Korean conflict. In
all, he spent 22 years in Uncle Sam's armed forces, then retired, a
grizzled veteran at the age of 40.

Always a man of action, Gaug then joined the racing division of
Goodyear where he's been fighting the tyre wars out of the
company headquarters in Akron, Ohio, for over two decades.
After 10 years in Formula 1, as Goodyear's Manager of
International Racing, Gaug is well-placed to put everything into
perspective. Lean and fit, and looking much younger than the
pensioner he is, he sees it all during his perambulations up and
down the pit lane, and he calls it like it is.

"A few years ago this used to be a gentleman's game, a rich
man's sport. It's not now. It's *big business.* It's big time
showbusiness. You've got to change with the times. We're in it, all
these big companies are in it, for the exposure. The publicity, the
goodwill. It's all about publicity and sponsors. And how do you
get publicity? You need heroes. If they aren't there, you *make*
them, you promote them. Everybody's got a PR man, writers,
photographers. And that makes it successful. You've got to. It's
part of the business. It's the most expensive sport in the world.

"Hell no! It's the most expensive travelling *circus* you've ever
seen. That's what it is. I mean, Sunday night they'll pack up and be
gone, and a week later they'll be somewhere else. They make
Barnum & Bailey look like a neighbourhood carnival."

Gaug describes his job as mainly a logistical one, looking after
the supply of up to 3,000 racing tyres to the Goodyear-contracted
teams at each race. Leading his army of tyre technicians he
accomplishes all this, the scheduling, transportation, provision of
different types of tyres and rubber compounds, with military-like
precision, but his position demands that he maintains a position of
strict neutrality.

"I don't take sides, don't play favourites. Treat every one of them the same. Sooner or later, if you get too close it's going to get you in trouble. So long as we've got all of them – I mean all the *best* guys let's say, under contract – you can't play favourites. It'll bite you because two years from now Ferrari may be beating the hell out of McLaren and you don't want them mad at you, you know. You can't just sit in McLaren's pit and baby them and forget the rest of them."

Gaug notes that he was one of the few who could sit down and talk (about tyres) with Senna and Prost – one on each side of him – during the height of their feud at McLaren. He doesn't care who wins, as long as they're on his tyres, and while he appreciates what the drivers do, Gaug is not overawed by them.

"I think a good race driver would make a hell of a fighter pilot, and a good fighter pilot would make a hell of a race driver. They have to be nervy, they have to have good co-ordination, they have to have competitiveness. And the wealthier ones all own airplanes. Flying airplanes and driving race cars I think are pretty similar.

"So in other words, I respect what they do, and I can appreciate the good ones from the not so good ones, and the ones that are really competitive and try, and the ones that are just out there to be a hero. But, they're just people, like you and I. I mean, some of them are spoiled young rich kids. In my estimation, some of them are. Some of them are level headed. But they're just people. Maybe because of my age and background I'm not overly impressed."

Still, on an international scale, Gaug thinks the Formula 1 drivers are the very best at what they do and he has theories as to why none of them are from his native land. "These drivers – the likes of Senna and Prost – are good, as good as anybody in the world, if not the best. My estimation is, among the young Indy drivers for instance, young Andretti and Unser probably have the best chances of coming over here. But they won't because they're over there, and they're pretty well established because of their dads and so on. But most of them would not make it here. Less talent. Lesser drivers.

"Part of it is that they can't start early enough. Most of your champions here have all started in go-karts when they were 10 years old. You can't get a driver's licence till much later back in

the States. Here, you've got Caffi, Bernard, Lehto, Alesi. Alesi is
the best young race driver since Senna. These kids are *good*. And
they're fast. And you couldn't get a handful like that in the States
and come even close to them in road racing."

"And as far as the press is concerned, Formula 1 is served better
than anything in America *ever* was. The people here do it year
after year. I've been here 10 years and I'm a new man compared to
a lot of these journalists. And photographers. They've been doing
it for 10, 15, 20 years. They know their business. They're experts
at it. They can look at a car, they understand what's being said and
done. This series has top notch, professional journalists. Dozens
and dozens of them. No question about it.

"As far as the States are concerned, there is no question that the
biggest race in the whole damned world is Indianapolis. The next
biggest is the Daytona 500. Formula 1 isn't near as important in
the States, and we realize that. But Goodyear is a multinational
company. We have companies in Australia and Japan, in Mexico
and Brazil, in France and Italy and Germany and England. So we
need Formula 1 for the rest of the world outside of the States."

BARRY GRIFFIN

*"I think one doesn't really look on this as a job. It's more a
way of life than a job to most of us."*

Barry Griffin is the Manager of International Racing Public
Relations for Goodyear. A fitness enthusiast, he often begins his
race weekend by donning his running gear and jogging around the
circuits for a first-hand look at the arena where his company's
tyres will perform. The rest of the time he circulates around pit and
paddock, wearing a seemingly permanent smile, probably because
he loves his work.

"The thing about it is the excitement, the speed and the noise,
which gets your adrenalin flowing, and being part of a high-profile
sport. And I think it's perfectly natural to appeal to lots of folk
with a sense of adventure, and maybe we all fancy ourselves as

potential Grand Prix drivers. I soon realized that I wasn't a potentially fast driver at all. Did a few rallies as a kid, essentially club rallies in a Mini, and soon found out that I was a very slow driver in comparison to most people. So, I got out of it before it cost me money or I wrecked the car.

"I've been in the racing division full time since 1979 and I would say I'm a genuine enthusiast for being involved in motor racing. Having been involved it would be very difficult, once you were out of it, to go back purely as a spectator. Here, you feel you're part of a very prestigious operation which one can derive a certain amount of pride from. And it goes deeper than motor racing itself. For most of us it is the opportunity to meet some wonderful people, travel to some wonderful places, and have some great experiences.

"But, having said that, I don't think there is much glamour here. I think it's perceived to be a very glamorous sport by those people who are not involved in it. Those of us who are involved in it, I think, essentially, take a pretty low profile. We come to work in the morning, we go home at night, we have a meal and we go to bed. There's very little partying that goes on. I think there was partying way, way back, but now it's a much more serious business.

"I'm happy with the business nature of the sport today because I think it's the only way motor racing could exist, and could have reached the heights that it has done. The thing that has gone away from it, I think, for those who have been here long enough, is the friendship of some of the drivers and other significant people.

"Part of my job is dealing with the press and I think the professional people who follow it continuously do an exceptionally good job. There will always be the occasion where a newspaper sends a man over and he's looking for something sensational. And if we happen to have a problem – oh well, there it is: Goodyear cost Nigel Mansell the race, or something like that. He's going to do that. I think that man does it unwittingly, without knowing the damage he does to a company like Goodyear.

"We take to every Grand Prix at least 2,300 tyres, and have done so for years, and years and years. And if you look back at the quality of the Goodyear product, the number of things that have gone wrong is a very, very small percentage. The problem with a tyre is if it happens to default it is usually very spectacular. But you have to realize, and I think maybe the inexperienced journalist doesn't always realize, that a tyre is just another component of the total package. And if you were to look at the rate of failures in motor racing I think you'd find tyres were one of most reliable components. But we expect to be noticed because we're on show. And I think most people respect us for being prepared to put our name on the line every two weeks of the racing year in front of I don't know how many million television viewers. We're pretty proud of our record.

"In the long run, I think one doesn't really look on this as a job. It's more a way of life than a job to most of us. In my own case, it means being away from home some 130 days of the year. It becomes a balancing act between your job and your obligations to your family. I happen to have a super wife who supports me totally. I think the hardest thing is leaving home, saying goodbye to your wife. Once you've done that and you're on your way to the airport you enter into a different phase of your life."

SIMON ARKLESS

"The people I'm closest to among the teams are all people who make things happen, who don't just let life pass them by."

Simon Arkless looks after Champion spark plug's interests in Grand Prix racing, a task that keeps him hopping along the pit lane since the majority of the teams use his company's products. Prior to joining Champion in 1983, Arkless spent 10 years with AP Racing (a supplier of brakes and clutches in Formula 1) and the reason for his longevity as a Grand Prix person is quite simple.

"I really love the sport. I used to race myself, in the '60s, in anything I could get my hands on. I would have liked to have gone on as a driver, but the cost became so prohibitive that it just wasn't possible. And now I suppose I'm a frustrated racing driver, and I'm still attached to the sport because it's what I enjoy doing.

"My main function is a technical one, to see that all the teams that are using our equipment have the right spark plugs. I do dynomometer tests at the engine makers' factories, Ferrari,

Renault and Cosworth, and places like this, where we evaluate certain types of spark plug and pick the best one for the use with that engine. I then go to all the Grands Prix to ensure that they don't have any problems, or investigate any problems that do arise. It's very satisfying to keep everything running smoothly, and there are other little job satisfactions as well.

"Most of the engine manufacturers are very secretive about what they do. And, very often when I 'read' a plug, I can detect that they have done something to the engine, that it isn't the same as it was the week before. It gives me a lot of satisfaction to be able to go along to them and say, 'Hey, you've changed this', or the fuel's changed, or something. They don't like me finding out, but it's enjoyable.

"I have to remain neutral to all our customers, and it can be difficult at times when, for example, Ferrari and Renault, who both use our equipment, are in adjacent garages. You have to walk out of one garage into the next one and you have to be very diplomatic. The teams must have confidence in you to know that you are not going to give away all their secrets. And, if they have any little tweaks and somebody is trying to find out about it, you can't say anything at all. Because otherwise, you just couldn't possibly do your job. The teams must respect you, that you're not going to give away their secrets. On occasions, certain teams have asked me to get information for them. And I've just said, 'Absolutely no way. Can't be done'.

"But basically, they are a great bunch of people here. There are some difficult personalities, certainly, but when times get really hard, they all stick together. I can remember a case in Portugal a few years ago. One practice morning the fog came down over the circuit and two or three of the teams were playing football in front of the pits when the police tried to stop them. One policeman took the ball away, and the guys who were playing football protested. And I think the policeman at that stage was probably a little bit frightened by the fact that so many people were asking for the ball back. He set one of the dogs loose. And virtually en masse, the whole pit lane, everybody from every team, climbed over the pit wall and everybody joined forces.

"I mean, it was a fantastic sight! The fact that everybody in Formula 1 stuck together. And whether it was McLaren, Ferrari,

Ligier, all of them, they were as one. The policeman backed down, he had to. He gave the ball back. It was incredible. So I think, basically, there's a very good camaraderie here. OK, there's a lot of internal politics, which do get a bit heavy from time to time, but the camaraderie amongst the teams is always very strong.

"But the sport has changed a lot during my time, probably the professionalism is the biggest change. With sponsorship, and so on, there's a lot more money now involved, and when a sponsor is putting millions of dollars into the sport, he's expecting a good return. And consequently, everybody has to be very professional about the way they go about things, because they are representing their sponsor, and having to put across a good image. And I think this has had a sobering effect on the overall image of the sport.

"In the early days there was a lot more of a party-type spirit. And that, unfortunately, has disappeared to a large extent. The drivers got a lot more involved with the social side of the team activities then. Now they tend to remain a bit aloof and a bit remote. They tend to disappear into all the motorhomes in the paddock, which is another aspect of the professional side of the sport. It does isolate the stars from the people who are paying the money to come and see them. Obviously it's not going to spoil the sport, but I think the sport would be that much better if these guys could socialize a bit more than they do.

"The people I'm closest to among the teams are all people who make things happen, who don't just let life pass them by. I think most Grand Prix people are like that. They have a goal, they have a particular flair for what they do, and they do make things happen. If there's a car to be got ready in two days, they'll just work until it's done. They don't sit back, they don't knock off at 5 o'clock and go home, they work until the job is done. Because with a race every two weeks, there's no time to waste. So if there is a lot of work that has to be done, they just go out and do it. And I think this is what makes a lot of them particularly special. They just put their heads down and go for it."

MICHAEL KRANEFUSS

"In Formula 1 some people have got this Dallas complex, whether they have seen Dallas or not."

About 35 years ago the man who is now head of Special Vehicle Operations for the Ford Motor Company used to hitch-hike from his home in Germany, in Westphalia, to the Nurburgring to watch the races. Michael Kranefuss recalls how his fascination with vehicles used for sporting purposes began, and where it has taken him since.

"My family had a dry cleaning and a laundry business in Muenster. My father was the oldest and got the business, and I was the oldest and was expected to take over some day, though I was never asked if I liked it. But the one thing I knew was that I loved cars. We had about 15 transporters, which I volunteered to wash on Saturday afternoon, so that I could move them around, just on the premises. Well, that was when I was 12, 13 years old. And it never stopped. I raced Ford Escorts myself for awhile before joining Ford in 1968. Now I'm still attending 30, 35 race weekends a year, including all types of racing. And I must say, I do enjoy most of them.

"In Special Vehicle Operations we are running the racing business primarily in North America and also doing Formula 1. We're providing the racing teams with the kind of pieces they need, to be able to race our engines, for which we are doing the development. Of all the types of racing we are involved in, Formula 1 is by far the most expensive. It's a high-pressure kind of a deal, where everybody sets his own goals. At times you're running up against somebody who just happens to have a different viewpoint about the value of the package, and spends maybe 10 times as much money as the next guy.

"Because it is financially less limited than anywhere else, Formula 1 is the pinnacle of motorsport. In terms of the technology involved, the engines, aerodynamics, materials, it is definitely the pinnacle and it's difficult to compare with any other series. The thing for us is to figure out what this whole thing is worth, and to what extent we think we want to support it. And then you have a problem, that if you're getting caught by somebody

305

who has a different opinion about the value of Formula 1, you're going to have to go back to your management and say, 'Hey, you know, unless we do something we're going to get our arses kicked'.

"But Ford Motor Company's motorsports programme goes into many, many areas, so we're not really only focussing on this one. Secondly, we have a long history in the sport, and we have seen it all, including our own attempts to win Le Mans. That was a no limit kind of a deal and we won it.

"But if you look at NASCAR in the States, it's definitely the best series in terms of racing. I mean, there's nothing close. And it's not very expensive, and the teams right down to the number 10 can make a halfways decent living there. But the series is run with a different intention. For Bill France, who runs it, the idea is not to provide exciting technology, the idea is to provide entertainment on wheels. And NASCAR has the most relaxed atmosphere in racing, certainly it is not as hyper as this one is. The teams help each other, whereas here the attitude is screw the guy who is next to you. Definitely everybody wants to win in NASCAR as badly as here. But it's not as driven as this. Again, it's all about money.

"For years I've said this cannot go on. Still it goes on – spending too much money. And you have to ask yourself about what the top teams are spending today. I know, for instance, what Ken Tyrrell is spending, and look what he's done recently. With a very minimal budget. Which may force some people to think before they spend so much money. Whereas if you have enough money you can pursue 10 different directions immediately, cut out eight and pursue two, and at the end of it all, one of the two might be the right one. And if not, you throw it all away and start all over again.

"I'm torn constantly between trying to be a good manager for the Ford Motor Company and putting things into that perspective, and on the other hand I love the sport. So I can sympathize with the kind of ideas some of the designers have, which do cost a lot of money these days. In Formula 1 a lot of things can be bought. But you still have to make it work and sometimes people who've got a lot of money still can't make it here.

"And all the money has changed the sport in other ways. I remember the years when we could hang out with Graham Hill and Jim Clark and they told wonderful old stories. And some of them were actually true! You could have a good time with those guys. And it was because there wasn't so much money involved, it wasn't so serious. Nowadays you can't get near the drivers. But the sport has never been more popular and today's drivers are still heroes to the public. If Bernie Ecclestone has done one thing right it is that he understands that the more difficult he makes it for people to get close access to Formula 1, the more they're going to lust after it. It's a very simple principle, and it works.

"Of course the press has a lot to do with the popularity. With the Formula 1 press you have to differentiate between the buff books and the general media. I think the buff book guys, most of them are well informed. Some have their biases and strange opinions. They might like one team better, and even if it's 20th they still like to believe they see all kinds of things happening there that nobody else sees. Or they like a particular driver, and they're very biased about him. And they're constantly trying to sell you those kinds of ideas. But once they get over this, they're well-informed.

"In the general media the easiest thing is to sell the little juicy things or spicy things that are going on. Somebody's in the shit with his team manager, or his wife ran away, or whatever. And they're making much too much out of those things and ignoring the racing. In Formula 1 some people have got this *Dallas* complex, whether they have seen *Dallas* or not. Where everybody screws everybody else. So there is plenty of that for the general press to write about."

PAUL TREUTHARDT

"It is clear that the press is disliked, and sometimes intensely disliked, inside the sport, in the inner circles."

Paul Treuthardt's business card says that he is Senior Consultant of Avenue Communications, a London public relations firm which represents Courtaulds' interests in Formula 1. But Treuthardt's CV is heavily biased toward motor racing, an interest which goes back to his boyhood in Australia when he first saw Jack Brabham race on dirt tracks. For many years he was an international correspondent for United Press and Associated Press wire services, usually working out of Paris.

"My normal beat was general news, though I became more and more involved in motor racing over the years. I was described as the guy who covered wars and motor racing, because I was on the fringe of a number of wars. I was in Jordan for the '73 punch-up, and I was in the Sahara when the Moroccans invaded the Spanish Sahara, though it was reasonably peaceable.

"Anybody can go to a motor race, look at the results, and say, 'So and so came first, so and so came second, so and so came third'. But to find out what's really happening, it takes years and years and years, especially in Formula 1 because it is so very cliquey. And I think probably the more I know about it, the more interesting it gets and the more fun it becomes. It's great fun knowing the people, and knowing the personalities and I still think it's a very exciting sport.

"But what I found most interesting, after leaving wire service journalism, was the opportunity to go on the PR side when I became the Tyrrell press officer in 1987. I discovered there's another world that the journalists don't know about. And I thought, this is fascinating, because here we all are, the inner circle of Formula 1 journalism, the plastic card carrying members, and we think we know what's going on. The day you join a team you realize how much goes on that the press never learns about. They're kept in complete ignorance of all sorts of things.

"The competition is so tough that the team owners say, 'We can't release any tiny thing, that it's so vital that we really don't want to tell anybody about it'. The other thing that I found was that you become a part of another inner circus. You don't go into anybody else's garage like you used to, unless you're invited. You're now in a team uniform, and so forth. On the other hand, you have a rapport with all the other team people that you don't have as a journalist. However well you know them, they look at you and you're one of the tight inner club. And that's fascinating, and I've learned a lot of things.

"For example, when I was a journalist I saw all these people being wined and dined in the motorhomes, in the Paddock Club, and all that. And it wasn't until I came in on the PR side that I realized how valuable that is. Because like most people, I thought that's just a lot of people having a nice weekend. But I've learned about what has resulted from these winings and dinings. I know that the people I work for now, Courtaulds, find that there are two major things that they are looking for out of sponsorship, besides the international exposure. Half of it is an internal staff thing, improving morale through their racing involvement, and the other half is entertaining customers. And it works. We are there to help Courtaulds get the best value they can out of their sponsorship, for their employees and for their clients, and Formula 1 really works in that way.

"This sponsorship factor has changed the whole sport out of all recognition. In the old days it was virtually people towing cars on trailers behind their private cars. The pressroom was a wooden shack with three telephones in it. The whole financial explosion has changed the thing out of all proportion. It has certainly made it less friendly in many respects. People used to stay around until Monday, and if you won a race, you threw a party where a lot of people ended up in the swimming pool and various hooligan-like activities went on. All the pressure now has changed that. The pressure for results.

"There are enormously more journalists than there used to be, and they have to be tougher. There were a lot of dilettante journalists, particularly some of the old boys in the English press. There were some elderly gentlemen who would say at the end of the race, 'I say, old boy, who won? What was he driving again?'. You can't do that any more. You've got to hustle.

"It is clear that the press is disliked, and sometimes intensely disliked, inside the sport, in the inner circles. For two reasons. First, they take up a lot of time, and it would be much easier if they weren't around. Second, when a story is wrong, people get furious, without accepting the fact that they are trying their hardest to conceal information, and the press is only getting what it can.

"The teams feel that the press don't understand the financial realities of the sport and can too lightly take the amount of sponsorship required, and given, without realizing how the sponsorship works. Just looking at the size of the logo on the car is really the tip of the iceberg. You realize more when you are inside that, while the teams are racing, they are also running a business. And the new factories and luxury motorhomes are all part of that business. They also have to be realistic businessmen and put 10 per cent aside as a reserve for next year, or whatever. And I don't think that always is perceived in the pressroom."

DUNCAN LEE

"I think the paddock on race weekend is absolutely the worst place in the world to have a business discussion."

"No." That's the word Duncan Lee finds himself having to say most often to those who seek sponsorship from Camel. As the Director of Sponsorships and Special Events for RJ Reynolds Tobacco International Inc, Lee finds this aspect of his job interferes with his enjoyment of a Grand Prix weekend.

"The most aggravating thing to me is when people find out who I am, and where I am, and try to give me a sales pitch on why our company should sponsor them and spend money with them. It's a case of when you get cornered by people you feel that you have to be polite and listen to them, and it just takes up time. You listen to the same things over and over again and you have to tell them the same things over and over again. Which is, basically, 'No'."

W. Duncan Lee would really rather be watching the racing, because he is an enthusiast. And, in particular, he would prefer to be following the fortunes of the teams and drivers wearing the Camel yellow and blue colours – those to which he has said "Yes" about sponsorship. Lee's fascination with motorsport began back in the American Mid-West from whence he came.

"I can remember when I was probably about 14 years old, I was in a local drugstore in this little town that I grew up in, in Missouri, and I was looking at the magazine rack for no particular reason. I picked up a magazine about custom cars which in the '50s was the big craze. I was taken by it for some reason, and so I started seeking out that type of publication and others on drag racing. And every Friday and Saturday night we had our impromptu drag races out on the black top road outside of town. We got maybe 10 or 15 cars and a lot of people watching it. I used to tear the transmission out of my father's car quite regularly.

"When I started to drive, my father had a Chevrolet stationwagon which I was mortified to have to go out on dates with, having to pick a girl up in a stationwagon! In that part of the country we also had dirt track racing, sprint cars and modified cars, so that was the next thing that attracted my attention. I didn't see a sports car or a road race of any kind until I went to Germany in the service.

"After graduating in journalism from the University of Missouri I went into the army and became a public information officer, based in Heidelberg. The Hockenheimring had just opened nearby, and I spent a lot of weekends out there. Friends and I would go to every kind of race, motorcycles, sidecars, sports cars, and the biggest thing they had there at that time was Formula 2. I was there in 1967 when Jimmy Clark was killed, a very sad day. I used to read everything I could get my hands on about racing, so even though I wasn't personally that interested in Grand Prix racing at the time, I knew who all the names were.

"I was in the army for three years, then I worked for the Department of Defence for another three after that. Then I decided to combine my interest in motorsports with the journalistic skills I had, and became a freelance writer and motorsport marketing consultant around Northern California. That led to a job as Public Relations Director for Sears Point International Raceway in 1976.

"Some of my favourite writers of the day were Charles Fox, Brock Yates and William Janes, who I thought was on the borderline of sanity, but he's a very entertaining writer. Another one was Henry N. Manney III, in *Road & Track*. But I always had the feeling that maybe writing about, or working in, motorsports wasn't quite respectable, it wasn't a real job or occupation. Maybe because it was so much fun.

"For a long time my real dream was to be a race driver, and I tried that a little bit. I debated on whether to go road racing or oval track racing, because I liked both of them. I made a decision, based on economics, that the most inexpensive way to do it would be to get a little circle track car because they were very inexpensive and cheap to run, so I did that for about three years, racing on dirt tracks. I did everything wrong, made all the wrong decisions, got involved with the wrong people, and spent my money on things I shouldn't have. My driving career ended when I ran out of money.

"The Sears Point job was quite an exciting thing for me, and really got me on the road to where I am today. We had an IMSA Camel GT event and through that I met the RJ Reynolds people. Working at a race circuit in those days was a little bit tenuous, you never knew who was going to own it next and where you were going to be, so I thought about looking for something else. I called some people I knew at Reynolds, and by coincidence they had an opening which I applied for and got. I worked on the Camel GT events and the NASCAR Winston Cup series.

"RJR International only came into existence as a formal company in 1976 and started growing fast. And in late 1982 they decided the strategy would be to make Camel a global brand. In 1984 they asked me if I would like to go work for them and co-ordinate that effort, and that's how the Formula 1 connection began.

"Formula 1 to me, and I guess to most people, is considered the ultimate form of international motorsports. From the standpoint of technology, it was and still is. But as a form of entertainment for a fan, I don't think it is. And I think the approach that the associations in the United States take is that motor racing is more entertainment than it is sport. But Formula 1 is very well accepted, especially in Europe and in Latin America. It is what it is. If the fans buy the tickets and watch it on TV, then why change it?

"But people always ask me about my favourite type of racing. I think the NASCAR racing is very exciting, but I always tell people my favourite is the half-mile dirt track stuff for sprint cars. I still think that's the most exciting racing. It's really very, very basic, but very spectacular. Not very sophisticated, but it's good fun.

"The so-called glamour, the mystique, the prestige of Formula 1 racing is in the minds of the fans, mostly. But for the people who actually work in the sport, on the teams, and the organizers, and people like us, the sponsors, after you've been in it for a few years, you get pretty cynical about it. You laugh about it being a glamour job. But, for the people who only see it once a year, it's there for sure. The research that we've done with our customers shows us that it's certainly there for them.

"People go to great lengths to get the right passes to get into the paddock and try to work here. Those that strive for attention are attracted to the sport, by the television cameras, the news media and the large crowds of people. But most of the team people I know are pretty professional at what they do. When someone on a racing team has a specific job but is more attracted to the glamour side of it, then they usually won't last very long. Because if they're paying more attention to watching the girls, or making themselves seen, or whatever, then they won't be very effective at their job.

"Sometimes it seems the sponsorship side of it has almost become bigger than the race itself. Even amongst the drivers, they seem to be more involved with the politics and their sponsorships, and that sort of thing. But on the other hand, once they get in the cars, they become real racing drivers. And I don't think their cars, the technology, would be at the level it is today without the sponsorship money that allows the engineers to develop this sort of thing. So I think from that aspect the sponsorships have been a great help.

"But sometimes it seems to me to be quite distracting to a team. I'll leave the drivers out of it, but if the team manager is preoccupied with taking care of sponsors, or trying to find his next year's sponsorship, or more money for the present year, I don't think they can really concentrate as much on the activity of the day as they should. That's just my impression. I think the paddock on race weekend is absolutely the worst place in the world to have a business discussion, anyway."

ALEARDO BUZZI

"Our sponsorship is not just a matter of commerce. It is a matter of love."

That the red and white corporate colours of Marlboro are such a fixture in Grand Prix racing is largely due to the influence of

Aleardo Buzzi, now President of Philip Morris International. A Swiss-Italian who was always a fan of motor racing, Buzzi recognized in Formula 1 an opportunity to market Marlboro internationally, in a very special way.

"What we wanted was to project an image of adventure, of courage, of virility . . . an image to match our Marlboro man, the lonely cowboy on a horse. We transformed the horse into a mechanical one. But our sponsorship is not just a matter of commerce. It is a matter of love.

"I love motor racing and I've been involved in Formula 1 directly since 1972, when we started to sponsor BRM. That year we had only one victory and it was with Jean-Pierre Beltoise at the Monaco Grand Prix. It was a good one to win, but we also had a bit of luck, because it was raining, raining, raining. Beltoise took the lead and it was impossible to overtake him.

"We were delighted to do something for motor racing and I think we can say today that we have done a lot. We've encouraged a lot of drivers and several teams. We have also helped finance the security on the race tracks. I think we have done also quite a bit for the journalists, providing them with better working conditions, and so on. But I am an enthusiast of the sport, and I think all our people who are involved here, they are professionals, of course, but they love it. And you can't do this if you don't love it. That's very important.

"Money is certainly also very important, because to develop all the Formula 1 technology you need funds, otherwise it is impossible. And it's a bit unfortunate, in one sense, that it is creating a big disparity between some teams. We are big spenders, yes, but we really try to spend our money in a very reasonable way. And I think the last four or five years have proven that we are successful, and we are doing it in a very responsible way, *vis à vis* the sport and *vis à vis* our shareholders. I'm particularly pleased about this, being a sportsman and loving motor racing. It's quite an accomplishment where you can marry both, the pleasure and the results."

JOHN HOGAN

" 'It may be a business on this side of the pit wall, but on the other side of that pit wall it's bloody well a sport!' "

An opinion frequently expressed along the pit lane, particularly by some purists who feel sponsorship has spoiled Formula 1, is that the sponsors are only there for the publicity and don't know, or care, about the sport. Perhaps the disparagers haven't talked to John Hogan, in charge of sponsorship for Marlboro . . .

"I still get excited, it's an extraordinary thing, but I still get excited the moment I come through that gate and I hear the engines. I can't help it. I'm actually 46 years of age, and I still can't help getting excited when I hear those engines. It started when I was about six years of age. I saw a film with Clark Gable in it and a bloke called Mickey Rooney. And I can't remember the name of the film, it was about single-seaters on dirt tracks, but that was what first captured my imagination.

"I've been with the Philip Morris company for 15 years, but I've always been sort of an inside enthusiast. I had friends who were Formula 3 drivers, or whatever. I've been a friend of James Hunt's for longer than I like to remember, and I've got a fair number of old friends here. On a race weekend, I particularly like the evenings, after practice on the Friday, after practice on the Saturday. I like sort of hanging around, basically talking to the mechanics and the team people, because I know practically everybody in the pit lane.

"They're a fascinating bunch. I think the most significant thing about the individuals, and also about the sport as a whole, is that it moves very quickly. It encapsulates things which happen in the outside world, and I think in the business world in particular. They happen here in a very compressed sequence of time. This definitely attracts extrovert individuals. I mean, it's certainly not the sort of business in which an introvert could actually survive.

"Everything here happens very quickly. I think you age very quickly. I think one of the interesting things that one sees from time to time, if you look at the photos in books about racing over the years, is that the drivers age so quickly in a very short period of time. I don't think it's just confined to the drivers. I think the whole process of life here just happens much faster, the result of which can be very satisfying. Because you can say that you actually pack a lot of action into a fairly short period of time.

"And every five to 10 years or so, something extremely exciting happens. It usually tends to be a driver or a technical breakthrough. I remember when Gilles Villeneuve came into Formula 1, for example. That was wonderfully exciting. I remember when Ronnie Peterson came into Formula 1. That was exciting. And I think you've got that in Senna now. And it's tremendously stimulating to actually have somebody of his stature around. To watch him, to be out there at the track when Senna's doing one of those ridiculous bloody qualifying laps . . . it's just amazing! It's something you'll only ever see every five or 10 years.

"That's the racing side of it. From the sponsor's side, I think Formula 1 provides a sort of vitality for the products that we make and support. It helps to sell our product. And I think it provides a degree of interest in the company, because everybody's interested in the sport. And it helps, in general, the morale of everybody in the company.

"People go on about all the politics in modern Formula 1. But, you know, I think the political intrigue has always been there. If you speak to some of the old Grand Prix drivers, as I do occasionally, Stirling Moss and people like that, the proportional finance wasn't available in their day, but there was still just as much intrigue. Whether you were going to drive for Jaguar, or Aston Martin, or this or that. I think there was a tremendous amount of intrigue.

"Everybody thinks that sponsorship is something quite new. It's not. It's always been there. The actual teams in the old days were sponsored by fuel companies, but they didn't say anything about it. Strange sort of sponsorship. Anyway, if you remember, certain drivers could only go to certain bloody teams, because of their fuel contracts. I understand that one of the reasons Stirling couldn't go to Ferrari was because he had a sponsorship contract with a fuel company which actually prevented that. Now that sort of thing today cannot exist. We've turned it round. We actually help people to try and get the good drivers.

"And people say the sponsorship has turned the modern sport into a business. Again, I think that's always been the case. I remember something Jack Brabham said way back in 1969. I remember reading it in one of his books at the time. He said something like: 'It may be a business on this side of the pit wall, but on the other side of that pit wall it's bloody well a sport!'"

AGNES CARLIER

"I think Grand Prix people are also very tough. I think they're very nice, but they have very good nerves and nothing can break their determination to be happy and to make it."

She always wears red and white and a serene smile as she goes about her business in the pressroom, pit lane and paddock. Agnes Carlier's costume reflects her allegiance to Marlboro, and her pleasant demeanour serves her well in her position as Manager of Press Relations and Event Marketing for Philip Morris Europe. A Parisienne, she is also fluent in English, German, Italian and Spanish, the main languages of Formula 1. Among her duties is the need to persuade the Marlboro-contracted drivers to perform public relations roles, and Agnes recalls feeling some trepidation when this first began.

"When I discovered I had to deal with Niki Lauda I was very afraid, because I used to deal with younger drivers who were very easy and friendly people. And I was so impressed with Niki that I thought I would never succeed doing that. Actually, he was probably the best driver that we ever had, because Niki is very direct. If he says 'Yes', he does it. If he says 'No', you won't get him to do it. But he's very organized and I really appreciated his professionalism. The best driver I had after him was Keke Rosberg, who must have attended the same school. If he says 'Yes', he does it smiling, and if it's 'No', he doesn't do it.

"It is difficult when a driver doesn't co-operate because sometimes the press do not understand that it is not the right time, or that the driver has a specific problem; it could be with the team or with the car, or even with his family. Part of my job is to interface the press with drivers, or with other famous people they want to interview. But the other part of my work is also giving service to the journalists.

"Meeting people and communication techniques is what I like most about my job. The good part about communicating is that you're never sure that you will make it. You're never sure that the driver will be on the front page of the newspaper. And that is the good part about communication, it's always a challenge, and never boring. The worst part of the job is all the begging. I'm not talking about journalists, but it's the fans that try to get a sticker or a cap.

"The best time during the race weekend is early in the morning, when I arrive before 9 o'clock, or at night after 7 o'clock, when all the non-professional people are gone. That's very pleasant, because it's like the family. And actually, for us it's not very bad to travel. People think it must be horrible to travel to a different city every week or every month, but in a way we're like gypsies. And we always travel together, and it's very friendly because at every race you meet the same friends again.

"I first came to racing by accident, because my husband was a motorcycle journalist. He introduced me to motor racing when it was so easy to be the wife of someone and just come there and watch the race for fun. And I must say it was the days when I had the most fun. It was also the good old times when you could have good parties, in friendly motorhomes. Now it has disappeared because everyone has become much more professional, and everyone has become much more precise. It's probably because there is more money involved and people are more responsible and they want to see results for the money they invest, so they are much more demanding.

"But even now, I think that once you are in the family, Grand Prix people are very warm and very friendly, especially maybe because they all have a difficult life in a way. I think Grand Prix people are also very tough. I think they're very nice, but they have very good nerves and nothing can break their determination to be happy and to make it."

ANN BRADSHAW

"You're actually working with people who have different languages, different cultures, the whole lot. You become more tolerant of people and you also have a wider spectrum on life."

"Ever since I was old enough to know that there was a difference between horses and horsepower, it's been horsepower for me. My family are motorsport fanatics, and I've been lucky that a lot of my friends have been people who have been involved in one way or another with the sport. I'm a journalist by profession, and left a local newspaper to become secretary to the executive director of the British Racing and Sports Car Club. And basically, that's how it started.

"I now work with CSS, a sports promotions agency, but I'm very much the Williams person there. We are the official sponsorship agents for Williams, and we also look after the PR for the team. So on behalf of all the sponsors I do a Canon Williams public relations and press-related operation. I make sure that all the journalists and anybody who's interested has all the information they want, both during race meetings and away from them, during the week, when people want to organize things. It might be anything from somebody just wanting a press pack to a journalist wanting to interview a driver.

"I write all the press kits and all the press releases, and anything else that needs writing about the team and its activities. But also I do specifics for some of the sponsors, like Labatt's, whom we look after on a more personal level. With sponsors like Labatt's, I'll help them if they want any special promotions, and at a Grand Prix they might want help explaining a bit about the racing to their guests.

"I enjoy it all very much. There might be moments, perhaps if the team isn't doing that well, when you think, oh gosh, there must be an easier way of earning a living, as you try to explain why we were 14th and not fourth. Fortunately, we're usually successful. But, a few years ago, when we weren't so competitive, I found it more difficult. I was lucky, obviously, to still have two good drivers in Nigel Mansell and Riccardo Patrese. They're both newsworthy, positive people, so it was made easier. But still, when you've been winning, then you're not winning, you're having to work a little harder.

"I find that with most people, if you smile at them you're half way there. Some of the male PR people say, 'Oh sure, you're female and you're blonde and you've got a head start', and I suppose you do have. But from an outside point of view, people tend to think that a female who is involved in motorsports is there for two reasons: to sleep with a racing driver and to be seen looking pretty in a pit lane. So, to me, the downside of my job would be people who aren't involved in Grand Prix racing who see my role as a bimbo! And there were people who used to do that, but you can't get away with that any longer. It's a myth, and that attitude, I sometimes feel, is a shame. But the nice thing is that nobody I deal with inside the sport feels that way.

"On a Grand Prix weekend, every Thursday is like a first day of term at school. You start all over again and the feeling of expectation builds up continuously. And I enjoy Thursday, because I have a chance to chat to people. People are more relaxed and I think that's what I enjoy the most. I think we all have to have a fairly standard way of looking at life. We all have to obviously enjoy what we're doing here, to be away from your home and family life. I think most people in Grand Prix racing now are very dedicated, hard-working people. We all have to think the same way and that's why I think that there are a lot of good relationships between everyone, the mechanics, the journalists, the drivers, the motorhomers. We all have to have that positive, hard-working attitude. And there are sacrifices. But there are also a lot of compensations for those sacrifices.

"We're travelling the world, seeing new places, having the chance to meet new friends. Though you can't spend great chunks of time with them, I think that's one of the nicer things, meeting people, getting to know them. OK, perhaps we're all a little bit incestuous in Formula 1 and we all tend to sort of cling together. But even then, you're actually working with people who have different languages, different cultures, the whole lot. You become more tolerant of people and you also have a wider spectrum on life."

DANY HINDENOCH

"Until '83, or '84, we had closer relationships. Because there were less teams, less people, less sponsorship, less tension, less money."

"At Ligier I'm in charge of the public and press relations, and also I'm in charge of the organization of all the travel and hotel accommodation for the team. I started a long time ago, as a journalist, and then I worked in the car industry for Chrysler Europe, in France, for seven years. I always was involved in motor racing; I was in charge of the rally programme of Talbot in the '80s, and when Talbot decided to go into Formula 1 in association with Ligier, I started to work here then. When Talbot stopped its Formula 1 programme I stayed with Ligier.

"Race weekends are a very busy time, but maybe Thursday night, when everything is set for the weekend, it's a good time . . . when there is no particular problem, when all the organization is ready to work for Friday morning, that can be a very good time. We have a dinner in a restaurant with Mr Ligier and the engineers, except in some particular places, such as Monaco or at the French Grand Prix, where we have a lot of guests. There is not too much tension on Thursday night. Then on Friday morning the tension starts and grows steadily until Sunday.

"I don't like the start of the race. I'm always anxious about an accident. This is, for me, the worst part of the weekend. After the first lap, then everything is OK. One of the worst things that I remember is the start of the Canadian Grand Prix in 1982 when Paletti was killed. And each time there is an accident at the start of the race I'm always anxious.

"But if you want to work in Formula 1 you have to be a motor racing fan. If not, it's impossible. Because it's so hard, nobody except the people really involved in Formula 1 can understand. It needs so much time and so much work that if you are not enthusiastic you can't do the job.

"We consider it like a big family, and I think that every Grand Prix weekend something happens to make a special atmosphere. And I think that the common thing between all these people is the fact that all of them like motor racing. So this is the strongest link

321

between all these people, who sometimes don't know each other, but I think there is a common feeling.

"It's very international and the differences disappear, but some people think Ligier has the best food. This is our reputation. In fact, along with Renault, we were the first to have a motorhome with food for the journalists and for the guests. It is true that we always made an effort to stay at a certain level, you know, and because of the fact that we are French and that France has a certain reputation in the hospitality field.

"The motorhome creates a very good atmosphere. For example, the journalists can have their breakfast with Ligier, lunch with another team, and have a drink with another. There is no conflict. The relations are completely open, and I think that this is probably one of the most positive aspects of this particular world – this camaraderie.

"But there is a difference today. Until '83, or '84, we had closer relationships. Because there were less teams, less people, less sponsorship, less tension, less money. So it was more friendly than it is now. I think this is the normal evolution of the business for all of us, and I think that all of us who have lost something have gained something else. It's another era, in fact.

"One thing that has changed is the fact that now, because there are so many sponsors and so many companies involved, there are some people in this big circus who normally should not be here. And these people are not professional. They seem to look like they're involved in the business, but in fact they are not part of the business. And these people are difficult to deal with. Sometimes it's difficult to understand how certain people get their passes."

ERIC SILBERMANN

"You can't describe Grand Prix people collectively and I think that is the good thing about it."

Given the success of Honda engines in Grand Prix racing it might seem that the public relations officer for the Japanese manufacturer might have an easy time of it. But Eric Silbermann finds that working for a frequent winner calls for a lighter touch, requiring perhaps a firmer grip on reality than if he were trying to make a silk purse out of a sow's ear.

"I can't be constantly banging Honda's drum and saying how wonderful we are. You have to tell it how it is and just generally be accepted as a reasonable source of information. You know, public relations is a bit of a nebulous type of occupation. I see my job as being here to help the press, and that's what I try and do.

"I've always worked in motorsport somewhere or other. Before doing this job, working for Honda, I was the assistant team manager for the Larrousse team in their inaugural year. I've been an enthusiast since school days and through university I started competing, in rallying, mainly. First as a driver, and then, when I realized that I was no good at that, as a co-driver. So it's always been something I've been interested in since I was a little boy. And I've been lucky enough to turn a hobby into a career.

"I'm still an enthusiast, but there are days when you have to remind yourself that you're an enthusiast. There may be trivial problems, like when it comes time to produce the team press release you can be sure that either the printer won't work, or the photocopier will go bang, or whatever. But, to be honest, there's very little I don't like about it.

"I have found very few people in this sport, certainly amongst the media, that I don't get on with. And of course, there are some that I know better than others, some that are personal friends, whereas others are just people I work with. I can honestly say that I can't remember a journalist being rude or offensive to me, or deliberately causing me a problem.

"You can't describe Grand Prix people collectively and I think that is the good thing about it. I mean, if you took everyone in the pressroom, and if you went down the line and asked them what their interests were, and their backgrounds, I don't think you'd find two people the same. And I think it's probably unique in that way.

"Referring to all the wheeling and dealing, and the intrigue, and the old adage that the real racing in Formula 1 takes place in the paddock, not on the circuit, I suppose that can be true. But then the other truism about motor racing is: When the flag drops, the bullshit stops. And all the wheeling and dealing in the world can't change the results of a race that's achieved through top-quality engineering and first-class driving. That's never going to change. And every Sunday afternoon, I think everyone still gets the same buzz, the same excitement, and remembers that, underneath it all somewhere, this is still a sport."

ORTWIN PODLECH

"There is nothing more exclusive than being able to go into a Formula 1 pit and talk to the driver and see the inside world of Formula 1."

In reference to former Grand Prix driver Keke Rosberg's entrepreneurial flair, it was often said (as it had been of Jackie Stewart) that his briefcase was as important as his helmet. The man who helped fill Rosberg's briefcase was his manager, Ortwin Podlech, who now represents the interests of the Belgian driver Thierry Boutsen.

Podlech was in the carpet business in Germany when he first linked up with Rosberg in the mid-'70s, when the Flying Finn persuaded him to help organize his Formula Super Vee racing enterprise. They became good friends and Podlech became more involved as Rosberg progessed up the racing ladder and into Formula 1. When Rosberg became World Champion in 1982 Podlech dissolved his outside business interests to concentrate on management. He no longer is involved with Rosberg (who now runs his own management company) and Podlech operates his company, Euro Sport Promotion, from the Mediterranean island of Ibiza.

"When I first started with Keke we made an agreement that I would get a management percentage for finding him sponsorship. Then it was just organizing the contact between the sponsor and the driver, and they sorted themselves out. When I began to do it full-time it was based on proper business methods, with proper contracts, lawyer-approved, and with input from tax advisers and all these kinds of things. It became very successful when he became World Champion and we expanded. We took on other drivers; Stefan Johansson was with us for three years, and we began with Thierry about the same time.

"When Thierry contacted me, we made the final decision only after he had been with me for four days. We had to talk about everything else besides racing, to find out if our understanding was good enough that we could work together. Because it is very easy to be a manager if somebody is on the way up and you just knock on the door and say, 'Here I am'. When you are already successful, the next team is already knocking on your door. It is very easy to play the very successful manager. Basically, then, in my opinion, you don't need a manager, you need an adviser.

"You need an adviser to tell you, 'Don't get over-excited, don't do it yet. It looks good, but don't do it'. I could give you a lot of examples where a young driver has made a lot of mistakes which I would not have done. And to find this understanding there has to be a lot of trust from both sides. I don't see my situation as just that I go around, find a sponsor, thank him for the money, put the logo on the driver's helmet and say that is a deal. I try to serve the driver, I try to serve the sponsor, and try to get out of this relationship something which establishes success from both sides.

"We have two sponsor types. One is the sponsor who supports a driver because he loves Formula 1, which is always the dangerous sponsor, because they can get tired of the idea and tomorrow they like football or horse racing. What I always try is to find a sponsor who I can persuade that the money is best invested if he uses the co-operation with the personality of the Formula 1 driver in the best possible way. And I always try to help them, or advise them how to do it.

"Even a smaller company which is unable to support a Formula 1 team, but can afford to support only a driver as a personal sponsor, they can make a fantastic use out of it. The product of the company does not have to be related to racing. It can be any kind of fashion, it can be high-tech computers, anything. Whatever it is becomes exclusive in the world. And for this sponsor to come as a guest of the driver to a Grand Prix race creates a very special atmosphere. There is nothing more exclusive than being able to go into a Formula 1 pit and talk to the driver and see the inside world of Formula 1.

"If we talk about a team sponsor, there is still the exclusivity and prestige, but mainly there is the worldwide mega promotion in Formula 1 from the TV coverage, even if you are not a front runner. If you are a front-runner the coverage which you get worldwide is outrageous in relation to the few pennies which you basically pay to get into Formula 1. One of our sponsors checked it exactly, based on only when their identification was readable on TV. They counted it up and found that the exposure from one logo in that Grand Prix, if they had bought the advertising time on the screen, would have cost them more than $23 million. That was in only one country. To complete the calculation you have to multiply by an average of 40 countries that see the race on TV live.

"On the Grand Prix weekend I am basically there just in the background for my driver. He knows I'm there if he needs me, but mainly I am working together with the sponsors because there are so many things to be arranged. We are very busy, but I wouldn't say the real wheeling and dealing goes on in the paddock because there, every wall, every motorhome, has an eye and has 10 ears. So I would say that the contacts are made there, but decisions are made somewhere else.

"I wouldn't over-estimate the power of a manager. Because even the best manager is unable to sell a bad driver to a top team. Therefore, the tool which you have to look after is the driver and the success relates basically to his performance. And you are only the background organization. I don't have any goods to be sold. I have nothing to deliver. The only thing I have is contacts and, lets say, organizational services. In the paddock, my office is in my briefcase. The most important item in my briefcase, I would say, is the small computer with all the telephone and address memories, and my diary."

TONY JARDINE

"When I walk down the pit lane, to me it's a sort of kaleidoscope of colour and activity."

Sociologist, psychologist, art teacher, political cartoonist, lorry driver, tyre fitter, engineer, design draughtsman, assistant team manager, public relations firm proprietor. Tony Jardine's broad experience and range of interests also includes music appreciation. When the din in the pressroom, along the pit lane and in the paddock begins to pale for him he wanders out to the edge of the circuit and clears his head by tuning in to the engine notes of the Lamborghini V12.

"Because it's just like music. And it has a particular note. In fact, even the Lamborghini engine in the back of the Lola has a sweeter sound than the one in the back of the Lotus. And I can detect all the different engines. I think it's brilliant since we got rid of the turbos, because Grand Prix racing is back with a real chorus of sounds."

The operatic allure of Formula 1 engines first beckoned to Jardine at the British Grand Prix at Aintree in 1959. So powerful was their attraction to the impoverished Liverpudlian that he circumvented the turnstiles to get an earful of the motors being conducted by the likes of Brabham, Moss, McLaren and Schell.

"As a good scouser you had to know how to get in over the fence without paying, and I knew how to do that. So that's what really fired me up, because at first I loved cars, and then, when I realized how they raced them, saw these characters, that's what really turned me on to it. But first I had to deal with the old man's plan, which was basically that if you get your degree, then I'll help you go racing."

Jardine dutifully got his degree, studying sociology and psychology, and majoring in art. The latter subject drew him into teaching jobs, first in Liverpool, then in an American university, then in the Middle East, in Iran and Kuwait. In the evenings Jardine also cranked out political cartoons for a Kuwaiti newspaper. Meanwhile, he kept his racing ambitions alive by knocking around in a Formula Ford and competing in rallies whenever possible.

While Jardine was filling youthful minds with the rudiments of art history, architecture, painting and drawing, his pay cheque was entirely inadequate for funding a major racing career. The lure of the open road, and more money, beckoned, and he traded in the teaching lectern for the front seat of a lorry and drove juggernauts around Europe for a time.

"And then I realized that with a truck driver's licence you could get into Formula 1, and I worked for Goodyear fitting tyres, and then they made me a temporary engineer. Then I joined Brabham and ended up working in the drawing office with Gordon Murray, because of my art training. And then I went to McLaren as assistant team manager to Teddy Mayer when Prost and Watson were together. Finally, I went out of motor racing altogether, because I'd got as far as I could get in the admin side of the sport, and I wanted to learn about marketing and things like that.

"So I worked for an American marketing company, and then CSS Promotions asked if I wanted to come back in the sport, but be involved with PR. I had learned a lot about public relations, which I enjoyed, because I used to look after a little bit of that when I was at McLaren. And I was just combining all the different things I had learned. I did five years at CSS, and in that time I ran all the JPS business, looking after Lotus sponsorship for JPS, their powerboats, their motorcycling, and so on. That was very busy and it took me around the world doing all sorts of events until I formed my own agency in 1985."

The clients of Jardine Public Relations have included Richard Branson, the British Government, the Guernsey Tourist Board, BP Oil International, Autoglass, and companies in a variety of other fields. JPR looks after the Camel sponsorships in a variety of motorsports, but his Camel Formula 1 connection keeps Jardine where he likes to be, though he sees room for improvement in his sphere of activity.

"What I feel is wrong in Formula 1 is that whilst racewise, and internationally, this series is the best, for the media in general, who we try to serve, it's very, very difficult for people to get the job done. And what has to be created by FISA and FOCA is a proper framework for promotional and PR events within the sport. For example, there has to be a set time when drivers are available at the end of the day, maybe for autograph-hunters. And the top three in each session must go to the press conference after official training, and after the race, and be available so at least the press know that they can get what they need from those top three people. I think that is where the sport can be promoted better. And you cannot take it away from the Americans, they invented PR. They do it fantastically.

"If I phone up CART and I want to know about a guy who might even be 32nd in the charts, I get everything, and I get it immediately. They've got a great media service, and if Formula 1 is to continue to grow, then it's got to be done here as well. I can do what I can individually with Camel, that's what I try to do, and I think we are certainly making inroads here. But, specifically, my area is not seen as a large contributing part to Formula 1, and that's got to improve.

"But we all love Formula 1, otherwise we wouldn't be here. When I walk down the pit lane, to me it's a sort of kaleidoscope of colour and activity. I am looking for any fizz or buzz going on in any one particular garage. I'm looking to see where any particular media attention is focussed, to find out what is going on. I'm going to look for key media people, to make sure that I am seen, can be seen, and try and communicate. There are some places when you walk down here that are very foreboding. They've got all their barriers up, they might have their garage doors halfway down, which says, 'Don't come in'. But then I can hear a car revving up, particularly now the Lamborghini, and I go and listen to that."

NORAH TYRRELL

"I have always thought they were a special group of people."

Ken Tyrrell's wife has been listening to racing engines for most of her life. For many years she was kept busy along the pit lane, doing the lap charts and timing for her husband's team. Now, she spends more of her time in the paddock, around the new Tyrrell motorhome.

"I've always supported Ken's motor racing habit. I first started coming here with him when the boys were in boarding school. I've always enjoyed it, but in a different way now. It has changed so much. When we started – and I'm particularly thinking about the Jackie Stewart times – all the girlfriends and wives were really responsible for doing the lap charts and the lap timings of the cars. The team managers relied on all of us to do that, and it kept you very busy if you were doing seven or eight leading cars. Those were the only lap times they had apart from at the end of the day, when the tower did them. Then we had Longines and Olivetti come in and do the lap times, so that made me redundant in that area, and about two years ago they improved all the lap chart electronics, so I don't do that any more, either. I miss that because, though it was hectic, you were busy. Now I have nothing to do.

"In the old days there was no such thing as a motorhome. All the girls used to congregate at the Dunlop or Goodyear transporter and get a Coke from them. So we were often together. Now, with the sophistication of the motorhomes, you don't really see quite so much of the girlfriends and wives. So that's changed and it's not quite as friendly as it was. But the people are still nice.

"I have always thought they were a special group of people. Years ago, you were thrown together more, and you knew them better. But the times that I do meet them now, there is no-one that I can say I'd rather not meet. And racing drivers are a bit of a special breed, I've always thought, a little bit selfish, perhaps, but I still find them nice people. I really like the whole scene here.

"I can see a day when I could get bored with it all, now that I'm not doing any work in the pits. And you don't see very much in the pits anyway, because you are not allowed to go to the wall. I still like motor racing, but I can see when I might say to Ken, 'I'll give this one a miss'. But I've never done that. I've never missed one race of the team.

"I don't mind the travel. Packing up and unpacking doesn't bother me at all. I think the longer you do it, the easier it becomes. When the end of the season comes, I think, 'Oh great, now we'll be at home for a while. But then, after Christmas and New Year, I think, Oh my goodness, how long is it until we go away again?"

PAM WILKIE

*"Everybody is under pressure. And people who don't work
well under pressure wouldn't enjoy being in Formula 1."*

"We're a bit like circus people really," says Pam Wilkie, "because
of the fact that you're going to an event, then setting it up and
entertaining people. Then it all comes down, folds away, and off
you go again to another event. And it's almost like a circus
mentality in that you look at the whole event each time and you try
to give it your best shot every day. That's what we're aiming to do
because the people out there expect it of you."

Pam Wilkie is talking about the roles she and her husband Dave
play in the catering side of the Grand Prix circus. Their
performance is played out in the ELF motorhome, and their
audience comprises the journalists, photographers and VIP guests
who congregate there for rest and refreshment during the race
weekend. The Wilkies have been running hospitality units for 15
years, beginning with the Tyrrell team. Now it's a full-time
business, which includes designing and building motorhomes and
providing the catering service under a contract with ELF.

"We didn't start off as racing enthusiasts, but over the years we
have become very interested in motor racing. It's very much the
lifestyle which is interesting, as well. It's a very exciting type of
atmosphere. I think there is glamour, too. There is a panache about
it all. If you look at all the teams, and all the motorhomes,
everybody is trying to be the best and look the best, and do the best
for their clients. So if you're doing that, you obviously want to add
glamour to the whole thing. Everybody's trying to make the thing
look glamorous, and however much hard work goes on behind the
scenes, that's not what's shown. It's the hospitality, the being
friendly to people, that's what you want to project.

"Very rarely are there things or people we don't particularly
enjoy, because I suppose we're lucky on this particular vehicle.
We do have a lot of contact with the people who are regularly
involved in motorsports over the years. They're the regular
journalists, the regular TV people, and so on, and therefore you do
tend to meet people whom you are getting on with anyway,
because they're within the general Formula 1 scene. I think a lot of

people, too, who come to Formula 1 just as a guest, they're quite overawed about it, so they don't tend to be particularly pushy. We haven't met many pushy people in our time. We've probably been very lucky.

"Everybody is under pressure. And people who don't work well under pressure wouldn't enjoy being in Formula 1. It's as simple as that. And I think also that they've got to be able to get on with everyone, because it's quite a close family, and if someone is a journalist who doesn't get on with the rest, it would be difficult. So it is very much a sort of person who fits in well everywhere that would like this type of life.

"Our job is looking after our client's image. As Formula 1 is the top of its class, obviously everything that we are doing for our client has to be to the very best quality possible. And that automatically puts pressure on you, because there's such a limited time frame in which you can offer a service for your client, and other people can see what your client's image is. So everything has to always be 100 per cent.

"Little details like flowers on the table. Behind-the-scenes things like making sure the electrical equipment is working, and everything else. The vehicles are obviously fairly complicated, and they're travelling from Grand Prix to Grand Prix, so there are always problems that are going to arise and you've got make sure that those are always being solved."

DIANA SPIRES

"I still get amazed when people I used to watch as a spectator just come up to me and chat and say, 'Hello' . . . it's just very nice. Like one big family."

To many of the people in the paddock, Diana Spires is 'Mum' and her husband Stuart is 'Dad'. They run the Benetton motorhome and dispense food, drink and hospitality to VIPs, mechanics, journalists and drivers, even those from other teams. Nigel Mansell was a great fan of Mum's tea.

"We started all this with John Surtees' team in 1978. Stuart and I had always been motor racing fans, even before we met. When we married we both had good jobs, I was a civil servant and he was a quality control engineer, and we spent all our money going to Grands Prix abroad. When the Surtees opportunity came up it was a big decision to make. But it took us about five minutes to decide!

"In those days it was a lot quieter, although it was a three-car team and Stuart was the tyre man as well, while I did the cooking and everything. The whole thing now isn't quite the sport that it used to be, because it's big business. But I still get amazed when people I used to watch as a spectator just come up to me and chat and say, 'Hello'. They're friends now, Jack Brabham, and James Hunt, and all these sort of people. So it's just very nice. Like one big family.

"I suppose they call us Mum and Dad just because we look after them. Sounds corny, but whatever they want, you try and do. Nigel, for instance, just liked straight-forward English tea. And Manfred, who is German and runs the Arrows motorhome, he comes round for tea because, although I've tried to teach him how to make it, he says he can't quite get it right. I don't suppose I make it any different to any other English person, but they seem to think it's special.

"Everyone among the motorhome people is friends. It doesn't matter what team you work for, we all work together, really. If you need to borrow something, you borrow it, and they might lend you something back. It's just a friendly atmosphere, and you get to know everybody at a different level. Take the drivers. You're with them a lot more than even the mechanics, and when they're in the motorhomes, they can relax a bit.

"Everyone in the whole show seems to fit in the same mould. Obviously the different nationalities make a difference, but we try and mix with all the nationalities. We're very friendly with Luigi at Ferrari, and Manfred at Arrows, and others. And if anyone new arrives, you try and help them, introduce them around, and so on. We don't feel any real competition to have the best motorhome. We just try to make it look nice, and we designed it to fit in with the team. Stuart did all the technical things, like where the water tanks go, and all that sort of thing. And we had the upholstery specially done for us.

"Before Benetton we were with Ken Tyrrell for one year and we were with Toleman in Formula 2 for a while, then Formula 1. Then we had two years at Lotus when Toleman had a few problems with sponsorship. But then, as soon as Mr Benetton bought the team, we came back, and we're very pleased to be here. We also have contracts with Ford and Leyton House, and provide people to manage the operation in their motorhomes.

"The only negative thing about it is when somebody gets injured. Obviously you get very attached to the drivers, and although they all know, and we all know, it's a risk, you still can't quite comprehend that when somebody just goes out and says, 'See you later', they don't always come back. They might end up in hospital or something. It's happened only twice to us, drastically. The first one was when Vittorio Brambilla was with Surtees and was involved in the Ronnie Peterson accident at Monza; Vittorio was in a coma for six months. He recovered, but then, unfortunately, Elio De Angelis was killed when we were testing at Paul Ricard. We'd had him at Lotus and were still very friendly. We actually sat outside the motorhome with him just before he went out. And that was dreadful. I said I'd never do it again. But you go on somehow.

"We keep saying, 'One more year' all the time, but I think we'll know when to stop. When you actually dread the first Grand Prix of the year, I think that's when it's time to stop. I'm trying to write a book about this when I get the time. I wrote an article for *Prix Editions* magazine which was a precis of what the book might be. The longer we stay here, the longer the book will be.

"We have no children, Stuart and I. This was a choice we made. This is our baby. We're Dad and Mum to all those 35 mechanics in the garage. And the drivers. And they *are* babies sometimes!"

DAVE MORGAN

"There are a lot more nice people here than there are the other kind."

Dave Morgan helps Mum and Dad Spires look after the Benetton motorhome in the paddock. But before he does that he has to drive the support vehicle there, along the motorways, autoroutes, autobahns and autostradas, from England to all the European races.

"On the long hauls on the road, I have a system for keeping going. If I have three scares in a row, then I pull over for a while. When you start to see bulls coming toward you, with lights on their horns, it's time to stop. On some trips you might have extra time and can have a bit of a lie-in at a hotel. Other times you've got to go like hell all through the night."

Morgan arrives at the circuit late on Tuesday, or early Wednesday morning, and then helps with the vehicle set-ups in the paddock. For the next few days he caters to the needs of visitors from dawn to dusk, then on Sunday night he packs everything away and drives off into the distance again.

Driver, roust-about, steward, chief cook and bottle washer, Morgan was a one-man show at the Goodyear motorhome before switching to Benetton in mid-season 1990. Previously he had worked with Dunlop, attending the Grand Prix motorcycle events for 10 years. At one stage he stopped his roaming to reconsider his future. But he came back to Formula 1.

"You just go back, don't you. I don't know why, but you just go back. I suppose I like the circus thing of it. It all sort of moves together, and you get to know people. It becomes more of your family than your family at home. Especially with the motorhomers. They depend on each other so much. If you go out and do a big shop, you always forget something. I can borrow a cup of sugar from anybody in the paddock. You've always got things breaking: your fridge goes, your hot water goes, your electricty goes, your hoses bust. So you help each other out, and everybody seems to get through the weekend.

"It's early morning starts. I set the alarm for 6 o'clock. When I've got everything ready, I can sit down and have my breakfast. During the day I can sit down for maybe five, 10 minutes somewhere. But usually you're on your feet all the time. Because there's always somebody who wants something. And then, when they've all gone at night, you can sit down and have a beer, and start to clear away. By the time you've cleared away, you're talking 8, 9 o'clock.

"The worst part of the weekend for me is after the race, taking the awning down. It's a son of a bitch. It's the awning and packing everything away again. It just takes so long, you've got to pace yourself. They're the scourge of the paddock, awnings. The driving is the least of my worries.

"The people who come to the motorhome I see as people I've got to look after. It's my job to do so. And I'll be professional enough to override any personal feelings about them, unless they get really rude, and really obstreperous, and then I put a damper on it. I'm employed to make sure everything runs smoothly, and they get something to drink, something to eat. So, I basically put up with any shit for four days. Sometimes I've got to bite my tongue, but you get that in all walks of life. But there are a lot more nice people here than there are the other kind.

"There's always the build-up to that green light on Sunday afternoon. I still feel it. And if you don't feel it, there's something wrong. You shouldn't be here. But you go out there into the pit lane, and once that light goes, there's that roar and that thrill and they're gone. I think if you've got an interest in the sport, it makes it easy. If you haven't got an interest in the sport, it's hard work."

ALAN WOOLLARD

"The motorhomes here are just superb, all kitted out in suedes and leathers inside. It's oneupmanship."

"In the paddock I'm responsible for parking it all, every vehicle in here, making sure they keep to the rules, making sure everyone gets a fair position, and so on. The teams park in the constructors' order, according to how the teams finished in the World

Championship the previous year. If you're one of the top teams, you get the benefits in every way, including where you park in the paddock.

"I started this kind of work a long time ago with a shipping and forwarding company and we used to shoot the cars around in those days on boats. Once Bernie Ecclestone formed the Formula One Constructors Association I was an obvious candidate for this job.

"I have no title, but I wear many hats. Sometimes it's a bit like a traffic warden. Sometimes it's a car park attendant, sometimes a security guard . . . whatever it takes to do the job. Everything from organizing the freight down to parking the motorhomes, to giving out credentials, even making the credentials.

"There are credentials for several thousand people at every single race. A race team takes 60 people and you multiply 19 teams times 60 to start with. There are about 1,500 journalists and photographers per race, about half of them with permanent credentials. There may be 3,000 Grand Prix people all told at a race.

"The motorhomes here are just superb, all kitted out in suedes and leathers inside. It's oneupmanship. Everyone wants to make their motorhome bigger and better than the next one. We try to control that and try to keep their feet on the ground. That's why we're not very popular at times. We just restrict them on the sizes, otherwise the big teams would have 10, 15-metre canopies.

"All this keeps me busy. The worst part of my job is the amount of hours you put in, the amount of walking. I'm always walking somewhere. Fast. Certain days you start at 6 o'clock in the morning, just to get in the gate before the crowd. I'm finished, maybe at 9 o'clock at night, even later sometimes. For example, when we first come in the paddock, often on Tuesday, if one of these trucks breaks down, it clogs up the whole system until we get it moving again.

"The whole thing is like a large family, on the move every two weeks. It's a good family. They're lovely people. I'm talking about the motorhome people, mostly. They have their ups and downs, as we all do. But, basically, everyone here, they're all living a gypsy life, because they're always going somewhere. In a way, they're all eccentric."

CHARLIE WHITING

"Sometimes you get so many people on your back doing this job that you think, Oh God, why can't they just shut up!"

"I'm a technical delegate for the FIA with regard to scrutineering, but I am very much an enthusiast of the sport. I used to work for my brother, who raced, and I started when I was about 15, preparing saloon cars and rally cars, things like that. Then I worked for him for about 10 years and we ran a Formula 1 Surtees in the British Championship in 1976 for Davina Galica. After that I got a job with the Hesketh Formula 1 team, and when Hesketh failed I got a job with Brabham, where I stayed until the end of 1987.

"I was Chief Engineer when the team stopped racing, and Mr Ecclestone, my employer, said there was a very good job for me within the FIA. They needed someone else on the technical side, and they felt they wanted somebody who had a good knowledge of Formula 1, so I took that job.

"In my early days with the Brabham team the rules were not so well written, and there were ways around some of them. Now, I feel the rules are written fairly well, and I think it's much more difficult to cheat. But, because I'm only one engineer, and in the pit lane there are 50 or 60 team engineers, they should be able to think of something! My job is to make sure people do keep complying with the rules. And to make sure the rules are applied in an even-handed manner, the same way all the time. I've tried to take out any ambiguities. It's not always possible, because however hard you try to write a rule, somebody will think of a slightly different way of looking at it.

"On a race weekend I enjoy Thursday best. I've got more to do on Thursdays with all the scrutineering, and that type of thing. Any problems usually occur on that day. Pre-qualifying is always quite interesting, and weighing and checking the cars during practice. At the start of the race I stay at the exit of the pits to assess anybody who might be starting from the pit lane, making sure they do it the right way, and then I just look up and down the pits.

"What I do miss now is the involvement with a team, and the feeling of winning a race, which is incomparable. What I *don't* miss is the aggravation on a team. It's just non-stop. It's very, very hard work. I mean, my job now is not hard work. It's not physically hard work. I make no bones about that. So I don't miss that side of it. Except that, sometimes I think it might be nice to go back and be involved with one team. Sometimes you get so many people on your back doing this job that you think, Oh God, why can't they just shut up!"

LUIGI SARTORIS

"If you did that for just the money it would be not enough. You need to have pleasure from the racing to enjoy it."

"My job is to co-ordinate the logistical and technical functions in the Olivetti and Longines teams. We at Olivetti are a partner with Longines, providing the data processing and the timing in the Formula 1 World Championship. On each car is a transponder, like a radio transmitter, each with a different frequency corresponding to the number of the car. We receive all this information and our job is to control it all and to distribute the results to everybody, in the monitors, on the television, in the press centre, everywhere.

"During the race this is a very stressing job. I must follow the race closely in the tower with our technicians, we are 16 in all, and see that our very high-tech equipment is working OK. I watch our monitors and also the television and suggest to the chief of television how to inform all the people in Formula 1, and the fans, about what is happening.

"I am very much an enthusiast of Formula 1. Before I worked with computers in rallying and when the opportunity came to work with Olivetti in Formula 1 I took it immediately. My home is in Italy, and of course Ferrari is the big favourite there. But at the Grand Prix we must follow every car. Back home I can watch the race on video and read the papers. Besides Ferrari and Prost, I think Senna is a fantastic driver. You must be an enthusiast for this work because we are busy at the race for 12, sometimes 14 hours each day. If you did that for just the money it would be not enough. You need to have pleasure from the racing to enjoy it.

"At the Grand Prix the best time for me is when the race is finished. Then we find out if our job is correct. Then we receive congratulations from the journalists, or from the teams. When they say everything is perfect, for us this is the best time of all. Then we must dismantle 1,200 kilos of Olivetti equipment and 1,000 kilos of Longines. It goes into 40 to 45 boxes. Then it's time to get ready for the next race."

FRANCESCO LONGANESI CATTANI

"Some people want the pass just to be part of the Grand Prix. They want to be in here. It is the forbidden city."

"I am Manager of the FISA Press Department. I like motor racing, of course, but I can't say that I am a motor racing enthusiast. And probably that's what allows me to do this job without getting too much involved in passion. Of course, being Italian I have a little bit of feeling for Ferrari, but it's more sentimental than anything else.

"Before doing this job I was *Aide-de-Camp* to Prince Rainier of Monaco for five and a half years. With the Grand Prix there, and so on, I was familiar with the sport. I worked a bit with Bernie Ecclestone, and in August 1989 they asked me if I could take this position and develop this department, which I am trying to do.

"Nothing about this work makes me unhappy, but sometimes the journalists consider the press officer at FISA as a pass distributor. I mean, this thing of the credentials is something that is extremely time-killing, and 90 per cent of my talk to the journalists is about passes, passes, passes – parking passes, pit lane passes, and this and that.

"Of course, the journalists are professionals, and they need a pass. The pass for a journalist is a working tool. Just like a hammer, or a screwdriver, for a workman. And I have exactly this conception that the pass is a working tool, that I supply it to someone who needs it. You are a motor racing journalist, you have a pass. Tomorrow, you will do something else, maybe you will be covering the United Nations, or whatever, and you don't need this pass any more. That doesn't mean that you are any better or any worse than before. You are just doing a different job. But you don't need this pass, and I won't give you this pass. But I will give it back to you as soon as you need it again.

"Some people want the pass just to be part of the Grand Prix. They want to be in here. It is the forbidden city. It is to be close to some of their idols, or some of the cars. There is a similarity to when I was ADC to Prince Rainier. You can say that people want to be invited to the palace, as people want to be invited in the paddock here. So the ones that think they can get in the palace, they do everything to be invited there. But you can't get there unless you're invited.

"The people in the paddock I think are beautiful people. This is a very colourful, sparkling, mixture of humanity. They are professionals, all are working on different things. You are working with a tape recorder, this gentleman is working with a wrench, the other gentleman is working with PR, there is a cook. I mean, it's like a little city, or a big family, if you want, with all the frictions and understandings, and the misunderstandings, that happen in a microcosm. And I think this is a microcosm where all the social classes are represented. And I think that it is all very fascinating."

JEAN-MARIE BALESTRE

"In the star system the Formula 1 journalists use they speak only about Formula 1 and forget all the rest. I do not agree with that."

The President of the *Fédération Internationale du Sport Automobile* (FISA), the governing body of world motorsport, has been involved in racing for over 40 years, most of that time serving in an administrative role. Monsieur Balestre has attended well over 300 Grand Prix races but, from the FISA headquarters in Paris, he presides over many categories of racing besides Formula 1, a branch of the sport which at times has been troublesome for him.

"Some people say I am a dictator. But that is not true because, although in motorsport the sporting power is very strong, we are very democratic. We have a governing body of 32 people, and each one is from a different country. We are really a group of friends with the same philosophy, and this policy is that the commercial interests must come after the sport. We are a non-profit association, and I do not receive money, except for my trips, which is normal. We are completely independent. And we love motorsport and we take the decisions with the sporting interests first. We completely forget the rest.

"Some of the journalists, I think they have been too long in Formula 1. They don't take the time to learn the rules and regulations and they make some mistakes. And I don't agree with the Formula 1 journalists because they use the star system. They ignore other motorsport. I am also the President of the French Federation. For me, motorsport in that country is a pyramid. The base of the pyramid is the amateur driver, and we have 100,000 amateur drivers. And if you have not this basis, you have not the World Champion. I use the same consideration for the amateur as for the professional driver, because we have in world motorsport only about 400 to 500 top professional drivers and a million amateur drivers. In the star system the Formula 1 journalists use they speak only about Formula 1 and forget all the rest. I do not agree with that.

"But I am an enthusiast of Formula 1. For me, the top time at a Grand Prix is the start of the race. Another very important time is the briefing for the drivers. In the morning of the Sunday we have a half-hour meeting with the drivers, in friendship, completely free, with the Clerk of the Course. It is a very important moment.

"I know all the drivers, and I think they are the same as my sons. I was the creator of the karting races in Europe in 1960, and I was for five years the President of the International Karting series to help prepare new drivers. And today we have very positive results. Nearly all the drivers in Formula 1 started by karting. But also during the past 30 years I have gone more than 30 times to the cemetary for the drivers who died: Ascari, Behra, Jim Clark, Depaillier . . .

"I think I love the drivers because they take risks, and I think they are very courageous. But one very important thing is, even though they receive a big amount of money in the World Championship, at the start of the race all the champions, all the star drivers, they forget money. There is only one thing in their mind. That is to win. That is a certitude at the start of every race."

ROLAND BRUYNSERAEDE

"It can be very dangerous, this sport. But I love this work. I don't want to sit somewhere in the grandstands."

The start of a Grand Prix is surely the most exciting moment in any sport. Everyone feels it, the millions of television viewers, the thousands of spectators, the Grand Prix people, certainly the drivers. And one of those most caught up in that scintillating moment is the man responsible for unleashing it: Roland Bruynseraede, the official starter of the race.

"Yes, yes, yes! I'm really excited! And I think if I am going up to the starting tower and only just pushing the buttons, forget it. Stop the business. Go home. I have given many Formula 1 starts, and in my whole career, in all kinds of racing, over 500 starts. And I still get excited. Every time."

Roland began preparing for his job nearly 30 years ago, when he was a flag marshal at Zolder in his native Belgium. He worked his way up to become paddock marshal, pit lane marshal, security chief, then Clerk of the Course at both Zolder and Spa. He also became a prominent member of the Royal Automobile Club of Belgium and, in 1987, he was asked by FISA to replace the retiring starter, Derek Ongaro. Besides his official starting duties, Bruynseraede is also the Race Director of each Grand Prix, and the track safety inspector.

"At the circuit I'm looking for everything. I'm looking for the track surface itself, the guardrails, debris fencing, tyre wall protection, gravel beds. Then you go into safety: intervention cars, rescue equipment, ambulances, removal cranes for the cars, spectator fences – all of those things. I do an inspection tour before every Grand Prix. I walk around for one, two or three times.

I always walk, because if you go with a car you don't see anything.

"The countdown to the start works like this. Say one hour before the start of the race, we make the last inspection lap with the stewards and we have a look if everything is good. All the marshal posts we pass, they give us a green flag, so then we know that that post is ready. Then the girls come on to the grid with the boards showing the car positions, and 30 minutes before the start I open the pit lane. Then everybody goes out for one, or two, or three laps, passing through the pit lane. Exactly 15 minutes before the start we close the pit lane. Then we have the boards displayed, showing 5 minutes, 3 minutes, 1 minute, 30 seconds. And then I give the green flag, and they do a formation lap and come back to the grid. When the last car is in position, somebody shows me the green flag, and then it's up to me. I put the red lights on, wait for three or four seconds, or even less.

"What makes me decide three or four seconds is something in my head. You hear, of course, the engines running, you see the first rows in front, all the 26 from one side, you see everything at once in only one second or so. And if everything is good, you put on the green and let them go. Seven seconds is the maximum. But you never go to seven. And in my head, it's not three or four seconds. It's a feeling inside.

"When the lights go green and the cars are gone, I can only pray after that. Because you're playing with lives. It's not us sitting in those cars. In Formula 1, you know all those drivers. And if you lose somebody, you lose from your family.

"And once they've gone, I stay up on the starting tower for one or two laps. I'm already in contact with the race direction and they tell, me, 'OK, first corner, no problem, second corner, no problem'. The cars come back and I count 26. OK, it's good, let's stay here one more lap. And then I come down and go in the race control tower to watch the different TV cameras that have all the circuit covered. And if something happens, I stop the race.

"It can be very dangerous, this sport. But I love this work. I don't want to sit somewhere in the grandstands. I must be involved with something, I must have some work to do, even if only as a marshal. But not as a spectator. Yes, my job, it's a dream come true."

SID WATKINS

*"I think, until you've seen the inside of it you have no idea
actually what goes on in Formula 1 motor racing."*

"I make a lot of jokes about the fact that as a neurosurgeon I
should hardly be required at a motor race because the drivers don't
have any brains, otherwise they wouldn't race!"

Professor Sidney Watkins is a neurosurgeon at the London
Hospital, where he is head of the academic unit which deals with
the whole spectrum of brain disorders and injuries. He is also
President of the FISA Medical Commission, Formula 1 Medical
Inspector and, unofficially, the "family doctor" for everyone in the
Grand Prix circus, treating any aches and pains that may crop up
on a race weekend. He has been to every event since the 1978
Swedish Grand Prix, on call to perform his most important
function: attending drivers who have been injured.

"To be serious, most of the drivers are very accomplished
people in terms of perceptual skill. And I admire their capability to
control the machines as they do. They have highly tuned sensory
skills, and obviously highly tuned motor ones, too, to be able to
drive the machines. But from the point of view of a neurologist,
they've got excellent computers up there, for doing what they're
doing. And I like most of their personalities.

"One of the interesting aspects of my presence at the races is
that the drivers who know me like to see the father figure arriving
and to know that I'm around. And that, I think, has helped a lot,
because in the circumstances of a big accident it's sometimes hard
for the driver to know who's actually trying to help him. Often the
drivers don't really know who is trying to do what to them, and
they're anxious that they don't get injured further than they
already are. So, there's a fair amount of anxiety and tension
around the situation at that stage, and my presence seems to help
control it.

"The racing is getting safer, but there's always a possibility that
something terrible will happen. It's always upsetting, and that
applies to all of them, even the people who have been injured
savagely but have not died. I'm always sad and upset when they do
get hurt, or worse. I remember when I first met Gilles Villeneuve,

he said, 'Prof, I hope I'm never going to need you'. Then, of course, when I got to his accident at Zolder in 1982 his injuries were such that he didn't need me. And that made me very sad.

"I suppose you could develop an argument that there's a conflict of interest for a doctor, dedicated to saving lives, to be in a sport that can take them. But if you believe in free will, as I do, then I think it's up to anybody to do what they need to do in life, and to recognize that there are dangers, and at times there are serious dangers. Besides, there's hardly a sport that isn't dangerous, except perhaps snooker, or something like that. But the physical sports, the contact sports, all have their injuries and their fatalities from time to time. And with regard to my own personal life, I've got a daughter who is a pilot, and a son who is a Grenadier Guard, both potentially dangerous professions. When they were younger, my two daughters were in horse show jumping and cross country eventing, and I used to get my heart in my mouth fairly frequently then. But I wouldn't stop them doing it."

When he was a boy, Sid Watkins spent a lot of time in his father's garage in Liverpool, often driving cars around the property before he was licensed to do so. He became interested in the competition possibilities of cars after the war, though his goal in life had always been to become a medical practitioner. He served for two years as a British army doctor in West Africa, then trained in general and orthopedic surgery to become a neurosurgeon. While working at Oxford, the proximity of Silverstone beckoned and his "obsession" with motor sport began. He became a medical officer at club events, then moved to Syracuse University, in America, where he also headed the medical team at the nearest circuit, Watkins Glen, for several years. Returning to England in 1970, he joined the medical panel of the RAC, where Bernie Ecclestone was impressed with his work. When Ecclestone asked Watkins to co-ordinate the medical side of Grand Prix racing, the doctor was only too happy to oblige.

At each circuit Professor Watkins first checks that everything in the medical centre is in order, the intervention vehicles and the rescue helicopter are ready to go, and the medical personnel are in place. Then, prior to the cars going on to the track, he takes up his station at the end of the pit lane, sitting in a high-speed intervention vehicle in his flameproof suit, helmet in hand. He remains there throughout practice and qualifying, keeping in touch with developments by radio, and ready to spring into action. At the start of the race, Watkins speeds into the wake of the storm, following the cars around on the first lap.

"You have to make rather quick decisions as to whether or not you need to stop when you see an accident. I suppose that's the most difficult part of it, really. But with regard to the confusion of the start, and the chaotic pattern that many of the cars produce as they leave, with bits of this and that flying around, and the speed, I think, as I've done so much of it, I no longer get involved in that aspect of it. I ignore all that part of it, and I'm looking for the accidents. If there is an accident, I try to make the right decision as quickly as possible, whether to stop or push on.

"The high point for me is at the end, when there hasn't been an accident and nobody's been hurt. And I get back in the hotel room, and have a shot of whisky and a shower, and then I'm always hungry, ready for a decent meal. I do keep away from most of the Grand Prix social life. I also disassociate myself from any particular relationship with any particular team. And I'm usually to be found hanging around the circuit, rather than in a motorhome. Although, over the years, the people at Goodyear have always been so nice to me, given me a sandwich and coffee, and a roof over my head when it's raining.

"While I don't participate in any of it to any degree, I think it's a very interesting and glamorous scene. I think, until you've seen the inside of it you have no idea actually what goes on in Formula 1 motor racing. It's a meeting of a large number of minds at all sorts of levels in society, even to the giants of industry, and a fair amount of wheeling and dealing goes on in the background. It's almost as if the sport were riding on the back of the entertainment, and a huge business system with a lot of corporate decisions being made."

Professor Watkins is over 60 now, and vows he will stay in the Grand Prix circus until he is "superfluous, extraneous, or perhaps a bit geriatric". When that happens, Watkins the enthusiast will still watch the races on television. But Watkins the neurosurgeon prefers to be on the spot and admits that a large part of his fascination is with the specimens he observes there.

"They're all very bright people, and they are very dedicated. I only do this job outside my professional life, and they are utterly immersed in it, the whole of their time. They are extremely single-minded. And I've always found them absolutely logical to deal with. We don't get any hysterics, we don't get any nonsense. They're exceptional people.

"Of course, Ecclestone himself is an extraordinary person. I think he has an exceptional brain. He's highly intelligent. He has a wonderful memory. He plays everything absolutely straight. He often knows ahead of the game what the problems are. He's almost got a predictive ability about him. And he's extraordinarily nice to deal with. If Bernie Ecclestone gives you his word that something will happen, then it does."

BERNIE ECCLESTONE

"They're all a bit mad! That's all!"

Bernie Ecclestone is the undisputed ringmaster of the Formula 1 circus, king of all the Grand Prix people. Officially he is President of the Formula One Constructor's Association (FOCA), representing the interests of the teams, and Vice-President of Promotional Affairs of the *Fédération Internationale du Sport Automobile* (FISA), the governing body of the sport. But Ecclestone exercises the ultimate authority over where the Grand Prix races are held, who organizes them, and how much it will cost them to do it. He is widely experienced in the latter aspect, since he personally 'owns' several of the events on the calendar. Few begrudge him that because Ecclestone's efforts are largely responsible for transforming Grand Prix racing from a relatively amateur pursuit into a polished professional enterprise of global proportions. Under his guidance it has become the most expensive sport in the world, a showcase for big-budget sponsors and a highly lucrative business for its practitioners.

Small in stature (he was once described by the diminutive Denis Jenkinson as being, 'like myself, about half actual size'),

Ecclestone's dapper figure can be seen darting about pressroom, pit lane and paddock throughout a Grand Prix weekend, with Bernie (as most people call him behind his back, though it's often Mr Ecclestone to his face) fixing his eagle eye on everything from the state of the toilets to suspicious-looking passholders in the pressroom. In the wake of his passage dirty toilets are quickly made immaculate and journalistic poseurs escorted to the other side of the fence, sometimes by the man himself.

When not conducting his whirlwind inspection tours, Ecclestone presides over his domain from behind the tinted glass windows of his mission control centre, the FOCA motorhome in the paddock. From the vantage point of this inner sanctum he observes such things as the way people dress. Personally fastidious and always nattily attired in freshly pressed blue trousers and immaculate white shirt, it is said that he sometimes despairs at the sight of certain grubby journalists.

"Like yourself, you mean? No, I'm joking. I suppose it's something that's always there and you can't dress all the press in a uniform. In fact I'd hate to see it. The journalists should be completely individual and remote and away from everything. I don't like to see any of them wearing a shirt with a sponsor's name on it.

"Really, nothing much bothers me about the press. They're doing a job in a way that they see it should be done, as far as their newspaper or magazine is concerned. So they report in the way they think their readers want to hear things or see things. Sometimes, perhaps they're wrong, and sometimes they're right. And sometimes they hand you the truth in a funny way. But lots of times they can't get the truth, so they speculate a little.

"What I don't like about some press people is they always tend to be negative. If the sun shines, it's no good. If it's raining, it's no good, and so on. I think the majority of the press is either a little bit lazy or a little bit cautious about trying to find out the real facts. They tend to read other people's reports. Anyway, I read very little to do with motorsport. I generally know all about it before it's written. I know the facts. So the fiction doesn't bother me too much."

Journalists seeking the facts about his background from Bernard Charles Ecclestone are often led a merry chase. He is a reluctant celebrity. ("The drivers are celebrities, not me. My private life is my private life.") Yet in the interest of preventing more fiction being written about him he acknowledges that he was indeed born in St Peter's, Suffolk, in the year 1936: His father was a trawler captain, then an engineer, and Bernie trained as a chemist at Woolwich Polytechnic, where he got a BSc in Physics.

The physical properties of racing machinery had appealed to Ecclestone from an early age, and he first defied the laws of gravity in competition when he was 14, astride a grass track motorcycle at Brands Hatch. He graduated to four wheels in the 500cc Formula 3 category, and raced around England in the early '50s. Meanwhile, he began to engage in the various entrepreneurial activities that eventually brought him considerable wealth. A motorcycle spares business, which he first conducted from his mother's kitchen table, blossomed into a chain of bike distributorships that became the second largest in the UK. His Weekend Car Auctions enterprise was sold to British Car Auctions at a hefty profit, and his forays into property development were equally lucrative.

Less successful was his first venture into Formula 1 team ownership, when he purchased the Connaught equipe. The cars were uncompetitive and a certain B.C. Ecclestone failed to qualify a Connaught-Alfa for the 1958 Monaco Grand Prix. In that year, also, Ecclestone's good friend Stuart Lewis-Evans was killed during the Grand Prix of Morocco, and Bernie dropped out of mainstream racing for the next 10 years. He returned to run a Formula 2 Lotus team with Jochen Rindt, befriended the Austrian, and was acting as his manager in Formula 1 when Rindt was killed in a Lotus at the Italian Grand Prix in 1970. The deaths of his friends caused Ecclestone to seriously question his involvement in racing.

"I was very close to both of those people, you know . . . had a great respect for them. And it seemed to me such a waste of life, particularly the way they both died. Both incidents were tragic . . . where they shouldn't have died. And for me it was a case of asking: 'What am I doing here?'"

It was a short dilemma for Ecclestone as he bought Jack Brabham's team (for $600,000) in 1970 and kept it for 18 years. "I bought it so I could retire from business and enjoy things. It didn't quite work out that way, but it seemed like a good idea at the time. Compared to what I do now, it's more satisfying, I suppose, to own a race team, especially if it's a successful race team as mine was. But even then, I was always in trouble because I was running the FOCA side of things as well. So I was always under an awful lot of pressure. Perhaps if I had nothing else to do except run a race team it probably would be much more enjoyable than the things that I have done. More relaxing.

"Now I get a different kind of satisfaction. I get satisfaction from trying to improve everything all the time. Sometimes I wish I had more free time. Then when I get it, I wish I hadn't got it. But I have three daughters, a teenager in school, another nearly of school age and a baby. So, you see, I must have some free time to have achieved that!"

Ecclestone is artistically minded and mentions architecture as a field of interest which he might one day pursue in more depth. His London mansion (purchased from Adnan Kashoggi for a reported $30 million) contains many works of art, among them a collection of netsukes, small toggles fashioned from ivory and wood. He designed the Brabham spitting cobra insignia and his aesthetic concerns extend beyond the sartorial presentation of the journalists to the image of the circus as a whole.

"Gradually I'm getting to all the people involved, and they understand what I'm trying to do. The organizers are now as conscious as I am of making sure their circuits, the paddocks and all the areas, are nicely presented, the toilets are clean, and so on, so we've got a Class A act.

"The teams and the drivers that compete, although they really are in showbiz, they're not very showbiz people. They're low profile people, really. They just want to get on and race their cars. But like other forms of racing, particularly in America, the sport is becoming more glitzy and showbiz and a little less sporting. Formula 1 is more exclusive, perhaps like ballet as opposed to some other form of dance. And for the hundreds of millions of people that follow Formula 1 racing, that's what they want. So if we try to change that image, we'd probably lose everything.

"Everybody says the old days are the best, don't they. That's because as you get older you like to think the old days were the good old days. But I don't think that way. I think each era has got its own special thing. Years ago, you'd buy a pair of shorts and some plimsoles, if you like, and you'd run a marathon. And now you see all the people running in high-tech shoes and uniforms with sponsors' names on them. If they play tennis, they've got high-tech racquets. The same with golf and other sports. So this is something that's inevitable. This sport, because of its high visibility, attracts people who want to put money in, to get coverage from it for advertising. It's not better or worse, just a change.

"Really, I think this is quite an infectious environment. And it seems the people that get involved, stay involved. For anybody who is a bit competitive, you get instant results, so you know how bad or good your job is on a Sunday afternoon. Then you move on to a different challenge, different race track, a whole different set of circumstances presented to you in another couple of weeks.

"We're all here for the competition, and the business factor doesn't change that. Business is about competition, and competition is about racing. I wouldn't do this unless I wanted to. I think I would only stop when I no longer wanted to be involved in any type of business. And contrary to general belief, I'm not motivated by money.

"I'm motivated by trying to do what I'm doing, and doing it well. That's what motivates me. If I was ever to decide to stop doing this I would make sure everything, from my point of view, was in good order for everybody else. I'm conscious of the fact that I need to tidy up everything in case anything terrible happens, if I need to retire, or am forced into retirement because I stop breathing!"

In the pressroom, along the pit lane, in the paddock, it seems everyone has an opinion about Bernie Ecclestone. And what does he think of all the Grand Prix people?

"They're all a bit mad! That's all!"